PRAISE FOR

Beyond Belief

"Jan Wojcik left the Jesuit order yet still became a holy father. In this charming memoir, refusing to weaponize fear as many books with religious themes, he finds different paths lead to God, even *Beyond Belief.* Along the way, he fishes, prays in colors, and sometimes dodges bullets.

"I wish I could have spent more time with him. Some of his passages resonated so deeply that I found myself returning to them over and over."

—**Becky Hepinstall, coauthor of** *Sisters of Shiloh*

"A candid and charming—often funny—memoir of a boy whose earthly sense of integrity compels him to become a Jesuit and, later, requires him to leave the order for the same reasons he joined it—to keep questioning the biblical literature about God, even as doing that might push him beyond belief. He can't stop anywhere along the line—or, in other words, he can't put a good book down. Neither could I his."

—**James Ritts, software engineer**

"I got to the end and was happy. It was just right for the story, funny and moving all the way through. A child grows to be a man, a Jesuit, a married man, building a valid philosophy out of what he thinks about what is happening to him. But then I was sad. There was no more story to read."

—**Robert Hans Neiderer, carpenter, building arts teacher**

"OMG the host down the cleavage episode had us in tears of laughter! Cradle Catholics would understand."

—**Natalie and Ferd Leimkuhler, photographer and professor and chair emeritus of the School of Industrial Engineering, Purdue University**

"A memoir—thoughtful, reflective, sometimes self-incriminating, and honest—that reads almost leisurely, this often reads like a novel whose characters are complex, fully developed, and very real."

—**Greg Fields, author** of *Through the Waters and the Wild*, *The Arc of the Comet*, **and** *The Bright Freight of Memory*

"A man withdraws from the Society of Jesus where he had been in training for the priesthood—withdraws without pronouncement or denunciation, or resentment, and as it happens withdraws into the lovely arms of a woman with whom he has two children.

"Prevailing against resistance is a recurrent subtext of *Beyond Belief*. The author and his wife, both full-time teachers, also manage to cultivate an active and productive farm in the hard-scrabble soil of the very northern reaches of New York State, providing the community with produce, animal meat, and an extraordinary array of cut flowers.

"The trajectory of the author's massive journey finds a fitting resting place in the author's later years—as a fisher of students. And the reader will very likely endorse with great pleasure the arc of this life."

—**Lee Perron, author of** *Pocket Poems* **and** *Celtic Light*

"Jan Wojcik left the Jesuits we lived in together. But we've remained brothers and friends for almost fifty years. The question that shaped his life and vocation is as he says in the epilogue of *Beyond Belief*: 'What if God has a sense of humor?'"

—**Joseph Appleyard, SJ, author of** *Coleridge's Philosophy of Literature* **and** *Becoming a Reader,* **Jesuit priest and professor emeritus at Boston College**

Beyond Belief:
Unexpected Biblical Wisdom from a
Former Jesuit, Teacher, and Fisher of Men
by Jan Wojcik

© Copyright 2024 Jan Wojcik

ISBN 979-8-88824-457-9

All rights reserved. No part of this publication may be reproduced, stored in a retrieval system, or transmitted in any form or by any means—electronic, mechanical, photocopy, recording, or any other—except for brief quotations in printed reviews, without the prior written permission of the author.

Published by

3705 Shore Drive
Virginia Beach, VA 23455
800-435-4811
www.koehlerbooks.com

Beyond Belief

Unexpected Biblical Wisdom from a
Former Jesuit, Teacher, and Fisher of Men

JAN WOJCIK

VIRGINIA BEACH
CAPE CHARLES

Christine
as long as I have words.

With thinking we may be beside ourselves . . . By a conscious effort of the mind we can stand aloof from actions and their consequences; and all things good and bad, go by us like a torrent . . . I am sensible of a certain doubleness . . . However intense my experience, I am conscious of the presence and criticism of a part of me, which, as it were is not a part of me, but spectator . . . When the play is over, it may be the tragedy of life is over, the spectator goes his way. It was a kind of fiction, a work of the imagination only.
—Henry David Thoreau, "Solitude," *Walden*

τί πρόσ σέ (*What's it to you?*)
—John 21:22

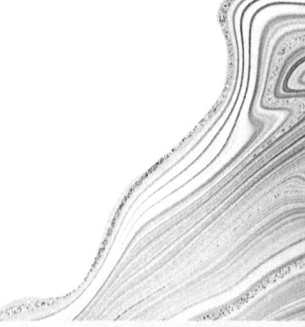

In the Lion's Den

1972

I was found innocent.
—Book of Daniel 6:23

"**M**y religious beliefs don't matter. But I know why you ask. That question always comes up."

Each student looked back like a wild animal you came upon by surprise in the woods: wide-eyed, curious, but alert and ready to bolt if needed.

Purdue University students were by and large from blue-collar families, the first to have matriculated to college. They had grown up on farms in Indiana's rural south. Or, at the other extreme, in the industrial northern part of the state dominated by Gary, Indiana—part of the Midwestern Rust Belt. They were earnest. Many had been raised as evangelical Protestants with strong presuppositions about what the Bible meant—and that meant what it *literally* meant, word for word.

Between the question and my response, most of the students missed my slight smile. I knew what *not* to say: that I had been raised Catholic, served as an altar boy, became a Jesuit seminarian for eight years, and had graduated from two Eastern universities, one of them Catholic. That would be enough for some of them to bolt. What was worse, by now I had no religious beliefs and was even mildly hostile to them.

I held up an edition of the Bible with a red cover that they had never seen before: the New English Bible with Apocrypha. It was well-worn. I used the same copy for forty years. I hoped some of them would hold on to theirs.

I elaborated. "My religious beliefs are personal and private, as I expect yours to be. That's the only way a course like this can work. We're not here to argue about doctrine or the theology of what religions teach. Rather, we'll see what the Bible as literature says before any of that stuff grabs a hold on it. Look, if anyone finds what we do uncomfortable, I'm happy to sign the forms for you to drop the course."

I could tell they weren't quite sure what to think. "But I know what you're worried about," I continued. "So let me give you an example of what I mean. Let's begin with Genesis. 'In the beginning . . .'" A few students smiled at the weak joke.

"Turn to page three if you've already bought the book. Or for this once, any other version you brought. The words will be virtually the same—where it starts 'The earth was without form' just wind and water. Anyone willing to read the first five verses aloud?"

A hand went up.

"Read," I said with a grin, "like you're standing in a pulpit." And she did.

"In the beginning of Creation, when God made heaven and earth . . ."

"Stop!" I said when she got to ". . . and morning came the first day."

"That's how creation starts, made in seven days, very orderly. God makes humans on the sixth day, after there's solid ground to stand on. 'In his own image . . . male and female he made them.' You can imagine God wearing a long robe, his arms outstretched, following some logical plan: a place for everything and everything in its place.

"Well, that's how the first creation story goes, but there are three of them. The third is weird, with the words, 'the sons of the gods saw the daughters of men were beautiful; so they took for themselves such women as they chose.' (6:1-3). You don't hear much about this passage, which sounds like it fell out of the pages of some pagan myth and got stuck there. And the question might be, why did the people putting Genesis together leave it there? You can say what you think about that later.

"For today, just for a few minutes, let's look at the second creation account that follows the first, starting in chapter two. We won't read the whole thing out loud. Everyone knows how this one goes from two thousand years of art and cartoons alone. Note God acts differently than he did in the first story. This time he makes a man before he has any proper earth for him to stand on. Then, as if the new man remains suspended in the air, God slips in ground for him to stand on. This God improvises. He doesn't make a woman for the man for another fifteen lines or so. God makes her up out of one of the man's ribs. I know a woman who, when she first studied biology, was surprised to discover modern male human beings were not missing a rib.

"Okay, we're not going into that right now. But in the next class, we are going to talk about why the original writers and editors of Genesis decided to weave three very different versions of creation together. Perhaps they were not interested in assaying biological or historical facts per se, but instead wanted readers to treat each story as providing a uniquely provocative way to think about what kind of god this God was—and why.

"For now, let's look at the second creation story. Like I said, this is the one you're probably most familiar with. It has the bits about the fruit and the snake and the tree and God finding out the first couple ate the fruit after he told them not to.

"Now we've all heard people say this story tells about humankind's first sin that cripples all of Adam and Eve's descendants to this day. Jesus died to wash the sin away, and so on. But note now, and check this out later when you can read the whole story closely, that the word 'sin' does not appear in the story."

A hand went up. "But isn't it a sin to disobey God?"

"Not if God wanted them to. Consider: God set the trap to lure the young couple into a necessary defiance. The bait was his telling them: 'eat anything you want, *except* the fruit of that tree.' The prohibition made the fruit look tantalizing. God then brings in a talking snake to tempt them to take a bite. Which they did. God suspected they had when he called them, and they cried out from undercover they were ashamed they were naked.

"'Who told you you were naked?' God said. And immediately added, 'Did you eat the forbidden fruit?' God's reasoning was, if humans could recognize the difference between naked and clothed, then they could see differences—to wit—*whether* to obey him on their own, or not. Unlike automatons who could only speak like ventriloquist dummies about what God had said.

"In other words, what if we read this story that God *wanted* them to disobey. Only if he knew they were capable of doing that, would any subsequent manifestation of human affection for him, or willingness to do what he wanted them to do—only then could he assume it would be sincere.

"If God had tried to build in free will from the start, it never would have been genuinely human. The original wide-eyed innocence had to be fragile enough for Adam and Eve to break through it into awareness.

"So, in fact, the story had *nothing* to do with 'original sin.' Instead, it was about original thinking. The question hung out before you today is: 'Do you want to learn to read like Adam and Eve learned to think?' If you do, there's a great ride ahead."

I looked out over the class. Their faces remained impassive. The same student who asked about my religious beliefs asked another impertinent question. "Why do you do this?" Not a question he would ask an engineering professor.

"The Bible is beautiful as literature. The stories are fun to read and invite you to think along with ancient writers who made stories to explore their special kind of God who talked to humans *and* expected back talk. A God who was writing a story himself—creating characters who had their own ideas of what to do in the story regardless of what the author might have intended."

Again, I did not say everything I thought about what I was doing.

Reading the Bible as literature *was* subversive. Make the Bible appear fascinating enough and the conventional doctrinal, sectarian dogmatic readings fashioned for Christianity by Saint Paul fade away. Paul quashes everything in the Bible down to the singularly flat story of human sins in need of a bloody redemption. *Surely*, I always say to myself, *many students sitting there must suspect this. After all, they've likely talked to other students who've taken the course.*

I heard from a former student of the class that the Catholic chaplain on campus began teaching a course on the Bible as literature through the Newman Catholic Center on campus.

"I've taken them both. Believe me, there's nothing the same about either one," he told me.

Which was fine. But I found it puzzling that the course had the same name as mine and was being offered for academic credit, as mine was. I went to the dean to ask if this was kosher. After all, I—not the chaplain—had earned a credential with a degree and earned an academic appointment.

The dean told me, "There is nothing that could be done. The Indiana State Legislature has passed a law that chaplains at state universities can teach religious courses for academic credit."

"And so, being a junior professor in a humanities department, I have no grounds for complaint?"

"That's right," said the dean, looking deadpan. "Aren't you lucky?"

"Did the legislature pass this bill because of the way I teach the Bible as literature at a state university?"

"I'm not going to say."

The dean was right. I'd always been lucky, beginning with the kinds of mistakes I made in the third grade. Beginning on another first day of classes. Which surprisingly enough to me, was the day I took my first steps toward gaining the credential and the academic appointment for teaching the Bible as literature. And as it would turn out, living on a road with men with guns.

Can You Tell Me Why You're Here?

1952

Become like little children.
—Matthew 18:4

I stood up next to my chair in a third-grade classroom of Marvin School on Second Street in East Norwalk, Connecticut. I had no idea why.

The other students bent over their desks writing. Miss Sonneberg, my teacher, had assigned an essay on what we did on our summer vacation. She had passed out writing paper. After a few moments of thinking about this, as the other children began to jot, I stood up and began to cry.

The other students didn't notice me. Miss Sonneberg walked quietly to my desk and, just above a whisper, asked kindly, "What's the matter? Does something hurt?"

I just shook my head, still unable to say anything, dazed.

Miss Sonneberg then turned. She spoke briskly to the rest of the classroom. "Class, just keep writing. We'll be back in a moment."

She took my hand. "Come with me," she said softly for just me to hear. "It's all right." I noticed the few students who looked up from their papers did not look curious about why she and I were standing there. Whatever my problem was, it didn't matter much. They had their vacations to write about.

She took my hand and led me to the large dark wooden door whose knob she opened with a small twist of her wrist. My ear was at the level of the knob. I heard a tick as a ring on her finger touched it. I liked the comfort of small noises I alone could hear. It made the place I was in intimate.

But we walked out of the classroom into a silence like a mood of doom I had never experienced in that space before. Usually the corridors and landings were full of children in colored clothing shuffling about and talking and laughing, gradually pulling themselves into the groupings of a class that went through its large, dark designated doors. I thought how strange it was to be the only student in the silent landing before all the closed doors, and to be with a teacher. There never seemed to be any adults around while children were moving toward their classrooms. The teachers were already inside the rooms. As if they lived there. Where all the learning was. Where the quiet calm was. Where was I now? In a darkling space with only myself and a woman taking me I knew not where.

As if she guessed my thoughts, Miss Sonneberg squeezed my hand to let me know she had the matter well in hand. She led me toward Miss Ferguson's, the principal's, office. Now for the first time I felt something more than just bewilderment. I was frightened. I thought of myself as a good kid who had never before been sent to the principal's office. Her large dark wooden door was always open. I had always hurried past it, lest she see me and beckon. Now Miss Sonneberg led me in. Miss Ferguson, very short, with thick gray hair pulled into a tight bun, always wore a long black dress. She looked up from her desk through her thick spectacles, which caught a sparkle from the sunlight coming through the window, and smiled. I could see her shift her eyes slightly from mine as she took note of my undried tears.

She said with what sounded like helpful concern, "Yes? What can I do for you? Sit down," she said, waving at a chair. "Can you tell me why you're here? What your problem is? Would you like a glass of water?"

What I found strange about her friendly greeting was that she spoke to me directly and didn't ask any questions of Miss Sonneberg. Without saying a word, Miss Sonneberg had already released my hand and had turned and gone through the open door to walk back to her classroom. Her footsteps faded. It was as if whatever was happening, however fearful it might seem, it was unsurprising to the god-like adults who ran my childish world.

Miss Ferguson didn't look stern. She gave me a glass of water. The sound of my slurp was comforting. She looked puzzled for a moment after I put down the glass with a soft bump. I blurted, "My family never takes vacations."

She continued to look at me with the same smile. "So . . ."

I continued after one final sob. "Instead, on his two weeks off, my father always paints one side of our house and then paints other people's houses during the daylight hours every day of the week between early spring and late fall. He never goes anywhere except up a ladder. Nobody else in our family goes on vacation either."

Miss Ferguson chuckled and said, "Well, this is a nice neighborhood to stay home in." She smiled kindly. "But you still haven't told me what's the matter with you."

I leaned toward her and whispered like I was telling a secret just for the two of us. "When Miss Sonneberg asked us to write about what we did on our summer vacation, I didn't know what to write. I don't even know what a vacation is. When the other children find out, they will make fun of me," I whimpered.

"Well, maybe they didn't go anywhere either. Vacation from school could mean just playing every day, swimming, riding a bike. Did you do that?"

"Yes," I said, "I rode a lot and swam and after a few weeks, the soles of my feet got tough, and I could go barefoot. I hadn't thought of that. I could have told about that. Now I feel silly."

I hadn't thought enough. Now my being upset shifted ground, but I still felt bad.

Miss Ferguson smiled. "Should I call your mother?" Miss Ferguson whispered, as if she, too, was in on a secret. What seemed odd to me was that neither the teacher nor the principal had corrected me. As if it was normal for a young person to feel lost.

She picked up the large black handpiece of her desk telephone and called my mother, who showed up within a few minutes. We lived just down the short Second Street from the school. As I listened to Miss Ferguson explain things, my mother looked puzzled at first, then frowned, then smiled. Miss Ferguson and my mother gave me a choice to go back to class or to go home. I chose home.

I spent the rest of the time of that school day in my room reading my favorite comic books about the Donald Duck family of Uncle Scrooge, Uncle Donald, and three child ducks: Huey, Dewey, and Louie. The kid ducks were of unexplained parentage. They addressed both the older ducks as "Uncle." It was always the children ducks who got their uncles out of scrapes. That reading was hopeful.

When I returned the next day, the other students shared in the conspiracy of silence or the indifference of my elders. They said nothing about the tears and disappearance. They probably had their own confusions to conjure with. Whatever the reason, I was happy and relaxed that no one had teased me. Maybe my agonies weren't all that interesting. It was normal to be confused.

From that incident alone, I became a disciple of Miss Sonneberg. My devotion deepened. Sometime later, I had been working away comfortably at my desk while the third grade was taking a mandatory IQ test. They were asked to identify common shapes like rectangles, triangles, and squares. I noticed there was a round figure that was mostly a circle but a little flattened at one end. And with what would now be called second guessing, I pondered whether it was really supposed to look like a circle but had been poorly printed. Assuming adults always got things right, I chose "circle." Later, Miss Sonneberg told me that was wrong. I tried to explain.

She smiled, and told me in her sweet teacher's voice, "Nobody gets everything right." Then she said, "And it doesn't really matter."

Sometime thereafter, I got up out of my chair again and brought a book up to her desk. I pointed to a passage and said plaintively, "Miss Sonneberg, this doesn't make sense."

And she retorted firmly, "No, it does make sense; you just don't understand it yet." That did it. Miss Sonneberg had hit two nails on the head. She'd given me two insights with which to negotiate the rest of a life that would last at least another seventy years. The idea here was it's normal to be ignorant. Even useful.

However, it was Donna, who became my first real friend, who helped me get unstuck and move along the rest of my errant life.

Donna had sat next to me for the first week in the third grade. She often wore gingham dresses with small brown checks. Donna had brown hair and lots of brown freckles, which sometimes looked like they floated off her face and then sprinkled onto her dresses. She had an extra yellow HB No. 2 pencil when I couldn't find mine. Up until this time we hadn't said much to each other. Just smiles. Even in the third grade, boys and girls had a sense that boys and girls belonged apart. More than that, she was calm, as if she had no need for inner agonies.

Donna started things off. She asked quietly, privately, looking around to see that no one was watching, "What was that about? Why did you cry? I never saw you do that before."

I replied, "Oh, I was just being silly." I looked down at my feet. I saw hers. She was wearing black Keds sneakers that looked funny with her dress. Like duck feet.

Donna persisted, "No. It's more than that. You were really upset. Why was that?"

I explained, "I had been embarrassed. I have never gone away on a vacation and didn't even know what the word meant. I saw you writing. You go on vacations, right?"

Donna nodded. "Yes, we do."

I paused for a moment. I didn't want to sound jealous, but as sincere as possible for a kid in grade three. "I'd like to know about them."

She smiled, put her finger to her lips to stop the conversation, and said, "Just be patient."

Later that morning on the playground, Donna told me, "At Christmas time my mother takes me on a plane to visit my uncle and aunt who live in Puerto Rico—where my father was born. My father died in the war."

I felt a pang. Compared to that, my own troubles did seem silly.

"I'm sorry to hear that. There're other kids in our class who have no fathers and live with their mothers or aunts. One father I know brought back a German Luger pistol. He also gave me a deactivated hand grenade. You don't hear much talk about the War. But what you just said means there's a lot of sadness in the silence."

Donna touched my hand. "That's nice of you to say. Thank you. My mother sometimes tells me about my dad. But we never saw each other. For me he's like a hero in a story book."

After a moment, with a brisk tone in her voice, she continued to answer the question about her vacations. "But during summer vacation from school, I go swimming a lot, mostly at the beach of the country club where my mother is a member. We love to sit together on the sand and watch the waves. Sometimes we talk about my father."

"You know," I said looking at my feet again, as if you were supposed to address a girl indirectly, "I feel a little ashamed that I got all upset about my father never taking us away on vacations, when you say you don't have a father to take your vacations with."

Donna nodded her head sadly. She said with a soft smile, "I'd rather have the father."

Donna and I didn't talk about vacations again until the next year, in the fourth grade.

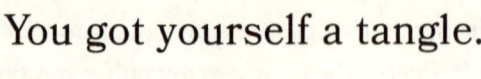

You got yourself a tangle.

1954

As she wept...
—John 20:11

Once more, the once dreaded question came up, as if it was the school year's introductory incantation: "What did you do on your summer vacation?"

Donna sat next to me again. However, this time I was primed. I'd already told her the story that I now sat tight to write out, and it came easily. Several days afterward, Miss Knorr, our grade four teacher, asked me to read the story out loud in front of the class. I stood straight.

"It was on a bright sunny day in July, when my father and mother and baby sister Jill and I took my grandfather's boat out to the second largest of the Norwalk Islands, Sheffield. It has a stone lighthouse. We did not stay in the lighthouse. We stayed in a large shack with gray, unpainted boards on the outside, near the lighthouse. We only saw the sun that week on the ride out and on the ride back. It rained every day. Wind blew through cracks in the outside boards. Sometimes I walked around wearing a sleeping blanket as a cape.

"Almost all the pots that came with the place were scattered over the floor under roof leaks—as the drops hit the water in the pots, they made the sound *plink*.

"One of my jobs was emptying the pots outside as they filled. I played in the water pots with my sister using little pieces of driftwood we pretended were little boats—not having brought any toys with us. On the second day my father went trolling just offshore—over an underwater shoal of boulders known locally as 'Tommy's Pants.' No one knows how the name came about. You couldn't even see it—it was all underwater. But very big striped bass lurked among its boulders. It was a favorite fishing spot of my father and grandfather, who owned our boat, and they often went there to troll and cast at night. That's where my father managed to hook one during daylight, which we ate for the rest of the rainy week. On the last rainy day of our time on the island, my father took me fishing for the first time. I didn't understand how to do it. He baited a hook with meat from some mussels we had scraped off the rocks. He added a weight, then threw the end of the line off the side of the boat. When the line stopped going out, he said, 'Okay, it's on the bottom. Here, take the pole. And jerk it up if you feel anything pull the pole down.' Immediately I felt the down jerk and did the up jerk. But then, nothing happened. My father looked over kindly and said, 'That's okay. You're just stuck on a rock.' He stood up and reached for the pole to work the hook free. I pulled the pole back. I said quickly, uncertainly, 'No, no, I felt it move.' He took the pole, jerked it up, felt nothing move, and announced, 'Nope. You're on the bottom.'

"'No, I'm not,' I insisted. Impatiently I grabbed the pole back and started reeling. And behold, I had pulled up a small striped bass of my own.

"'Good going, kid,' my father said with a laugh. 'That'll teach you never to listen to anything from your father.' A few minutes later, this time after baiting the hook myself, I caught a second one without my father doing anything. He just watched and then said happily while netting the fish aboard, 'Beginner's luck.' He slapped me softly on the shoulder. We took my two fish home with us the next day.

"I remember one nice moment when the rain thinned to a drizzle that hissed on a boulder at the end of the stony shoreline—there was no sand—and watching the tide sloshing and swirling gray and white, a sound of people mumbling in a foreign language. And my sister sitting next to me, babbled back. On the sunny day we went back home, the four of us sat close together and close to the engine for warmth, as all of our clothes were damp. My father smiled and said, 'Well, I wouldn't have been able to paint the house this week anyway.' And sure enough, after we got home, my father started painting the house again the next day. The end."

The other kids in the fourth grade thought the story was funny and laughed, especially at the parts about Tommy's Pants, playing boats in pots of water, and the part where my father went back to painting houses. I felt great. I finally had a story to tell.

Donna of course liked the story too. "That's a real vacation all right," she said with emphasis. "It had everything—a cruise, a house on the beach, all the water anyone could want to play in. And you learned how to catch a fish. What more could you ask?"

"It wasn't like going to Puerto Rico in the winter to go swimming," I replied ruefully.

"Of course not," Donna answered, "but maybe just as good."

"Give me a break."

Then, once again, Donna said just the right thing to make me feel good. "Do you like swimming too?" she asked, looking me in the eye.

"Yes," I said eagerly, "a lot really, just like you when the water warms up. Usually just around the block from our house, in a small space between an oyster company dock and an electrical way station. At the end of Second Street. We call it Second Point. Only the neighborhood kids swim there. It's stony, with lots of crabs, broken oyster shells, and no sand—but you dive in quickly and get out into the channel and out among the boats moored outside the channel. You have to watch out or you'll get pinched by the rock crabs all over the bottom who eat hunks of cleaned oyster bits tossed there by the Lovejoy Oyster Company. So, you dive right in and swim. No beach-blanket stuff."

Then I experienced something new: an expectant pause. What I had said prompted, it seemed, what she would say, as if I had intuited what she was thinking and then given her the space in time to say it. I was learning to play music at the time. Later, when I thought about this hovering moment, I likened it to a "rest" in music. A temporary silence that gathered the music before it into the extra pause it needed to push ahead with vigor. The rest made music too.

Rest. Donna insisted, "Take me there."

I was happy. No girl had ever asked me to do anything before.

I chose the date of the big swim carefully. I wasn't sure how Donna would react to seeing traces of the neighborhood's hardscrabble surfaces. The discarded oyster bits drew rock crabs, all right, which were repellant to look at: short, squat, with tiny scuttling legs; but what was worse, fuzzy seaweed algae on their shells made it look like they were disintegrating. The huge piles of oyster shells next to the shucking house still had fleshy residues that attracted sea rats. Sometimes when you looked at a pile, the shells were stirring on the surface, almost as if they were alive; but actually, they moved because rats were scavenging just under the surface. The rats were everywhere. Feral cats prayed on them. The cats were scrawny and furtive; they denned under stairways and porches and in driftwood shelters. The neighborhood kids teased them with sticks when they were defending their litters with wild eyes and hisses. Sometimes a cat walked backward, dragging the carcass of a rat to feed its young.

The rats had another predator. Joe Dugan was the most eccentric of the local army vets from World War II—a fog which lingered over the neighborhood even seven years after it ended. There was another man who had been severely wounded. He spent every sunny day sitting on the concrete steps of an apartment building, smiling and waving, almost never moving.

Joe often wore an Army shirt with sergeant's stripes on the sleeves. He also wore a stained New York Yankees baseball cap.

Joe was about the same age as my father and the other adult men vets in the neighborhood must have been. But he looked older, with deep furrows of age and worry on his head and neck. His eyes were moist and turned downward as if he was sad. He'd cobbled together a houseboat by nailing two-by-four studs to the sides of a large rowboat, using gray driftwood planks for siding and brown rusty scrap metal panels for a roof. He moored his boat fore and aft with ropes tied around big rocks on a tiny strip of shoreline between the oyster company docks and a restaurant that apparently no one cared about or claimed.

I liked to stop and chat with Joe, who was at ease being alone. Hearing my footsteps, Joe would look up and smile. "Oh, it's you. Have a seat. There's always room."

The inside of Joe's boat was mostly a place for his bed and clothes hanging from nails. He had a hot plate. There was no sign of a toilet. When I asked him once if I could go to the bathroom, Joe reached into the back of the boat for a white plastic bucket, which he waved toward the pilings along the shore crusted with barnacles at low tide. "Rinse it out afterward," he said.

Joe had fashioned a little porch off the stern where he'd sit in a plastic chair with a .22 rifle over his lap. He shot the rats that ran across the shoreline below his boat at low tide.

The day before the scheduled swim with Donna, I walked along the shore to pick up trash at low tide. I walked by Joe's boat. Joe looked silently out at the tidal water running into the cove he could see off the stern. At the high tide scrum line of seaweed high up on the shore, I could see rat bodies Joe had shot in gray heaps, with a few pink feet sticking up.

I knew the high tides rinsed away the rats. Then blue crabs ate the dead rats. The cove's bottom crawled with beautiful blue crabs, which had fins on their back legs that enabled them to swim all the way up the East Coast from the Chesapeake Bay. Here in the little cove, they spawned where they fed and molted during the summer before swimming back to the Chesapeake again. The first money I earned was selling the Blue Crabs I netted off the pilings that supported many waterside buildings that overhung the water. The real prize was bagging two at once: a soft-shell molting, with a hard shell straddling it with its claws held out and menacing for protection. I could sell the soft-shells for a dollar apiece to the neighborhood restaurant. Big money then. The plenitude of rotting rats on the bottom is one reason the cove teemed with blue crabs all summer long. Watching this local natural cycle was fascinating and even lucrative for kids in my neighborhood who grew up with it. I feared whatever she saw of it might be repellant to Donna. I fixed the swimming time to coincide with high tide when the ample, smooth surface of salt water kept this activity mostly under cover. Adding to my decision to take Donna swimming only at high tide, I decided to lead her on a route from which she wouldn't see Joe's boat.

Still, for all my plans, I felt uneasy early on the appointed day. I wanted things to go well with my new friend. The sun was shining. It was a warm September day, when the tide was full, when Long Island Sound was still warm from the summer. I rode my bike down the street to the fancier part of the neighborhood. I met Donna on her bike at the bottom of Pine Hill Ridge, from the top of which, where her house was, there was a view over to the waters of Long Island Sound. As I rode behind her to Second Point, I watched her feet. She'd brought a pair of old black Keds sneakers to wear while crossing the stony beach I'd told her about.

"Barefoot is only for sand," she said as if it were a rule when I complimented her about her sneakers.

Standing at the water's edge, she took off and wrapped the sneakers up in a shirt she wore over her brown bathing suit with small yellow polka dots. She tossed the wrap high above the high tide line and then dove out into the deeper water without "striking her foot against a stone," as the Bible says (Matthew: 4:3). I dove in and followed quickly after her.

As we came up for air, I told Donna, "You're really smart bringing the sneakers. I have tough soles instead, and you have big feet."

Donna gave the water a big kick. "I'm part duck." We swam across the channel and among the many moored boats tied at the bow to buoys. The boats stayed still while the ocean pushed by. The two of us swam among the beautiful white skipjacks—vintage oyster fishing sloops the Lovejoy Oyster Company brought up from the Chesapeake. They used them along with their usual diesel boats—also painted white with black stripes of trim. "Shipjacks were magical boats: forty feet long, broad bottomed, with a centerboard that could be pulled up in the shallows, and the jib fastened to a long bowsprit. The main sail was a very large squat triangle, curved like a sheet in the wind on a clothesline under sail. All this designed for dredging oysters in shallow waters—stable, but nimble. And by law, at least in the Chesapeake, with no engines, so with built-in environmental, competitive constraints. By using them for the elegance of their laboring, the Lovejoy Oyster Company lived up to its name. It gave me a warm feeling to think about that. That day, the sailing and motoring fishing boats comfortably pulled their mooring lines straight against the incoming tide, like swans on leashes. What wonderful company.

Donna and I swam behind a small cruiser, and a man leaned out and asked earnestly, "Hey fellas—can you give me a hand?"

With only wet plastered heads showing above the surface, we both must have looked like swimming boys. The man explained, "I was coming back to shore this morning. I think I overran a mooring line that got twisted into my propeller. You two look like good swimmers. Could you dive down and see?"

We dove down and found the rope was really twisted around the prop tight like a balled fist. We were okay with swimming underwater without goggles—where everything underwater looked green. We came to the surface. Donna blew her nose free of water and laughed. She said to the man, "Yes sir, you got yourself a tangle."

He asked for a second favor, holding up a rigging knife, "Do you think you could use this to cut it free? I'll pay you five dollars."

"We'll give it a try," Donna and I both said at the same time, which made us both giggle. We repeatedly dove and surfaced for air—and with some effort found that, with Donna pulling any loose part of the line taut, I could saw away at the knot ball with the knife the man gave me. It took a while. It felt great when the rope suddenly came undone—like pulling striped bass aboard after a fight. Donna surfaced, holding the cut-up rope in the air like a trophy, and hollered, "TAH-DAH!" The man clapped.

While we were still treading water, the man said he would pay us the five dollars. Donna was quick to say to him, "No, please no, the bill would be wet before we got back to shore."

I thought, *Well, maybe the man could mail us the money.* But I gave Donna the lead—a good decision for the rest of my life with women.

I could see the man looking down at our bathing suits. Donna was wearing a brown single piece with yellow polka dots; I was wearing black shorts. On closer look, it was hard to mistake that we were obviously a girl and a boy. The man apologized for calling Donna a fella.

"I've been called worse," Donna laughed.

He asked, "Are you brother and sister?"

Donna replied sharply, "I wish, but now we're friends, which is probably better."

The man said with feeling, "Well, I can at least give you a soda."

The man pulled us both up by our arms. We clambered into the cockpit of his cruiser, shaking off seawater, little drops of which hit each other. The man insisted we drink a 7-Up with him.

He thanked us over and over. "I really thought I had messed up bad this time. But you two swimming along made this my lucky day!"

When the water dried on our bodies, we dove back into the water and swam back to Second Point. Donna swam faster and stronger than I could or would even try to do. Swimming behind Donna, I saw a pair of lively fish splashing playfully on the surface next to her two remarkably large feet. When we got back to the shore, I walked on my tough soles across the rugged shore to fetch up Donna's shirt and sneakers.

When I turned and walked toward her, I saw her standing there, one leg straight in ankle-deep water, the other bent with her bare toes on point, her tan body radiant and glistening from the vigor of the swim, waiting for me. Her lips were pursed in a shy smile. I thought,

She sure is pretty. I remembered the scene when years later I stood in the Uffizi Museum in Florence before the massive Botticelli painting of the birth of Venus on the seashore. Great art does that to you.

When I bowed and, with a flourish, handed Donna her black Keds sneakers on the stony shore of Second Point, she said graciously, "Why I thank you sir, and now, like I said to the man, we're friends."

A few weeks after our swim together at Second Point, Donna's mother called my mother. They knew each other. It was an odd connection. Donna's mother was my mother's gynecologist. When Donna introduced me to her mother later, she laughed and with a sly smile said, "We've already met. I helped your mother give birth to you." But it was more than that. Our mothers had discovered they were neighbors in East Norwalk.

When my mother came back home from a doctor's appointment with her, she would say things like, "Donna's mother is very friendly, and we talk about how we like living near Long Island Sound for the salt smell in the air and those mornings when the fog softens the streets with gray, and everybody drives slow for a change. I like her."

On the phone, Donna's mother asked mine if she could take the two of us to the country club beach for a day. "The Sound is still warm enough. Our kids like to swim together," she said.

My mother was happy to say yes. When she told me about the invitation, she added with some pride, "You and Donna have both made good friends."

When I heard this, I thought, *Even our mothers like us.*

This time there *was* a beach blanket and no rock crabs or broken shells. Instead, smooth tan sand ran all the way to the water. Instead of moored boats, there was a diving raft offshore. We clambered aboard and immediately dove into the water again. I climbed up the ladder and stood and watched as Donna continued to climb out of the water and dive again with no hesitation, like a turning pinwheel.

"When you dive, there's a sound like a slurp through a straw. Little splash. Even with your big feet."

"It was more fun diving down to free that propeller. At least we had something to do when we got to the bottom of the dive. I found out that day how long I could hold my breath down there—next to you—who really knew how."

I thought happily, *She thinks I can do one thing better in the water than she can!*

We raced each other swimming around the raft, and it was never a question of letting her win. Donna was a really good swimmer, and when she got into race mode—it was almost as if her body came out of the water—her legs and arms moved like churning oars. It was mesmerizing watching her from a short distance behind. I forgot for a moment to use my arms and sank.

When we came ashore, we shook the water droplets at each other as if we were wet dogs. Some drops had rainbows in them like they'd had in the cabin cruiser. We giggled again and walked back to the blanket. Donna's mom handed us towels.

She asked with the tone of someone asking a serious question, "Who wants an ice cream cone?"

"I do," said Donna brightly, "but I can only speak for myself."

With a sweep of an arm and bowing chivalrously, I said, "After you, ladies."

She bought the cones at a stand on the edge of the beach. We brought them back to the blanket to eat. I took care not to drip. I wanted to feel like I belonged in their elegant company.

"It's a beautiful day," Donna's mother said. "I am really happy we could all come here together. We've stolen a warm early autumn day off the lap of the gods."

What she said puzzled me. "What do you mean by 'stealing from the lap of the gods'? I've never heard of there being more than one God, and I could not imagine him with a lap. In pictures you usually only see him looking out of a cloud with a big white beard and only from the waist up."

She laughed merrily and explained, "It's an expression that probably comes from mythical literature or Greek legends. The old gods were selfish and greedy most of the time, and you had to fake them out if you ever wanted to sneak anything away from them."

"I'll try to remember you can do that," I said inanely. All three of us laughed.

We sat quietly together on the blanket for a while, just watching the sparkles on the water. I enjoyed the sensation of salt water drying on my body as it tightened on my skin. I did this medicinally when I had a bad poison ivy rash—which I got a lot. The salt drying on my skin soothed and squeezed the resin from the blisters. I could hear my skin sigh.

I took a deep breath . . . and a chance. I turned to Donna's mom. "Donna told me her father was killed in the war. I'm really sorry to hear that. It must have been just awful." I hesitated to intrude into another person's private life—and an adult's. But in the hesitation, I felt the gambit would be fine.

Her mom took my hand and then squeezed it gently. She smiled. Looking into my eyes, she said, "Thank you for saying that. You're very kind. Donna has been right about what she's said about you."

She sighed and looked out at the water. "It seems like it happened a long time ago. He died the same week Donna was born, and she's been his gift to me since then. But he wasn't actually 'killed in action.' Rather, the official explanation is that he remains 'missing in action' because his body was never found. He was a doctor in the Army and was operating in a hospital tent during a big battle, and the tent took a direct hit from a powerful shell, and nothing was ever found of anyone who had been in the tent. They vanished in the air. I've heard other war widows say it's worse to know someone is missing in action because it either holds out the false hope he'll be found alive someday or because it's too painful to think of someone you love getting evaporated in an instant—into a mist.

"The terrible news was awful when I heard it—and as sad as it is for me to think about him dying that way, I actually have come to feel at peace with the idea that he became a spirit without a body. Now he's with me in the air I breathe anytime I think of him. And I think of him whenever I look at his gift to me of my daughter—your friend Donna."

When she said this, I looked at her face quickly. I thought, *Her mother doesn't look like Donna at all. She's beautiful too, sure. But her skin is fair, not tan like Donna's. She doesn't have freckles. Her hair is short like Donna's, but blond, not brown. Her eyes are blue. She has a winning look when she smiles and bows and turns her head sideways when she talks—like she's being modest but clearheaded. She's not like Donna, who blurts out what she thinks. Perhaps because of what her mother said about Donna reminding her of her husband, he must live and breathe in his daughter. That's one of the things her mother loves Donna for.* "The spirit of a brave man?"

Both Donna and I got tears in our eyes. Her mother's eyes moistened when she looked at us.

Listening to the Ruffled Waters

1955

Build yourself an ark.
—Genesis 14:7

I stood on Second Street in front of a neighbor's yard on a cool early spring day. There was a for sale sign on a decrepit twelve-foot sailboat. Its paint flaked off at the touch of a fingernail; there was a nasty looking split in the hull; it had oar locks and oars that showed it had been cobbled out of a rowboat like Joe Dugan's home. Its centerboard trunk had been crudely cut into the bottom with the base smeared with caulking—a telltale sign it wasn't tight. A rudder had been dropped in the bottom of the hull, along with a boom and a canvas bag with a single sail—a cat rig. There was no mast.

I had begun to realize that my family wasn't going to go on any vacations again after the rainy, cold, gray week on Sheffield Island. I had to take matters into my own hands.

I bought the boat in exchange for mowing the lawn of the owner every week for that summer. I christened her *Flotsam*, a fitting name, as it looked like she had come ashore after a storm as a floating mess, probably filled with seaweed.

I walked and hauled her home by hand on my grandfather's trailer that was empty because his boat was at its mooring for the summer. I tried hard to make her look as good as she could; I sanded and caulked and painted. I admired the wiggle of light the brush strokes on the paint created with the sun.

With my father's help, I fashioned a spruce two-by-four as a mast. I launched *Flotsam* at Second Point (at the other end of Second Street from where Marvin School was). I figured out how to sail alone in the cove. Even after all the caulking, the sailboat leaked freely; I had to bail frequently. Once, I heard a loud popping sound and looked over to see water leaking through a new split in the hull. I sealed the crack with the bubble gum I was chewing—and the patch held out water from then on. *Flotsam* still leaked from the base of the centerboard trunk, however, and my bottom got wet sitting on the bottom.

I came up with the creative solution of screwing together a lattice of slats to sit on that kept my rear end above the water on the boat's bottom. The angles were tricky. There are no straight lines on a boat. By trial and error, I fitted four separate grids to fit on four sections of the curved boat bottom, each pane in the lattice different, none precisely square. But together they did the trick.

With the lattices installed, instead of needing to keep bailing out the leakage while I was sailing around in the cove, I could sit high and dry. Once the bilge water started to rise into the slats, I'd sail to the nearest shore. I'd step out, brace my feet, grab the gunnels, and tip the hull sideways so that all the water would pour out at once. A pleasing gush of water would pour over the gunnels and sizzle on the sandy shore.

Flotsam didn't weigh that much. This procedure would buy at least another hour's sailing time. I had to sail close to shore or to sandbars. My system was satisfactory. I enjoyed looking at the edge of the sea on the shore on one tack—as much as looking out at open water on the other tack.

After a few weeks of sailing almost every day, I mapped out a series of little islands, sandbars, peninsulas, and empty beaches that I would zig and zag between. I'd look around to see if there was any interesting driftwood to pick up. One piece that looked like an arrow I mounted as a weathervane on the garage roof back home. I found that by reading cloud patterns, checking a barometer I bought (it still sits on my desk after almost seventy years), knowing the tide charts, and which way the wind was blowing, I could predict the weather for any day's sail. If mackerel clouds built up in the slot in the sky between Long Island and the Connecticut shore to the southwest, starting to appear as wisps of white on the horizon, no matter how blue the sky was elsewhere, the clouds portended stormy weather. I'd sail before the wind turned ugly back to a mooring in the cove. I knew when to quit.

Mine was rudimentary homegrown meteorology. But I found most people with boats didn't do it. As a teenager, I had a job dispensing gasoline to large yachts that would pull up to a fueling dock at a marina. One customer, after swinging his arm at the blue sky, exclaimed. "What a beautiful day! The weather forecast says it's going to stay like this all weekend."

I responded matter-of-factly (you shouldn't usually second guess customers), "No, it's going to start raining at 2 p.m."

He replied with mock sternness, "That's not what my trusted weatherman promised."

"I'm sorry. It's going to rain at 2 pm."

Looking at me with a grin, the boatman asked, "Want to bet?" I looked him in the eye and said firmly, "Sure—five dollars." We shook on it. That was big money in those days—but I trusted my simple tools, and yacht owners always had the money. This time, without Donna around, I would get to keep it.

That evening we met on the dock. The boatman handed me five dollars. He said with amazement, "We were cruising along at noon without a cloud in the sky. I said to my wife, 'The kid was wrong.' Then she pointed out clouds starting to coming up out of the southwest. They gradually thickened. I looked at my watch. As soon as the hands read two o'clock, sprinkles started and then became a downpour. But don't tell me how you knew it. I want to think of you as some kind of magician."

I liked sailing by myself. There was never anyone around to laugh at what I had to do to keep a leaky boat afloat. I was the only spectator and was content to stay seated and dry.

For several years, until I needed to get that job at the marina to keep a car on the road, I had lots of times like this. I wasn't really good at land sports that required running after balls. I swam and fished and sailed and rowed. I often trailed a fishing line off the stern and trolled at sailing speed, sometimes catching porgies or snapper blues or bunkers. If there were no boats with engine noise, the sound of the wind and the water and the stretch of the sails and the slosh of the bilgewater sounded like one breath breathed.

I loved listening to the ruffled water of Long Island Sound sidling along the hull of *Flotsam* with a sigh, gulls almost always calling—it didn't matter whether to me, or to themselves, or just laughing about how much prey was swimming around just under the surface, as if served up on plates.

I daydreamed. Because of the softness of the water and wind sounds, and the lack of engine noise or human voices, I'd find floating into view images of my father and grandfather fishing at night at Tommy's Pants or Donna swimming in the cove off Second Point or sitting with my sister on the edge of the shore on Sheffield Island listening to the water slosh around the stones. Stringing these images together was giving them second thoughts—how did all of them, different moments, events, look when brought together in a second thought? Certainly, they all had in common my love of being on or in the water and sharing moments with people I loved who also loved the water. But, could these thoughts start talking to each other as part of a conversation about what the water had to do with love or why people who usually live in houses or walk around on the land were drawn to the sea? In the early pages of *Moby Dick*, Ishmael gives an image of a city dweller who finds himself walking down to the docks. With one arm hooked around a piling, he looks silently, motionless, agog at the sea. What could such a person be thinking?

There's something uncertain and melancholic about second thoughts. There's wondering about what really happened or what it really comes to mean—later on—consequent to your experience, your memory, and your ruminations. But of course, any questions about them that second thoughts might stir up, they at least bring your experiences back to life; deep pleasures.

The Sail to the Sandbar

1955

You will make a catch.
—John 21:6

I sailed by the country club beach at the beginning of the harbor and saw Donna in her brown bathing suit with the yellow polka dots sitting next to her mother on the beach. I sailed toward the beach and pulled up the centerboard and rudder to sail over the roped and buoyed square that marked the swimming area. As soon as I got inside the square, I saw a lifeguard get down from his chair and, with a stern look, point, shout, and start running. Even at a distance, I must have looked like one of the "unwashed" outsiders the ropes were meant to keep out, as much as to keep the member swimmers in.

"Uh oh."

But I saw Donna's mother get up, walk over, and talk to the lifeguard. He shook his head, then marched back to his chair, turning around with a dirty look. Did he give me the finger? After Donna's mom turned her back on the lifeguard, she and Donna walked to meet me with smiles as *Flotsam* touched shore.

I asked her mother earnestly, "Can I take Donna for a sail just out to the edge of the harbor? We both swim, I have an extra life jacket, and we won't sail out of sight. Just to that sandbar out there," I said, pointing. "I want to show Donna something."

Her mother smiled, nodded, and probably stared at *Flotsam* wondering if the proud but leaky sailboat would ever return.

"Okay," she said simply after a moment.

I explained to Donna the lattice system and how I could turn the boat on its side to pour out the leakage when we got to the sandbar. She didn't tease me about my leaky boat. She noticed I was trailing a fishing line off the stern of *Flotsam* and had a small bucket for fish. She asked, "Do you fish because your grandfather and father fish—like you said in your story?"

"Well, I certainly know about fishing because of them. But they never took me with them. They go out at night and use heavy split bamboo boat rods my grandfather makes and Monel lines that never break."

"What are those like? I never heard of Monel."

"It looks like regular braided line, but there's a steel thread running through it, so if they ever hook one, that's *it* for the bass. They sometimes fight the fish for an hour, just standing in the boat, pumping the rod until the fish surfaces. Then they stick it with a huge hook on a pole called a *gaff* and haul it to the hull, then hold it there to hit on the head with a club. Then they haul it into the boat with the gaff."

Squinting, Donna said, "That doesn't sound very sporting."

"I don't think they do it for fun. In fact, I'm not sure why they do it. They never eat them. They say they don't taste good. But my mother and sister and I ate a small one I caught last month, and we thought they were delicate and sweet. Instead, they sell them to a Japanese restaurant that we never go to."

Donna said brightly, "Maybe our moms could take the two of us there sometime."

I was a little embarrassed and confessed, "You know, I've never gone to a restaurant."

"Oh well," Donna said soothingly, "maybe we'll go to one together when we get older." (We would, once.)

"My grandfather is fierce about fishing. My bedroom window is on the second floor, over the back entryway. One morning I was awakened by him cursing—in Polish—and making loud thumping noises in the backyard under my window. I looked out to see him emptying a wheelbarrow full of huge fish. That night he had tucked into a huge, ravenous school of very large striped bass at Tommy's Pants. But he had to quit catching them after his arms grew numb fighting, clubbing, and pulling in four of them each over forty pounds. After he got back, he walked to our house for a wheelbarrow to haul back his catch. As he threw each carcass to the ground prior to cleaning them, he cursed his diminishing strength. He barely spoke English, and I knew only a few stock phrases in Polish. So, I could only imagine what he was saying to himself, thinking he was alone: 'In Poland, I was young, strong. I should have stayed that way. Damn a country that makes you old. I could have caught all the fish in the sea. Damn my age.'"

Donna gasped. "Wow, what a great story. Sometimes I think you live in a movie."

"Well, maybe. But I'm not sure what the movie is about. Gramps and I live at the back of the house, and we keep a door closed between our rooms. He lives like a monk. There's only a bed, a dresser, and a closet door that also opens onto a staircase that goes up to the attic. Gramps has a picture of Jesus on the wall and a photograph of his wife who died before I was born. And that's it. We never talk much. He never learned much English and, to my regret, won't teach me Polish. He tells me if I learn to speak Polish, I'll never go to college."

Donna giggled, "I don't mean any disrespect, but I don't think what your grandfather said makes sense."

"No, it really doesn't make sense," I agreed. "But you don't know my grandfather. He and my father have this other idea. They won't teach me to use hand tools. They're afraid if I learn, I'll wind up working in a factory like they do, and again, that I won't go to college. My father should know better. But he was raised in Brooklyn before my grandparents moved to East Norwalk. And he spoke only Polish even in this neighborhood—until he went to the first grade in the same school we go to now. So maybe their strange ideas come with the language. Anyway, when I decided to make the lattice to sit on in *Flotsam,* I secretly bought myself an electric drill and kept it hidden. This way I could drill the screw holes. I think they've both seen what I did, but neither of them said anything about it. So now I leave the drill right on their workbench in the basement."

Donna said with a sly smile, "So, you're not only handy with tools, but you're also a rebel. I'm impressed."

"It makes me really happy to hear you say that. But I do know one Polish phrase by heart. Evenings before dinner, my father takes a bottle of rye whiskey out of a cupboard and pours himself and Gramps a hefty shot of rye—half a tumbler each—no ice or water. They clink glasses, salute each other with *na zdrowie*—"to your health" in Polish—throw the whiskey down with one gulp, grip the back of their chairs against the hard knock of the alcohol to their stomachs and brains, expel air, soften their eyes, and sit down. 'Polish cocktail hour' my mom calls it. She's not Polish and just looks down at her plate."

Donna said, "Wow! I'd like to see that. Invite me to dinner some night."

"You wouldn't like it," I said, feeling a little embarrassed I'd said too much about my family life. I was sure hers was more elegant with her mother. "Gramps doesn't want us to talk at dinner. He came from Poland—and he starts almost every sentence by saying, 'I was born and brought up on the other side,' to explain what he has to say. I guess over there having a full meal was so rare it was almost a solemn rite. If we start talking about something, he growls, 'Shut up and eat.' He knows that much English. My father and grandfather eat meat and potatoes every meal, the potatoes mashed. My grandfather covers the mound with pepper until it turns black. From *Flotsam,* I troll for fish like snappers and bunkers, and sometimes go after eels and flounder bottom fishing, but only my sister and mother and I will eat them. I fish for the fun of it but really for something else to eat instead of meat on Fridays since we're Catholic."

"This is great stuff," Donna said enthusiastically. "You should write some of these stories down, just like you did with your vacation story."

"That's nice of you to say. But who would ever read them? Who wants to read about the way poor immigrant families act stupid at dinner?"

Donna said brightly, "Well, me for one. Tell me more about your grandfather."

"Even if I don't fish like my grandfather, I like the way he does it because it seems to me Gramps fished the way he *was*. He fished his stubborn, bullheaded character. Other people fish differently because they're different. Every summer there's a tournament for flounder fishing. There are tons of them spawning and grubbing in the shallow water mud flats in Norwalk Harbor. Boatloads of men compete. A real circus. The winner will catch sixty fish. They drink beer. Every year there's a piece in the paper about one of them being hospitalized for severe sunburn. They'll fish all day in the sun, some just wearing jock straps."

Donna laughed. "Yes, I've read about that too. My mother, who works in the hospital, tells me—maybe it's just a joke—that they start preparing special burn beds for those fishermen guys the day the tournament starts."

"I've sailed among the boats fishing in the tournament once, and although I found it funny to watch them whoop it up and fall down and laugh, I thought it was pretty stupid. However, what I found, thinking about this, is that I could ask myself, *why do I fish the way I do?* If I think about that, do I find out who I am or who I think I want to be? Not to say my way is better than any other. Well, no, I really think my way is better. But what's useful for me is to go a step further in thinking about it. Those guys do seem to be having a lot of fun for themselves. What's wrong with that? But then—if I decide that's not for me—I can ask *well, why not? Who do you think you are?* I'm not sure yet. But I'm working on it. The nuns in catechism class are always warning us not to look down on people who are different from us. Does any of this make sense? What I'm trying to say is, however odd or silly you think the other kind of fishing is, you know your own way of fishing as a second thought you can ponder."

Donna said, "That sounds useful. Keep working on the idea. The nuns are right of course. What they say is part of why I like you. But you'd better not ever invite me to go fishing with you in that tournament."

"I promise," I said. "And besides, we're both still too young to drink beer. And unlike my grandfather and father, I keep what I catch to eat with my sister and mother on Fridays when we can't eat meat because, like I said, we're Catholics. My father and grandfather eat the quahogs my grandfather digs on another island. There's always a wet net bag of them in the refrigerator. Quahogs give me a stomachache."

Donna said, "I can see why you like to get out of the house a lot. On the other hand, there certainly is a lot of stuff going on inside."

Just at this moment, my pole bent over. I grabbed it with both hands and pushed the tiller over with my elbow to point *Flotsam* into the wind to stop. A sail makes a sound like slapping clothes drying on a rope when a boat points directly into the wind. You really don't need any skill fighting a mackerel. You just reel them in. When it got close enough to the boat, I could see it was a pretty good size.

As I put the fish into the bucket, Donna said, "It's impressive that you can manage to sail and fish at the same time. In fact, I think it's impressive you can sail. I can't figure out what you're doing pulling on these ropes and changing the side of the boat the sail hangs over."

"I'm not sure myself how it all works. I taught myself how to sail puttering around in the cove for a few days until I found how to get the boat to go in different directions depending on how the wind was blowing. I got a book on sailing from the library and found out the words for the different ropes—you call them *lines* on a boat. And the difference between a *tack,* when you zigzag because you want to go directly in the direction where the wind is coming from, so you have to do it by angles, or a *run,* where you just hang the sail over the side and have the wind blow and push you along from behind.

"My favorite is a *reach,* where you have the wind hit the boat sideways, and you just hold on to the sheet line that's attached to the boom and sail the fastest the boat can go. I mostly go on reaches, since *Flotsam* leaks and has to be bailed out on shore. I rarely really get anywhere in particular. I sail just to see what's happening with the wind and the water and what fish are in the harbor and what the gulls are doing. What's great is you usually can only hear one sound wind makes with water."

Donna said, "I like that idea of just sailing where the wind takes you instead of trying to get anywhere. Now that I think of it, most motorboats go straight."

"That's right. They get where they're going too fast. And all the people on board can hear is the motor. If you just sail around in the same big circle, you get to see the different things that are going on as the season is always changing. A few weeks ago, the day was perfect for my kind of sailing, with a strong wind out of the south and no hint of bad weather. And so, I sailed on a reach for the first time out beyond the Norwalk Islands—my first time out beyond the edge of the open waters of Long Island Sound. Then wow! I saw a magical thing—*I think*. A whale's fluke came up straight out of the water at the end of a long, almost funny-looking thin pole of a tail. I gasped. That's all I saw. It was over in a split second. It was so amazing I wondered if I had really seen it—since just a few minutes before that I was thinking to myself, *Someday* I'd like to see a whale out here. And then, bang! Poof! There was this tail. And it disappeared so fast I couldn't be sure I had really seen it, or my mind just filled in the blank of what I was thinking about with a picture of it."

Donna paused for a moment. "Two things I'll say to that: One, if I have a vote in the matter, I vote to say you saw the whale. Why not? There was no one else around to tell you hadn't seen it for real, right? Two, let's not go out that far today. This is my first time sailing."

"No problem. The wind's not right for doing that today anyway." But then I gasped, "We don't have to—if you want to see something cool—look at that!" I pointed to a large patch of rippling water. "A school of mackerel is in, and the bluefish are having at them!"

Donna was puzzled. "All I see are those gulls diving down into that big circle. They're crying out, and the water's boiling like it's being heated up. What's going on?"

"Now is the time in the summer the mackerel come into the Sound in huge schools; voracious bluefish like wolf packs follow after them. You know where they are first because you see the gulls from everywhere coming together into a frantic bunch diving down. Watch closely! You'll see the gulls never come up with a whole fish—they grab gobs of mackerel the big fish are chopping up as they feed. The blues herd the bait fish against the shore sometimes to pack them up. But when they catch their prey out here in the open, they bunch them up against the ceiling of the air and have at them with great sweeping silver swoops. I saw this twice last week."

Donna gave a wicked laugh. "These fish have dinner like your family does. Just shoveling it in. Whoops, I'm sorry, that wasn't very polite to say."

"That's okay. There's something to what you say. Maybe that's where we learned how to do it. But you described the way the fish feed perfectly. The water froths like it's boiling in a pan. The gulls make a racket diving into the foam. And it's funny. You never see the fish. Everything's going on beneath the surface. And like I said, you only see hunks of flesh in the seagulls' beaks because that's all they can carry, and they let the blue fish do the cutting for them."

I kept pointing *Flotsam* into the wind for the sails to luff. We both watched the slaughter in the sea going on without saying anything and without hearing any cries of anguish from the fish—just a jagged exaltation of gulls.

After maybe ten minutes, with a sly wink, her head bent down, and a smile, Donna asked, "Do you think bluefish are Catholics?"

"Well, I have heard that people sometimes call Catholics 'mackerel slappers.'"

Donna laughed, "I think the term is mackerel *snappers*."

After we had said that, we each took a breath at the audacity of what had been said. We laughed. I shook a finger. "You're wicked witty."

"You're a pretty good sport," Donna retorted.

We watched the ruckus for a while. The mackerel slaughter was the same as the oyster shell-rat-cat-crab cycle in the cove. Donna wouldn't have minded if I had told her about it on the day we went swimming at Second Point.

Then with the tiller, I pushed the bow of the boat off the wind and filled the sail for a reach. "Well, that's enough excitement for today. As it turns out, I do have a place in mind to go, and am happy to see I could get there on one reach right from the country club until—here!"

Flotsam scraped her bottom on the edge of a sandbar just breaking the surface about a half mile offshore. What I wanted to show Donna is what you could see standing on the sandbar just above water at low tide.

"Look, over there," I cried, pointing to a nearby island with men on it, playing basketball on an outdoor court, dribbling and passing back and forth between baskets. They were wearing white T-shirts. All wore black shorts and black Keds sneakers. "Those are Jesuit priests! Look. They're playing basketball!

"This sandbar is the exposed end of an underwater shoal that's attached to what's called Manresa Island. My father told me about these men. During the summer, members of the Society of Jesus from New York City to Boston come to Manresa for *villa*, as they called their vacation. My father met some of them having a picnic once on Sheffield Island—you remember, the place where my family had its one vacation so far. Isn't this fascinating to see this? Priests playing basketball? It's like nuns wearing swimsuits. I never knew priests could do this. The priests in our parish just walk around outside reading from a black book, wearing a long black cassock that reaches to their black shoes. They have bellies. These Jesuits have muscles. I wanted to show you this because of what we've said to each other about different kinds of vacations. Before I saw this, I never would have thought about any people having this kind of vacation. Maybe only Jesuits do. They do two kinds of vacations at once. They move from one house to another Jesuit house and then take it easy playing around the second house."

It seemed a long time before Donna said anything. I thought she was looking too. The men at this distance looked almost all the same. None were fat or too tall. Both teams dressed the same in white and black, so the players must have known who each other was. They played hard. One got knocked down. And another, hard to say whether a teammate or not, pulled him up and both started running right away.

I could see different hair colors: blond, black, and brown. There was one Black player. I had never seen a sports game with the players stripped down to sameness so all you noticed was the game they played.

Finally—and because of the sharpness of her tone, it must have been almost immediately in real time—Donna spoke.

"But," Donna cried, "forget about the Jesuits for a minute. Look at this! What about this? All these brown horseshoe crabs swimming about in the low water?"

She pointed to dozens and dozens of paired crabs—the smaller males, she explained—hanging on to the big brown shells of the females—as they maneuvered around to get traction in the sand for mating with each other. Their spiny shells looked like tiny shark fins breaking the surface. I knew about horseshoe crabs, too, but had never seen so many at once.

Donna exclaimed, "It looks just like the beaches in Puerto Rico at Christmas, with couples hanging on to each other all over the place. And what's nice is the crabs are having sex while those Jesuits over there aren't supposed to have any. They play basketball instead. And watch this!" Donna picked up a large female by the tail and flipped her over so the crab's feet and claws were writhing like a huge spider on its back, into which Donna laced her own fingers.

"Don't do that!" I said in horror.

"Don't be silly; they can't hurt you." She saw me flinch. She grabbed my hand and pressed it down into the writhing feet and claws. She held mine there with her own hand. Once I got used to it, it was like a silly way of shaking hands—like when one person's fingers tickle the other person's palm.

"You have no fear of creepy things," I said admiringly.

We improvised a race. We drew a large circle in the sand, and each put a crab into the center. The winner would be the first one to crawl out of the circle to get back into the water. We got into the water and swam with the mating crabs. I pretended to be a male crab and hung on to Donna's big feet while she swam. "Watch it," she warned, turning around and giving me a cross look, "we're not even going steady." (Several years later, Donna summed up our eurekas on the sandbar. "It's clear that after our sail I went with the horseshoe crabs, and you went with the Jesuits.")

Afterward, we sat on the sandbar next to each other as the tide rose and the sandbar grew smaller, and horseshoe crabs kept milling around a little farther away from our spot.

"We should be getting back to your mother. The wind starts to die down later in the afternoon, and we want to ride a nice reach back."

"Okay," she agreed readily. "But let's take a horseshoe crab back to show her. She likes them a lot. And she's the one who taught me how to shake hands with them."

After we pushed *Flotsam* back into the water and got back inside, Donna lifted a lattice loose so the crab could stay wet in the leakage water on the way back.

After we sailed a quarter mile offshore, we saw a speedboat bearing down straight toward us. I tried to turn *Flotsam* away, but the other boat just changed course and kept coming at us. I had already learned a trick about sailing or boating. If you saw another boat heading your way and lined it up with something on your own boat, like a cleat or a shroud, and the boat stayed right in line with it, that meant you were both on a collision course indeed, as we were. Although this boat, when it drew alongside, stopped short with a surge of wake off the bow that rocked *Flotsam*.

I cried, "It's Dwayne!"

Donna knew him from the country club and said with disgust, as the roar of the speedboat died down, "That creep! He'd push you off your bike if he was riding nearby. He never stops to talk. He's the neighborhood bully and is conceited because his father is a dentist. You watch," she said grimly, "he's going to do something mean."

Sure enough, after he'd pulled up short, he revved his engine and started running circles about *Flotsam* so she jostled in the wake and knocked us from side to side inside.

"Dwayne! Stop it. That's stupid. We could capsize!"

When Dwayne heard my voice, he squinted as he looked into *Flotsam*. He recognized both of us. He pulled his lips into a sneer and, pointing in disgust, yelled at Donna, "What are you doing out here with him?"

Before I could say anything, Donna grabbed the horseshoe crab by the tail and, standing up and holding onto the mast with one hand for balance, she threw the crab perfectly into Dwayne's boat so it fell into the seat right beside him, upside down, with its feet writhing like a spider on its back. Dwayne was terrified. He slowed down and came over and begged her to take the crab out of his boat.

Donna did and snorted, "You creep. If you ever do anything like that to me again, I'll tell your father."

I was breathless with admiration for what Donna had just done. With my arm resting on the tiller, keeping the boat pointing motionless into the wind, it was as if I were a spectator at a game or a play, watching the scene that was happening too fast to be able to think about it.

"Look at this! The shell of the crab isn't cracked! You got it to drop onto the upholstery of the seat next to where Dwayne was sitting. He was sure it was going to bite him. How did you manage that? Do you toss crabs a lot?"

Donna replied, "Don't be silly." Then, still breathless from her feat, she said, "You've got to be lucky to be graceful when you're doing something righteous."

On the sail back to the country club, we didn't say much. I was not sure what was on Donna's mind. I was associating again: the Jesuits playing vigorous basketball silently—at least at the distance from the sandbar to the basketball court—the crabs swimming silently, the swishing sounds against the small hull of *Flotsam*, gulls again; Donna just looking out at the water with the sun sparkle on the surface casting reflections on her freckles that made them seem to shimmer on her pretty face. All these images blended together—perhaps—just for the pleasures of what I felt sampling the images without the need to understand any of it.

Unexpectedly, my daydreaming broke with a jolt. Why this assault on my and Donna's serenity? Dwayne appearing out of nowhere with the wish to cause anger and pain to someone else? Was this just because Donna and I were in a homemade sailboat at the mercy of the powerful engine of his expensive speedboat? Why would anyone want to ruin the pleasures of another person? Certainly, Donna's family, like Dwayne's, was richer than mine—but there she sat, silently smiling, running a hand in the water past the hull of *Flotsam*, and just as content being there with a kid like me as I was with a kid like her. More than that. She was telling me something about myself: that I meant more to her living near Second Street than Dwayne did living near her on Pine Ridge Road.

What happened at that moment laid down slats of the lattice of the rest of my life. It was the first time I watched *myself* having second thoughts. Dwayne squatting in his boat, his head ducking down. Donna standing, holding the mast, tossing the horseshoe crab. Me just sitting in the boat, with my arm on the tiller as an astonished spectator to the scene. It was as if I stood miraculously on the water outside and watched myself thinking.

Now a rush of other thoughts tumbled out. I understood why I had cried on that fateful day in the third grade. It was the first time I realized I was poor—my family was too poor to take vacations. But what was worse was that apparently everybody else in the third grade was rich enough to take vacations. But another thought immediately tumbled in behind after that one. Dwayne drove a much finer and more powerful boat than *Flotsam* because he was rich like the other kids in the class must have been. And in his mind, when he saw me in *Flotsam* and recognized the difference, he did something mean about it to show me how much better off he was than me. That explained that. But there was more. Another thought tumbled out. But Donna, when she had asked me about my crying in the third grade and heard from me why I thought I had cried, she, whose parent was a doctor, and who lived on Pine Ridge Road like Dwayne, had spoken nicely to me to make me feel better. She didn't think me ruined or a second-class person. I realized that despite my outburst in class and my anger in *Flotsam*, if we were poor, maybe it didn't matter much—at least to people like Donna and her mother, who liked my mother. Even though I was thinking these thoughts to myself, I felt excited and a little stressed.

Now something happened that took all the images I'd just shuffled together and put them up against *another* image.

At just this moment, a small school of porpoises surfaced on both sides of *Flotsam* and for a moment kept pace as if they thought she was one of them. I pulled in my troll. Porpoises hunt snapper blues too. I wouldn't steal their food—or worse—hook a porpoise who'd grabbed a blue I'd hooked. No Dwayne-like assault on their serenity from me. Or from *Flotsam*. Unlike Dwayne's speedboat, she had no growling propeller.

I always treasured their appearance in the harbor. Every time, the abrupt emergence of their shark-like fins on the surface would frighten me for a moment until I'd recognize they were porpoises. Their smooth, synchronized rolling just under and just over the surface, as if dissolving in and out through a mirror, showed they loved doing together whatever they were doing. Either for migration or feeding or whatever—maybe for the sheer exuberance of it. It was infectious joy.

"Oh wow!" Donna cried. "Listen to them breathe!"

As each shining black back broke the surface, we could see the blow-holes on the back of their heads expand and blow sprays of water with an explosive exhalation of breath. The drops hit our faces. We both breathed back at them, making the same sound. And then, in a twinkling, the porpoises were gone. Either they had surfaced just to say a brief hello or were startled to see us and dropped out of sight. Either way it was a friendly gesture.

Immediately after they disappeared under the surface, they rose again in my memory, now juxtaposed to another memory less than an hour old: Dwayne running at us, then around us, rocking our boat out of spite. The porpoises running alongside us, mingling their wakes with ours, sharing bliss and meaning and movement even if just for an instant.

The porpoises dissolved any funk. And then and there, I added porpoises to the string of images—now Donna and horseshoe crabs and Jesuits and porpoises and the whole nine yards between then and now. Altogether, these events came in rapid fire. I gazed at them—dazed—taking them in visually, mesmerized as if at the movies. No stopping for a freeze-frame assessment—me, a seated spectator to what kept moving by.

I had achieved kid nirvana. I would never experience happiness *this* deep. It could not be any deeper.

It helped to brighten even this high mood that Donna's mom was walking down to meet us with a big smile as we approached the beach at the county club. Once again, I pulled up *Flotsam*'s centerboard and rudder to slide over the rope around the swimming section.

I took a quick look at the lifeguard, who didn't move off his chair this time. Although even at a distance I could see him scowl. Another finger? What could he do when one of the members of the club was obviously happy to see us coming?

"What's this?" was the first thing she said, pointing at the horseshoe crab Donna was picking up by the tail while I was pulling up the gunnels to dump out *Flotsam*'s bilge water that the crab no longer needed to stay wet in. "I know it's a horseshoe crab, of course. But why did you bring it back? Is it for me? As a souvenir of your cruise?"

"That's right. But you can't keep it. I wanted you to be the one to let it go back in the water as an honor the brave crab has earned." Then she told her mother about our encounter with Dwayne on the open seas, and how she and the crab, working together, had managed to fend off his attack.

"That Dwayne. He's always been bad news from the moment I had to help deliver him trying to come out feetfirst. At the time, I thought he wanted to kick the doctor."

I broke in, "You should have seen it. Donna's throw landed in

Dwayne's running boat perfectly. It was the most beautiful, athletic feat I've ever seen."

Her mother changed the subject. "From what I could see as you were both heading back here, it looked like for a while you were sailing in a school of porpoises. Is that right? That must have been much more fun than running into Dwayne."

Donna exclaimed enthusiastically, "Yes, that's exactly what happened! It was magical. They were breathing out their blowholes right next to us, so sometimes we could even feel the spray hitting us. And we also saw the water all roiled up where gulls and bluefish were in a feeding frenzy with mackerel, although we never saw the fish. And the sandbar was covered with horseshoe crabs, couples swimming around to start mating with each other—like this one was until we brought it back with us to show to you."

Donna's mother noted with a smile, "My *my*! All this going on in what looks from here like a calm day on the Sound. Who knew?"

I added, "We also watched Jesuit priests playing basketball on Manresa Island, which you could see from where we were standing on the sandbar. That's actually what I took Donna to see, since we talk sometimes about different kinds of vacations people take and I thought this was an interesting one. Although so far, we haven't said much about it to each other. She was more interested in the horseshoe crabs."

Donna's mother repeated herself, "My, my! What do you know? Even Jesuits are out there having a good time. You certainly picked a good day to go exploring. Let's get some ice cream cones and we can sit on the blanket while you tell me more about all of this."

"I would really love to do that. But right now, I have to sail back up the cove, otherwise my boat will have a hard time sailing against an ebbing tide. With the wind letting up now, you might see me sailing like I'm making headway, when I'm really just stuck staying put over one spot on the bottom while the ebb tide rushes by."

We said goodbye to each other several times while I pushed off and sailed for home.

You had to Listen

1955

Train up a child the way he should be...
—Proverbs 22:6

I stood close to my mother at the sink while she was shelling peas after I got home from the sail with Donna. I started nervously tapping on the pedal that made the top on the kitchen waste garbage can go up and down.

"Stop that," she said sharply, annoyed by the clunking. When she was really mad, she'd growl, "If you don't stop that, I'll break your arm off and beat you over the head with the bloody stump!"

The first time I heard her say that, I was a little stunned, not because I thought she'd do it, but because I'd never heard anybody say anything like that. I got used to it. All it meant was that she really meant what she was saying.

As we both calmed down, I told her about Dwayne and the lifeguard.

"Do people not like us because we're poor? They can't stand having us around? They think if they ever got close to us, we'd smell bad?"

"Just forget about stuff like that," she said sharply. This time she didn't say anything about breaking off my arm. She looked me straight in the eye with the cool look she used when she was serious. You had to listen.

"There are always people like that, and they're just assholes who are mad because they can't figure out how to stop being assholes—but other people like us can. We're not poor. We have plenty to eat and a good roof on the house that your father makes sure stays painted. You just had a nice boat ride with your friend Donna, right? What could be better than that? The next time you meet someone like those guys, say to yourself—like it's a prayer—'Hey, here's another asshole, and thank you, God, I am not.' And if you really think it will help—say the prayer out loud so that the asshole can hear it."

"Thanks, Mom," I replied. "You always know the right thing to say to make a guy feel good."

"That's what mothers are for," she said as she kissed the top of my head.

Later at dinner, the family silently passed around a bowl of peas (Gramp's orders). I thought, *This kind of stuff gets to her more than she admits*. I remembered a time we were in the supermarket together. She must have felt slighted by something a very expensively dressed shopper had said or did. The lady was wearing a mink coat that reached to the floor. Accidently, my mother rammed into her from behind with the shopping cart, then overly effusive, overly dramatic, apologized. Then she had turned and whispered to me, "Asshole."

Another time, we were in a fabric store. My mother was a great seamstress and made a lot of the clothes that she, my sister, and I wore. The year before she had taken a night course on sewing. For the final exam, she was supposed to appear in a fashion show before the class wearing a dress she had sewed. She'd gone over the top. She took my sister and me with her on stage. Everything all three of us wore—except for socks and shoes—she had made by hand herself. Needless to say, she had swept the field and won first prize. My mother took sewing and fabric seriously. So, it was not surprising that when we were in the fabric store this time, she grabbed a whole roll of some fabric she wanted that was leaning against a wall and slung it over her shoulder like she was carrying a log. Once again, in some way I hadn't noticed, she must have felt slighted by some other customer. Like a clown act in the circus, she swung the fabric roll around and hit the woman in the side of the head. Immediately the store manager yelled at my mother, "Get out of here. I told you, never come back to my store." That must have meant that my mother had done something like that before!

My mother had to be bothered by people who thought they were superior to her more than she was willing to admit. After dinner, while I was standing next to her drying the dishes she washed, I brought up the subject again. We spoke in whispers while my father and grandfather were shouting at each other angrily in Polish in the next room.

"Okay, if we're just as good and rich enough like other people, how come we've only ever taken one vacation? People like Donna and her mother take one every year, and everybody else at school seems to take at least one. You never take me anywhere. Are you ashamed of me too?"

My mother looked at me sharply, like she was about to start in with her mantra about breaking off my arm. Instead, she said in her best imitation of a New York City street accent, "Yeah, you wanna vacation? I give-a you vacation."

The very next weekend, we took the bus that stopped on our block at Cove Avenue on Second Street and rode to the South Norwalk train station that took thousands of commuters, usually dressed in nice suits and hats, into Manhattan every day of the week. The cars were almost empty on this Saturday.

"Because those fancy businessmen are sleeping off their hangovers," my mother spat.

I had been to the station only once before, sitting on my father's shoulders. It was during the presidential election of 1952.

Both candidates had made a whistle stop at the South Norwalk Train Station. I remembered seeing General Eisenhower holding his homburg hat in his hand, standing on the platform at the end of a train giving a speech about why he wanted to be elected president. I didn't remember seeing Adlai Stevenson give his speech. But I did remember being the only kid in school who didn't wear an *I Like Ike* button, because everybody in my family said to never vote Republican.

We rode the train to Grand Central Station that was remarkably just forty minutes away.

"Look at all the junk," I said. It was amazing to see how trashy the back side of fancy Connecticut commuter towns like Darien, New Canaan, and Greenwich looked along the tracks.

"Everybody shits once a day," my mother said.

The train slowed down as it traveled alongside the tenement buildings in the upper Bronx, where I could see sad-looking people looking out the windows. When the train hesitated once, I looked right into rooms with broken furniture and bare lightbulbs hanging over tables with the dishes left over from breakfast. I nudged my mother and pointed wordlessly.

"Now those people are poor," she said. "I used to live in a building like that—as you'll see."

First, she took me to the top of the Empire State Building. I was amazed.

"Mom," I cried, "you can hear city traffic almost a mile above the streets!"

"Cities," she said, scowling with disgust, "never stop to take a breath."

Then we walked all the way downtown. We bought sandwiches and Cokes and sat on a bench in Battery Park. She smoked a cigarette. I didn't cough in the open air like I sometimes did at home when both mother and father smoked at the same time. Nobody gave a thought to what smoking might be doing to my asthma. Or to my father's, who eventually lost a lung to it. Once, when I was two years old, an asthma attack from secondary smoke almost killed me and I was rushed to the hospital.

We looked at big cargo ships in New York Harbor. I tried to imagine what one of them would look like moored among the little boats in the cove back home. There was a bigger world out there than would fit into the one I lived in.

Then we took the subway uptown to Harlem, where I saw something I couldn't wait to tell Donna about.

Who Could Ever Forget You?

1955

Today is a special day for me.
—Esther 5:4

I stood next to Donna a few weeks later during recess on the playground. We hadn't seen each other since the sail to the sandbar. "You look great," each exclaimed to the other simultaneously, and then also simultaneously, "I'm very happy to see you again." Both of us giggled.

Donna asked with a wink, "Well, it's time to ask again: did you sneak in another vacation this summer?"

I replied promptly, "Yes, I did. And I want to tell you about it. But, girls first." I continued in a mock-formal voice like a teacher at the head of a classroom. "What did you do on *your* summer vacation?"

"My mother and I went to the Adirondacks again, where it's funny when you swim because there's no salt in the water, and you sink deeper down, and your arms and legs feel heavier. Even you might even be able to beat me in a race in fresh water. Now tell me about your vacation, because I don't think the teacher will ask us to write about it anymore."

"Let's hope," I agreed. "But actually, I would be happy to write about mine. My mother and I had a great day by ourselves in New York City. We took the train. We went to the top of the Empire State Building and then walked all the way downtown. We ate sandwiches sitting on a bench in Battery Park. The highlight of the trip was what happened next. I think it was what my mother had really taken me to see. We went up to Harlem. We took the subway up 8th Avenue to 125th Street. 'Much cheaper than a cab and faster than a bus,' my mother said emphatically, 'and it's where you see what city people really look like.' It was amazing. Everyone just stared like they were looking far away but not seeing anything. Some had suits. Some looked like they just got out of bed still wearing pajamas. 'Don't look,' my mother warned sharply when she caught me staring. 'Somebody will punch you.' It occurred to me when she said it that although she looks good-natured on the outside, she is always primed for a fight."

Donna chimed in. "I probably shouldn't tell you this. But that's what my mom says about your mom. 'She's a fighter,' she says, 'and that's why I like her.'"

"I don't need to tell you this either, but I think your mom's pretty sharp."

I took a breath. "Then we came up the stairs out of the subway station in Harlem. It was like we were emerging from a cave into a completely different world—certainly from the other places in the city we'd seen, but it was like no place I'd ever seen. Just about everybody you could see was Black and well-dressed—women wearing dresses and hats with flowers and men in suits and fedoras. They were talking and laughing with each other and didn't seem to notice we were the only White people on the street. A lot of the stores had neon lights turned on, even though it was daylight—advertising 'shoes' or 'drugs' or 'here's the place.'

"My mother took me by the hand and led me off the avenue to a side street. We walked past an old Black man sitting on a stoop wearing a Yankees cap and Keds sneakers like yours, and he didn't look up at us. He was staring blankly, like the people on the subway. My mother pointed up to a second-story, fire escape landing and told me, 'When I was a little girl, four years old, I was playing up there and I fell over the railing down to the sidewalk where we're standing right now. I could hear people shouting and running over to see me, but I just got up and ran off as if nothing had happened. I was actually afraid people would be mad at me.' As she finished telling me her incredible story, the old man who had been listening to her jumped up and cried, 'Little Loraine! Is that you?'

"And she turned and said to him with surprise, 'Do you remember me?'

"He cried out happily, 'Who could ever forget you?' They started hugging and laughing and talking about the people in the neighborhood they once knew. She introduced me to him, and he said, 'What a fine-looking boy. I hope he's a fighter like you.' And she said, 'I'm working on it.' I stood by my mother, smiled, and shook his hand."

Donna exclaimed, "Ah-ha! There it is again. 'Fighter' is the same word I've heard my mother say about your mother too. It's like that saying, 'Great minds think alike.' I'm not sure about whether the same word goes with you yet. But we've really just become friends. I've yet to see you in combat."

"So anyway, after that, we took the train back to Norwalk, and we didn't even have to go back to Grand Central. There's a train station in Harlem at 125th Street too. So how about that, my dear friend? Did I have a vacation like you?"

"Your vacations are never like mine," she said matter-of-factly. "Or like anyone else's I know. You leave home for worlds few people know exist. You must find it strange coming home afterward."

"I can't take credit for this one. I'm just my mother's son."

My mother Lorraine *was* a fighter to the end. Years later, after I had left the Jesuits and married, my sister Jill and I visited our mother just before she died in hospice care in Connecticut. A nurse took me to her bed. I watched her sleep.

The nurse spoke softly. "Wake up. You have guests here to see you."

Our mother smiled without lifting her head from the pillow. We had just finished whispering hellos when nurses walked into the large open room. There were perhaps a dozen hospital beds, each surrounded by a rack of curtains, most of which were partially open so you could see in, and wave at other patients who sometimes waved back. A nurse pushed our mother's curtains aside, grabbed hold of the front of the bed, which was on wheels, and ordered, "Come with us—there's going to be a concert."

We followed our mother's bed into another large room, where it was positioned in a row with others in front of three music stands. Three musicians from the Yale School of Music stood nearby, holding their instruments. They smiled and graciously introduced each piece before playing, telling the patients what to listen for. What was astonishing was that during the concert, a patient would shout out some demented words or another would retch loudly as a nurse ran over to put a basin under her chin and start to clean her up. The elegant musicians continued their bowing and expressive swaying as if they were entertaining in a formal setting.

Afterward, Jill and I stood around her bed again.

"I'm really not as sick as all the other people in here." She pointed to a nearby bed. "This one's got dementia, and that one over there has bad cancer. I think they're going to send me home in a few days. I'm just here for a rest." Then she turned to me and said, "When I do finally croak, I want to be cremated, and for you to bury my ashes in your back pasture by a stone under a tree, and I want a plaque on the stone that says: *When the wind is in the trees, I wave in the leaves.*"

"I will do that, Mom," I said quietly, sadly, "but that's not going to be for a long time."

Afterward, we asked the nurse questions about our mother's condition. As my sister and I listened about how dire it was, we would start—then stop crying. It was astonishing. The moment one of us would start, the nurse would start crying too and continue to cry while she continued answering questions matter-of-factly. Then she'd stop crying the moment we stopped. Her deep human empathy and her professional demeanor remained in perfect balance.

The nurse called me later that evening. My mother had died,

apparently, before anyone else in her ward. At her funeral I told the story about her winning the sewing class fashion show when she, Jill, and I each wore the clothes she'd made. When I mentioned the wonderful pies she made for family get-togethers, there were sighs of pleasure rippling through the room. I finished the eulogy with the story of meeting the old Black man in Harlem and concluded by quoting his words to her: "Who could ever forget you?"

I interred mother's ashes under an apple tree in my back pasture, her poem on a plaque on a nearby rock. And years later, at her request, I buried my sister's ashes next to our mother's. I attached a new plaque to a rock between a hickory and an apple tree, this time with both their names and dates and a change in the epitaph from a singular to a plural pronoun.

When the wind's in the trees,
We wave in the leaves.

I Saw His Ship Go Down

1955–1958

You shall be the father.
—Genesis 17:5

I stood looking down at my father, sleeping off his evening drinks, sitting in a chair with his mouth open. My mother and I had just gotten back from the visit to New York City. She looked at her husband, shook her head, and went right to bed.

I never asked my father why he never even took weekends off like my mother would. If he ever went out on Long Island Sound, he was either fishing alone at night or working as a licensed captain on a charter boat. When he was at home in the evenings, he usually sat quietly in an alcoholic stupor. He had been in the Merchant Service during the war and saw ships in his convoy blow up and sink near him. I only heard him speak about that once, when he told me why we always went on Christmas Day to visit an old couple who had emigrated from Poland with his grandfather. There were always wonderful Polish pastries to eat. On the way home one time my father told me, "My only friend as a kid was their son. I saw his ship go down. A U-boat got it. I never stop seeing that image of fire in my head. He was inside."

One time, when he was drunk and asleep in his chair, I said, "Dad . . . ?" He woke up, started to cry, and said, "Your mother never lets me make love to her." I was stunned and until now never told anyone else about what he'd said.

We never talked much, partly because he thought Polish fathers should be stern and partly because he had a bizarre conviction that the only way to afford college would be by playing accordion in a Polish polka band. He forced me to take lessons for seven years and insisted I practice one hour a day. I found practice agonizing, especially if I could hear kids playing outside or birds singing. I did try. I was never any good. I could not reach the level of skill at which point, for genuine musicians, music becomes a pleasure and a passion. In my father's estimation, I just didn't try hard enough, so for punishment he rarely spoke to me. The only project we ever worked on together was when he helped me bring *Flotsam* back from the dead. I did get from that daily accordion practice hour, I think, the stamina later in the Jesuits to sit kneeling at prayer for an hour in the morning when I really didn't feel like it. Or later, when I was writing a dissertation in graduate school, how to force myself over to my desk every day to keep writing. Or as a teacher, sitting before a stack of student papers to read.

In my elementary school years, 1949–1958, most of the veteran fathers in the neighborhood were weird in their own ways. This was my father's way of being sullen, maybe because he thought his friend should have survived, not him.

My father's love for his automobile was different. The only time I saw Father excited was when he took the car out for a spin. The family drove a fancy-looking gold Plymouth Fury with high tail fins. He'd drive around until he got to be first in a row at a traffic light. He'd be looking for some teenagers in a car in the next lane over. He'd challenge the other driver with a two-finger wave, which was taken as a challenge to a drag race. When the light turned green, he'd slam the accelerator and have a fiendish-sounding laugh if he managed to beat the other car off the mark, which he almost always did. He took me with him a few times. It was terrifying to hear the tires squeal and feel the back end shimmy. The car made a roar like Dwayne's speedboat. The car would lay a scratch of rubber, the other car eating its dust.

When he was home, my father frequently walked across the street to a bar on one corner of First Street and a liquor store on the corner of Second. Once, he fell into step with an old Black man who was walking down Cove Avenue to the segregated Third Street. My father heard him cough.

"Asthma," the man said when my father looked at him quizzically.

"Wait right here," my father told him. He crossed the street and went into our house. He came out with a plug-in air filter he had in his and my mother's bedroom. It hadn't worked for him. Maybe because he never stopped smoking.

"Here," he said to the Black man, thrusting the machine into his arms and curling up the hanging electrical cord to pile on top. "Take it. It'll clear the air."

The man said nothing, shocked by the gift as much as by a friendly encounter with a White man in his neighborhood. My father waved to me as I waited across the street, standing over my bicycle.

Another time my father passed in front of the house directly across the street from ours. A Jewish family from Holland lived there. Rumors said they were Holocaust survivors. They spoke no English. The only people who ever entered their house were other Jewish people who patronized a small dress shop the woman of the house ran, specializing in the clothing girls wore to synagogue. The wife had recently died. From the sidewalk, my father heard the man keening and sobbing in despair from inside the house, even with the door closed. My father just listened. Afterward, he looked up the number of a synagogue in Norwalk and told someone there about the bereaved man. Shortly thereafter, people came to the house. They must have taken him away since the house was soon up for sale.

With me my father was silent, grim, and always looked angry. When I started high school in 1958, I sat at the kitchen table with my mother.

"I've met the fathers of some of my new fellow students. I am surprised to see kids talking with their fathers routinely, as if it is normal, and they look like they enjoy it. Maybe it is a lot simpler for those kids like Donna who have never known what a father could be."

"That's it!" my mother cried sharply, slamming her hand on the table. "There's going to be no more of that damn accordion in this house."

A day or so later she spoke with a new tone of defiance toward my father. "I got him to say you could quit the accordion lessons. It's up to you whether you keep playing or not."

It was like slipping a backpack off my shoulders after a long day's hike. An extra hour of the day was mine. My father never said one word about quitting—or pretty much about anything else.

Several years after I left home and joined the Jesuits, my mother became a fighter for real. She was arguing with my father about his constant drinking and how she was going to leave him if he didn't stop.

He ran down into the basement and came back up the stairs with his pistol. He pointed it at her and yelled, "You wouldn't dare!"

My mother tackled my father, who was smaller than her. She knocked the pistol out of his hand. She picked it up and then left him on the floor crying. She drove to the police department and turned the gun in, and then instead of going back to the home he'd grown up in, she moved in with my sister Jill and her husband Sal.

On the Porch with Gramps

1955

A wise man advances himself.
—Ecclesiasticus 20:27

I stood at the end of the porch, pausing a moment before walking over and talking to my grandfather. It was several weeks after the train trip to Manhattan with my mother, still the middle of the summer with flowers in bloom.

My grandfather "Jimmy" was doubtless the best person in the family to teach me how to handle class shaming. He was completely oblivious to it—the perfect example of heroic independence and resistance to anything that would ever threaten his serenity. When he wasn't working at the tire factory pulling hot tires off molds, he was fishing, digging clams, or puttering in his little yard. He also groomed an impressive boxwood hedge along the sidewalk out in front that had a big bulbous half ball clipped at the entrance. He had built a stout grape trellis in the backyard, and as fertilizer he would put a fish in the ground at the base of each vine every spring. In the summer he gave me a penny for every Japanese beetle I plucked off the leaves. Gramps cultivated a bed of roses in the space between the house and the driveway. Without asking permission, I clipped off a rose to give to my grade three teacher, Miss Sonneberg.

My grandfather built trellises for raspberries, and I wondered if

I was the only one to ever eat them because there was never any left. In memory of my grandfather, I still cultivate a bush of raspberries in my garden.

Gramps stored his boat for the winter in one bay of the garage, next to where my father parked the golden Plymouth. Every winter he took apart all the mechanical parts to clean, oil, and where needed, restore. He sanded, revarnished, and repainted every surface.

There's no shimmer to his paint job, I thought admiringly, looking at the hull in the garage. *It's a mirror in which I can see my own smile.*

Gramps had the boat built to his specifications designed for trolling for large striped bass at night. The rudder was attached to the outside of the stern. It had a tiller he could hold and shift between his legs so he could keep both his hands on the fishing pole. He was proud that its custom builders with a shop in Norwalk hailed from the coast of Maine. It always shined brand new since he washed the sides with fresh water from a hose before and after he took it out every time.

For stability, it was round-bottomed like a bottle; its engine centered deep in the hull. It could only go slow. He would say to me, "I like that it takes so long. I think then."

I found Gramps sitting on the front porch behind another trellis that he'd made. This one was entangled with glorious purple wisteria clusters, so thick and luxurious he could not be seen from the street. He sat barefoot wearing shorts, in his strap undershirt, with the build of a stout barrel. He would spend hours just looking through the spaces in the leaves and bloom clusters. Now there were two sparrows flitting in the branches, tweeting their own language to each other.

I thought affectionately, *My grandfather always calls me maly wrobel* ("little sparrow" in Polish). As I never learned much Polish, and my grandfather, after forty years living in America still only spoke rudimentary English, we never really had conversations. He addressed me with long sentences in Polish, which must have been affectionate, while he was smiling and sometimes holding my hand, and he would repeat several times the Polish for "little sparrow." He'd also kiss me on the lips, which I never got used to.

Neighbors called him "Jimmy" because they found his real first name, Wladyslaw, unpronounceable. They mostly smiled at him when they met him on the street. He never learned much English, and he was the only Polish immigrant in the neighborhood.

As I stood near my grandfather that summer afternoon on the porch, as I had with Donna's mom, I took a chance with the question, "Gramps, do you like it here? Do you even want to go back to Poland or move someplace else?" It was the first time I'd ever asked him anything personal.

Gramps patted a spot on the porch swing to sit. He told me the story I had heard before about growing up "on the other side" and coming to Ellis Island at twenty-one years of age in 1910. His first job was working as a garbage man in Brooklyn. In 1920, he moved to East Norwalk to work in a factory—at the invitation of the local Democratic Party as part of its successful program to recruit immigrant voters to oust the Yankee Republicans that had ruled Norwalk without question for decades. Like my mother, he hated Republicans and talked about Roosevelt as a god. The reason he told this story over and over was because it was the only extended story in English he had managed to learn. Or maybe our family had heard it so many times we filled in the blanks.

In his broken English that only four people in the world understood, Gramps mumbled, "I've been places. Not good like this." He waved at the walls of his wisteria cave. He patted my knee. "I'm not going."

This conversation on the porch is my favorite memory of him, not like when he'd cursed his ebbing strength after catching his bodily limit of striped bass. Now Gramps was relaxed and satisfied.

I should have spoken more with my grandfather. How did he become a charter member of the East Norwalk Yacht Club? Its building perched right at the edge of Seaview Avenue, a major connector between East and South Norwalk. It ran over a drawbridge still opening and closing to accommodate industrial boat traffic from the Sound up the Norwalk River to an industrial hub of coal and oil depots in Norwalk proper. He and other immigrants and working people had built the clubhouse and dockage themselves on a muddy end of the East Norwalk cove. All its boats were short, like his, at the most eighteen feet long. There was a large porch overlooking the water with almost always a handful of people sitting on old couches chatting happily, always greeting Gramps and the rest of us.

A picture on the mantel in the clubhouse room, again furnished with hand-me-down chairs and sofas, shows the original members. Some, with comic smiles, held tools in their hands they had used to build the building. The picture shows three rows of people: men and women, with foreign faces and haircuts—like the European poor they once were. Face furrows, unkempt, teeth spotty. Gramps sits in the front row, his arms crossed. His head is tilted to one side as if he's sizing up anyone looking at the picture. In the picture on the mantel, my father, his son, then about eleven years old, with a shock of Polish blond hair and what must be blue eyes (pale even in black and white), sits at the feet of my grandfather, who's sitting on top of his world.

The group named themselves the East Norwalk Yacht Club. They even had an iconic pennant designed that every boat carried at its bow. Was this all done with a wink and a wiggle of the fingers at the nose toward the upscale wealthy people's big yacht clubs?

Years later Gramps was still living in his house with his own son when my father died of alcohol poisoning. When I went back to East Norwalk to make funeral arrangements, I stood with my grandfather out on the porch with the wisteria vines. We talked about the arrangements needed for my grandfather to keep living in his house.

Abruptly, Gramps turned and strode through the front door. He grabbed a photograph of my father off the wall and broke it out of the frame. Shouting in what sounded like a Polish curse, he tore it to pieces, batting the fragments with his hands as they fell to the floor.

Gramps's handmade cane boat rod with a large, black-and-silver Penn reel hangs on the wall of my farmhouse in Northern New York. Several years ago, I received a message from a woman he knew from

First Street in East Norwalk, with the query whether she had finally, through Google, traced back to find if I was, indeed, the grandson of Jimmy Wojcik.

"Would you like to have it back? We think you should."

She explained that my grandfather had given the rod to her father—one of his best friends—when Gramps could no longer fish by himself in his boat, which was the only way he would fish. She offered further that *her* son would take me fishing with the pole in Long Island Sound if I chose to make the trip. I caught a large blue fish with my grandfather's handmade pole. Years later my son Vlad, Gramps's great-grandson and namesake, took down the pole from the wall and flexed it.

"This is the one thing I want to inherit from you."

Such a lovely stick with which to reach back to poke a loving memory.

The Mass Was Full of Nice Moments

1955

I will go up to the Altar of God.
—Psalm 43:4

I stood outside the door of the vestibule at Saint Thomas Church on East Avenue in East Norwalk. It was after Sunday mass in early September 1955. School had started.

I knocked and heard the priest inside shout, "Come in." I stood quietly for a moment inside this holy place.

"I'm eleven years old. I want to become an altar boy," I told him.

The assistant pastor, Father Finnegan, of my family church, Saint Thomas—the "doubting disciple"—handed me a red paperback book. There was a stack of them at the end of the large recessed table where priests put on vestments. The book had all the Latin phrases altar boys needed to know and their cues. Father Finnegan told me to come back after memorizing them all.

Father Finnegan was a stickler about Latin pronunciation. It took several test sessions before I was pronounced fit to serve. Then older altar boys taught me the moves: when to kneel and stand, how to pour the wine and water, how to ring bells at the right time, and how to take the priest's biretta—a funny black hat with three wings on top the priest wore out to the altar. The priest would hold it by the middle wing then hand it to the altar boy standing to his right to take by a side wing and carry over to a special table, where it would stay until the mass was over. At the end, the altar boy would hand it back so the priest could grab it by the middle wing. It was all so new; nothing seemed odd.

I particularly liked pushing the button by the open door between the vestibule and the sanctuary that alerted the congregation with an electronic jingle that the mass was about to begin. The button made a satisfying click when pushed, with a moment before the bells chimed. It was the first time in my life I had the power to tell adults what to expect.

The Latin words were like reciting the words to a song that had cadence and sonority without the need to make any sense. The priest would intone: *Introibo ad Altare Dei* . . . "I will go up to the Altar of God." The two altar boys, in unison, would respond, *ad Deum qui laetificat juventutem meum* . . . "who brings joy to my youthfulness." This was a fun thing for a young boy to say. I particularly loved the bouncy rhythmic— you-ven-too-tem-meum. You could almost sway to it. The Mass was full of nice moments like that, and I was always a bit lightheaded from the fasting without breakfast so I could take communion.

As much as the Mass, I liked the bike rides down Gregory Boulevard heading for the Catholic Church at 6:30 a.m. in the winter when it was dark with very low-lying stars overhead. I could take my eyes off the road and, by lining up a star with a chimney or tree, pretend I was navigating at sea by the stars. Some mornings there was the morning star, Venus, that I could line up with the top of the mast of a telephone pole. Sometimes I rode through thick fog that rolled off the Sound, especially early in the mornings. The few cars would first show up as gray ghosts and houses as fairytale cottages with a few lights haloed in mist. It was easy to imagine that the people inside the houses were content with where they lived and what they lived for. There was little movement, no agitation. All was calm on the streets. I knew where to ride.

I liked the holy communion and the bike rides for the opportunity to string images together again—houses, rocks, gulls, silence, light, fish, the borderless blend of gray sea and sky, and the sound of water and wind. There were pleasures here full enough to still the mind either before or after any "understanding" Miss Sonneberg had counseled me always took time to gather.

There was, however, one startling moment that punctuated the serenity of religious service—something like the intrusion of Dwayne and his speedboat. One Sunday morning, Father Finnegan gave the sermon at Sunday Mass, with the pews full of people, while the altar boys sat on a side bench and waited for the Mass to resume. The priest was red in the face and started shouting about how modern culture and entertainment really got his goat—like Milton Berle dressing in drag for one of his comedy routines on TV or Elvis Presley swiveling his hips or Marilyn Monroe appearing in a low-cut dress. He actually used the word "goat" in church.

One song really got him going—the Big Bopper singing "Chantilly Lace" with the line in it about the (sinner) singer "feeling real loose, like a long-necked goose." Father Finnegan apparently thought the goose neck stood for an erect penis. I looked over at Father Finnegan at this point and thought irreverently, *Finnegan looks loose, like a red-necked goose*, which was probably close to blasphemy.

We had no TV at home at the time, and I hadn't seen or heard about any of these performers who enraged Father Finnegan. However, I enjoyed watching him pitch into it. *The red face goes nice with the black hair*, I thought. Father Finnegan then recited part of an angry diatribe of Jesus from Matthew's Gospel about an empty house filling up with devils. It seemed a strange man finds his house empty and so he opens a door and invites a bunch of devils to come inside. I wondered, *Does Father Finnegan mean TV is like a door that opens up to let the rock-and-roll devils into the house?* This didn't make sense. Neither did Father Finnegan's sermon.

Instead, I started reading the Gospels in translation on my own. There was an old Bible in the house that no one ever read.

I found a lot of stories I had never heard about in catechism class or in sermons, certainly none of the ones like Father Finnegan delivered.

There was a great story in Mark about Jesus asking a blind man he's just cured what he saw. The man said, "Men, like trees . . . walking." Wow! Well, sure. That's what a man might see if, in a flash, he first saw the light after being blind for a long time? Why didn't anyone preach about this? Or Jesus turning water into wine. Or walking on the water. Or feeding people bread and fish. Or miraculously appearing out of thin air to meet his frightened disciples in a closed room. Or disappearing into thin air after having a meal with two strangers he met on the road.

I probably should have thought more about what a sermon like Father Finnegan's might portend about the Catholic Church and its persistent, sickly preoccupation with sex. As well as about the crisis with a female communicant and her troublesome cleavage.

During the communion service, the altar boy's job was to hold a small bright brass plate called a paten under the chin of the communicant in case the priest should drop the host. Once during another full house at Sunday Mass, Father Finnegan was in the process of putting the host on the tongue of a woman kneeling at the altar rail. Perhaps rattled by what he could see of her cleavage at the front of her dress, the host slipped out of his fingers. His altar boy—me—tried to move fast but missed it with the paten. The host fell into her cleavage. It was the only time I ever heard a congregation laugh, if nervously. Father Finnegan laughed, too, and told her so everyone could hear, "Come into the sacristy afterward." His voice almost sounded seductive.

Later, out of the sight of the parishioners, the priest gave her some kind of sacred linen cloth. Women were not allowed to touch any host, especially a sanctified one, and of course the priest wasn't going to go digging after it himself. She couldn't quite figure out how to work the cloth.

"Do you have a glove?" she asked plaintively.

And Father Finnegan, trying to be patient, spoke slowly: "No. Just try not to break it. We don't want to deal with crumbs."

Both giggled at that. The priest and the woman communicant were enjoying a one-of-a-kind moment—and so was I. It seemed the one time when it was okay to keep your eye on a woman's cleavage, even in church. While she was digging away, I almost said aloud, but managed to keep it only to myself, *It's like a living Madonna and Child with Jesus at her breast.*

Happily, she dug out the host, handed it back to the priest, who said the words of sacred distribution again and this time didn't miss her mouth. The three of us had a good laugh. It was one of those moments of sexual titillation (even in a church) that was "on the house."

Some time after this memorable event, I had served an early morning weekday Mass with another altar boy, Johnny Gagne. He and I were just starting off in different directions on our bicycles. Johnny always wore a baseball cap with the brim rolled into a cone.

Johnny yelled. His "hey" had a nasty edge. It was always clear Johnny hated me. He was tall for our age, and strong, and a good athlete who played Little League baseball—a game that I could never play. I suffered from asthma, and several times, starting when I was two years old, had to be rushed to the hospital with horrifying asthma attacks. Despite my affliction, my mother and father smoked in the house. Probably as a result, I was slight and occasionally some kid would taunt me by snarling, "You'd make a good-looking girl."

This time Johnny couldn't contain himself. He shouted with a nasty edge, "You're a fairy!" There it was again. Something about sex in the churchyard.

In the quiet early morning air, I looked over at the service station in whose parking lot he stood. I could see men inside using tools I could not hear. So, none would hear what I said.

"Okay, if I'm a fairy—what are you?"

"Well, I'm a man," he said, and he pounded a fist on his chest, which must have sounded silly even to him since we were both twelve years old.

"Well, if you're an example of a man, I'd rather be a fairy." Not great wit, but at least I'd said something.

Johnny paused for a moment, gave me the middle finger, and peddled off.

Curious Kids From Everywhere

1956

Was blind, but now I see.
—John Newton, *Amazing Grace*

I knew giving the finger was an insult. But I learned more several months later.

This was the year of a great national Boy Scout Jamboree. Fifty thousand scouts from all over the country converged on Valley Forge, Pennsylvania, to camp out for a week of contests in fire-building and sharpshooting and winning cooking merit badges (a four-course meal, including bread, cooked over a fire started without a match, served to eight people). I won the badge on a hill in Pennsylvania.

I had never traveled any farther than Manhattan. I was curious to meet with other boys from very far away, just to see what they were like—were like me or like Johnny Gagne?

I asked scouts from Michigan if they knew what the word *fuck* meant or what giving the finger meant, since I wondered whether the word and gesture were just local to Connecticut.

They laughed at the question and said that sure, they knew the word and the finger. They then tried out several other curse words and gestures to see if *I* knew them. Later I asked the same questions to scouts from Nevada and got the same response. Ah-ha! There was a common kid culture, and it was mostly jokes.

I asked one, "How does Pennsylvania compare with the way Nevada looks?"

The scout told me that it was his first time away from home, too—and he was astonished at how green everything looked.

He spoke, waving his arm, "There are trees and plants everywhere. I still can't get over it. Where I live, everything is always brown, and you can see brown clear away to the horizon. In Pennsylvania, you can only see as far as the green trees let you."

I liked hearing that where I lived was someplace special for all its fog and water and green trees. It was also good that there were kind, curious kids from everywhere, many like him, among the fifty thousand young boys encamped in the huge verdant valley where Washington had set up winter quarters for his army.

Adults could be as mean as Dwayne. My troop was bused to view the Liberty Bell and other patriotic sights in Philadelphia. There were Boy Scouts in mufti uniforms everywhere. Like ants at a picnic.

I got to the head of a long line waiting to use the public toilet. A homeless man was sitting inside the stall for over fifteen minutes.

"I'm going to let the little bastards wait," I heard him say.

The boys behind me twisted in agony. Finally, I begged the man to finish. He shouted obscenities. And when he finally did exit the stall, he cursed and slammed the door. He pointed to me at the head of the line and complained to the troop leader how rude I was. Luckily, the troop leader said nothing, perhaps allied with sympathy and our common uniform.

What was worse was what happened after I'd signed up to serve as an altar boy for one of the Catholic chaplains at the Jamboree. After the Mass, we chatted in the priest's tent. Out of the blue, the priest asked prurient questions about what I thought about the scandal in the newspapers about the baseball star Ted Williams being arrested for visiting a prostitute. I admitted to the priest that I hadn't heard about that story. I lacked the nerve to tell him that I had no idea what the story meant or even what a prostitute was. Instead, I felt confused and uneasy. I bolted from the chapel tent.

It was only years later that I would understand what *prurient* meant: to fully recognize this instance for what it was: the uneasy mix of Catholicism and predatory sexuality, plus the perverse prejudice of people like Father Finnegan and Johnny Gagne toward any hint of what they considered abhorrent sexuality. My uneasy ignorance then made me itchy, literally.

Later that day I felt a rash on my face. There were creepy parts of the pretty green landscape, too, just like the snarly nooks in East Norwalk with their cats, rats, and crabs. My troop's campsite had been bush-hogged flat, but alas, the brush had contained poison ivy plants. Fragments covered the ground, and many Norwalk scouts got bad rashes. One day my face swelled up to the point where for several hours I couldn't open my eyes. No saltwater cures in Pennsylvania. I thought, *Like that blind man in the Gospel. If I'm just patient, I'll get to see the trees again.* It was the first time, I think, words from the Gospels consoled me when I was having a hard time.

The Boy Scout Jamboree ended well. The last night, the valley was filled with scouts sitting on the ground up and down the hills to watch fireworks where each volley was better than the finale in Norwalk's Fourth of July celebration. At the Jamboree, the finale went on for so long that I lay down and closed the thin slits of my swollen eyes, listening to the booms that caused the ground to vibrate. I wondered, *Are these the pleasures the blind man got in the story in Mark's Gospel when his eyes first opened?*

By the time the Norwalk-based scouts got off the train in South Norwalk, my face was pretty much back to normal. There's evidence. A photographer from the local paper, *The Norwalk Hour*, was there, along with my mother, who had just greeted me with a kiss on the cheek. The photo with us both—open-eyed and smiling—was on the front page the next day with a caption about the local scouts who had attended the Boy Scout Jamboree. Once again, Mom to the rescue.

Back home, I was left on my own, curled in a cocoon of curiosity. I read the New Testament on my own. It was quiet there, no odd priests or hostile altar boys intruding into the scenes. I replayed the scene from the sandbar of the Jesuits playing basketball silently because of the distance away.

What if I got a closer look? The Jesuits ran a high school in Fairfield, Connecticut, several towns down the road from Norwalk. I knew I could learn Greek there. That offered a closer look into the Gospels. In the spring of 1958, I passed the entrance exam for the Jesuit high school Fairfield Prep.

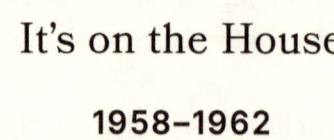

It's on the House

1958–1962

Treasure my teaching as the apple of your eye.
—Proverbs 7:2

I stood in the South Norwalk train station. For the first time I waited for a train going north, away from Manhattan, up the line toward Boston with a stop in Fairfield, Connecticut. A small crowd of young men my age stood by dressed in coats and ties—required for students like us attending the Jesuit high school Fairfield Prep. A few smoked. After a week of classes, I already knew some names.

It was exhilarating that social class distinctions appeared to disappear under the common dress code. Students took buses and cars and trains to get to Prep from all over the southern part of the state, from the fancy towns of Greenwich and Westport and the smoky towns of Bridgeport and Norwalk. I quickly mastered the art of using trains to travel around and visit friends, and even sometimes to travel to Manhattan just to wander around the city by myself.

I traveled further in learning Latin and Greek. Greek especially took me deeper into the Gospels. Jesus sees two brothers fishing from a boat and says to them, "Come, follow me, and I will make you fishers of men." It's fascinating the word for *fisherman* in Greek Jesus uses in the Gospel; it's a less commonly used word for it—*halieus*—whose root word is *hal*, "salt," perhaps because these men are fishing in the salt-concentrated Dead Sea. You could almost translate Jesus's word into English as "salters," or "old salts." My favorite fishing story is when Jesus has risen from the dead and, despite the miracle, his followers are back to work fishing when he appears on the beach. This is Christianity at its most pure. Miracles are taken for granted—a formerly dead man alive on a beach is no big deal. People still have to make a living and there were no priests or popes yet. The "old salts" don't recognize him at first, probably because they believe he's dead.

Jesus must've sounded authoritative when he shouted, "Throw the net on the right side of the boat," and when they do and they net so many fish, the old salts have to jump out of the boat and haul the net by hand to shore, for fear it'll break if they haul it into the boat. The story says they wind up counting 153 fish, all big ones, which proves they are real fishermen who always count and measure! And what a climax! When the fishermen walk over to Jesus, they find he's cooking fish for them over a fire for their breakfast. By the simple act of eating together, he shows them he is real. If he had been a ghost or an illusion, the fish in his mouth would have dropped to the sand. That was as good as the stories about appearing and disappearing into thin air. Jesus knew his way around fish. He used magic. Useful tools for fishermen.

I began to read other fishing stories by bringing them together out of the order in which they appeared in the printed text. In one story, Jesus takes two fish and five loaves of bread in hand and after blessing them, gives them to his disciples to distribute to a crowd of five thousand sitting by a lake to listen to what Jesus has to say. No explanation of the logistics. Do the disciples hand someone a fish and then magically find another fish appearing in their hands? Does a piece of bread magically grow back on the loaf after it gets broken off? Do the disciples get used to what's going on and start hamming it up? But it's a great scene to imagine the people happily fumbling around.

I was struck by the phrase: "I will make you fishers (old salts) of men . . ." I thought that Jesus didn't mean to *hook* or *net* or *haul*—or what would be worse, *gaff* like my grandfather—anyone into his way of looking at the world. Or to push them around or hurt them. Let's say Jesus wanted to make people content with a life of water and fishing and familiarity, and also being skilled at something pleasurable and nourishing. That sort of fishing could often include *releasing*—like sharing in the life of the fish and holding it affectionately and letting it go on its way. So, for Jesus, feeding people fish and bread was a gesture of generosity in the abstract, but beyond that—practically—it was satisfying people's real hunger.

Still, the darker shadows of Catholicism reached into the sweetness and light.

Three months into the first semester, the religion teacher gave all the students a retreat. This meant several days free of classes. The students sat in the school chapel to listen to the religious teacher talk about our religious obligations as Catholics. There was lot of doctrine that was easy to ignore. It had to do with arguments among Catholic adults who lived far away and long ago. What got everyone's attention was when the priest went into detail about how young people could commit each of the seven deadly sins—such as overeating or getting into fist fights. The topic he came down on hard was masturbation. He had all the lights killed. In the temporary dark blindness, he lit a candle on his desk.

The shadows gave his face ghoulish furrows. Then, histrionically, he lowered his outstretched palm onto the candle flame and held it there for a moment until it appeared to burn his flesh. At which point, he gave a loud yell and yanked his hand out of the flame in theatrical agony.

He shouted, "And that is but a tiny prick of the hell fires you'll feel all over your body forever if you die with the mortal sin of masturbation on your souls."

Students laughed or recoiled in horror. The shock of his words deadened our minds. Afterward, I heard one classmate ask another, "What's masturbation?" and the other one gave him precise instructions on how to do it. I listened in for any pointers.

But the horrific shadows the religious priest had cast were

overwhelmed by the zest and vitality of a new kind of young Jesuit: John L'Heureux. He wasn't ordained yet. But he wore a habit and a Roman collar and spoke with the voice of the angels of light.

On the first day of his class, he admitted that it was also his first day of classroom teaching. That was startling to hear. Most students thought most teachers had been doing it forever.

John L'Heureux went on to say, "This means, if I'm going to make any mistakes, I'm going to do them with you. You can leave right now if you don't want to take the chance."

That had to be rhetorical of course. The students had nowhere else to go. They sat in alphabetically assigned seats in assigned classrooms in every class they took, so for four years, as someone whose last name starts with W, I sat in the last seat in the row farthest from the door, against the back wall.

Then startlingly, L'Heureux said, "I hate the assigned English literature textbook you've already bought. Its selections are too religious—which real literature never was.

"So," he announced to his enraptured class, "I have received permission from the father principal to go through the required text in one intense month—you can quit and transfer to another class if you think you can't take the heat. Instead, after we dispose of that, you'll read the kinds of stuff I'm going to assign. You'll have to buy the books yourselves. But, don't worry, they'll all be cheap paperbacks. I'll find the money myself if anyone needs it."

The students hardly knew what to expect. The first month, the class raced through the originally assigned literature that L'Heureux taught them how to despise for being sentimental, like Joyce Kilmer's "Trees" or any poem with daffodils in it.

"I refuse to have you read any poems about daffodils," he snorted. Still, a great moment occurred during that first month of "romping through the garbage," as he put it.

The class read the poem "Barbara Fritchie" by John Greenleaf Whittier.

"The only good thing about Whittier was his middle name," said L'Heureux caustically.

That's the poem about an old lady who hangs out the Union Flag while a unit of the Confederate Army is marching under her window. An officer looks up and tells her to take it down. And she looks down and says the immortal words: "Shoot if you must this old gray-head, / but touch not a thread of your country's flag." The officer leaves her be.

L'Heureux made fun of the poem. He said it illustrated the sentimentality he was always warning us about. But what happened next was priceless. Tom Baker was already my good friend, who, because of *his* last name, got a seat in the classroom in the first row, by the door. Tom sat right next to the cork bulletin board. At that time, the company that sold Playtex Living Bras used an advertising campaign that would show a model wearing just panties and a bra hanging from a tree, or a building, or in this instance, a flagpole. The idea was that wearing such a bra made a woman feel free as a breeze. The next day, Tom brought in a full-page ad from *The New Yorker* that he pinned on the board and then for a caption, used the famous line from the poem, "Touch not a thread of your country's flag." L'Heureux came into class, and he saw it.

He cried out, "That's hysterical. And I'm not even going to ask who put that up."

Everyone enjoyed a good laugh. But things got really good in the next period when the same religion teacher who had given the masturbation retreat came into the classroom—students didn't change rooms; the teachers moved from room to room.

When he saw the picture, he bellowed, "That's obscene! Who put that up there?"

Nobody said a thing. He stomped over to the bulletin board and made a big dramatic gesture out of ripping the picture off, and then, tearing it into pieces, he tossed into the wastebasket. He batted the pieces as they fell.

None of the students paid any attention to what he said. They all made a point of looking at their shoes all during his class. As soon as his class was over, Tom Baker rushed out of the room, found L'Heureux in the hallway, and breathlessly told him what had happened.

"He can't do that. That's my classroom."

"Yes, I can," shouted the religious priest, charging into the hallway. "It was filth."

Hubbub in the hallway. Students milled about while the two Jesuits shouted at each other—something hitherto unimaginable. When somebody shouted, "Let's ask the principal," the whole crowd, with the two Jesuits in the middle, moved down the hall toward the principal's office.

Everyone ignored the bell announcing the next class period. After half an hour, L'Heureux emerged from the principal's office with a big smile and both thumbs pointing up. The students cheered. The religious priest did not reappear.

In the next class with L'Heureux, Tom had replaced the picture of the woman hanging in her bra from the flagpole. He fixed Fritchie's words to it again as a caption. Everyone cheered when L'Heureux entered the room.

He held up his hand for silence and said imperially, "We shall speak no more of this. I refuse to have a battle of wits with an unarmed man."

The students gasped, then laughed uproariously. No teacher ever had a more loyal class than we were now. We would have followed him over the barricades.

L'Heureux did have one more battle of wits with the religion teacher, although this one was much more subtle. Someone must have told him about the priest burning his hand during what the students referred to as "the masturbation retreat." One day in class, apropos of nothing we were reading, he looked at us with a mischievous smile and said, "Men, if you ever find yourself having an erotic dream, and the dream gets to the point where you're about to ejaculate, and just at this moment you wake up and you think, *What am I going to do now?* my advice to you is to let it rip. It's on the house."

For most of the semester the class read astonishing literature. Comic novels by Waugh: an English book that also could be hilarious? Also, *The Stranger* by Camus; *The Lord of the Flies* by Golding; and *As I Lay Dying* by Faulkner. It was dense—but he led us through it. Poems by Marianne Moore, Emily Dickinson, Allan Ginsburg, Pablo Neruda, Richard Wilbur, Karl Shapiro, and Langston Hughes.

I said to myself, "What a world awaits beyond these walls."

Time Out with Dave Brubeck

1961

Jesus . . . saw the flute players.
—Matthew 9:23

At the end of the spring semester, on a swimming date with Donna, I told her these stories about John L'Heureux. By this time, she and her mother had moved to a grand house in Westport, one of the fancy towns, after her mother got a job in the hospital there. The two of us were sitting around the pool with our feet kicking the water in unison.

She told me, "Well, one thing our English teacher did was give us a class period about sexual innuendos in Shakespeare. In one of the sonnets he says, 'Flesh stays no further reason; But rising at thy name, Doth point out thee as his triumphant prize.' Which I memorized, since I thought he was saying it was okay if you did it with your girlfriend in mind."

"I think L'Heureux would agree with you."

Donna and I insisted to each other, and to our mothers, that we were just good friends.

Donna turned to me and said, "Why don't you stay for dinner? I'm going to cook for my mother when she gets home from the hospital, so I know we'll have plenty to eat. And she'd like to see you. And by the way, I was thinking of asking you if afterward you'd like to drive the two of us to a concert tonight. My high school gave away free tickets for anyone who wants to hear a jazz concert tonight in Westport by the Dave Brubeck Quartet—people say it's the best jazz group around. What do you say? A real date?"

"Sure," I said readily, happy to be back in touch, "as long as you don't mind what my car looks like. I left it parked outside. You haven't seen it yet. It looks a little like *Flotsam*, and both leak—this time the car from the inside out."

Donna laughed, "Your wit's still dry."

I also confessed, "I really don't know what jazz music is."

"All the more reason to let me take the lead," Donna said decisively.

She laughed when she saw my car and said, "You were right. The car does look a little like *Flotsam*, so I should feel right at home. And this time we won't have to stop to bail the water out."

We found seats in the high school auditorium and settled in; we chatted for a few moments about what our different high schools were like. Donna asked coyly, "Do the Jesuits at yours still play basketball?"

"Yes, they do. And they're all elbows under the boards."

A hush fell. We watched four men stride across the stage, already set up with drums, a piano, and an upright bass. It was like a procession from the sacristy to the altar at the opening of the Mass.

A Black musician, Eugene Wright, led a blind White man wearing sunglasses, Joe Morello, by the elbow to the drum set and helped him settle in. Then Eugene walked over and embraced his double bass. Another musician, Paul Desmond, stood in the curve of the piano and tootled a few warm-up notes on his tenor saxophone. Then, Dave Brubeck sat at his piano, turned to the audience with a huge grin, and started to talk about jazz.

He played different riffs in Desmond's original composition "Take Five" to explain what jazz improvisation is. Paul Desmond on saxophone echoed a melody Brubeck had played on the piano to show how other players would carry on a conversation about the melody. They varied the chord structure that held it up. Then all four launched into playing together.

I thought it was like spring plants pushing and shoving each other out of bare ground. Porpoise fins breaking water or a thousand horseshoe crabs crisscrossing a sandbar. All through the concert, I kept seeing the image of a Black man leading a blind White man to his drum kit. An old Black man in Harlem hugging my mother. My going blind at the Jamboree.

Could sound, too, evoke reminiscence? Was making music for the blind drummer like seeing in another dimension like Jesus with the blind man in the Gospel?

I was mesmerized. Suddenly I thought, *The Gospels are composed like jazz! Stories follow stories as if improvising on their meanings simply through the juxtapositions of different stories against each other. Jazz and the Gospels flow along like continuous second thoughts!*

I didn't say this out loud. I only grasped the validity of the comparisons several days later when thinking about them. But I grasped Donna's hand and held it.

After the concert, Donna declared, "Let's get a pizza."

While we waited at our table I said, "Thank you very much for asking me to this. I've never heard anything like jazz. Brubeck with his big grin, teaching about improvisation so that you could really hear what he was doing. What he said about jazz music really hit me. He was saying that once he got the theme going, or the melody, what the jazz musician did was weave together different ways of imagining how it could be played—each riff, as Brubeck called it—making sense or music out of what it did with the riff before and after."

"I thought you'd like it. What you just said about the music reminded me of what I've heard you call reminiscing or having second thoughts. That's when you say you run different memories or scenes together and find yourself discovering what they mean when strung together. It's as if jazz is a continuous music of what you call second thoughts."

"Thanks for saying that," I said a little sheepishly. "It's nice you remember my idea. I still often have very happy 'second thoughts' about swimming and sailing together with you. But it's a little embarrassing.

The comparison you make is much more flattering to me than to Brubeck. He's brilliant at what he's doing, pulling all that beautiful music out of his head. And not only his head, but the heads of the trio of his fellow musicians. They're all presenting second thoughts about what they're hearing the other players saying to each other."

"Okay, I get your point," Donna said, squeezing my hand. "But don't you think we do something like that when we talk to each other about crabs and Jesuits and Dwayne and porpoises and with my mother on the beach licking an ice cream cone? Maybe jazz tells us we should all revel in the play-by-play with our friends and the land and the sea."

"That's pretty poetic," I said with admiration, "and I like what you say. We're sort of doing jazz, talking about ourselves and the great men up there on the stage. I'm not sure what Brubeck would say about our comparison. For me, it's just the way I'm working out what he said in my own terms. It's only my first time hearing this stuff. If we told Brubeck what we thought about his jazz, I think he'd just smile and nod his head. He'd know he had us hooked."

"Oh, happy fish!" said Donna as she hooked her index finger into mine.

Afterward, we drove down to Westport Beach, sat on a driftwood log, and took our shoes and socks off to dig our feet in the sand—even daring to cross toes. We were still on fire with the notions of improvising as we went. We necked, which was new for us. For the first time ever, I dared to unbutton a blouse to touch a woman's breast—to finger a stiffening nipple. I looked at Donna questioningly.

"That's okay," said Donna, "that feels good."

Then she pulled her head away and asked abruptly, but with a smile, "Are you still a virgin?"

A little sheepishly I admitted, "Yes, I am."

Donna replied meaningfully, "You should stay one for at least another night."

We both giggled. "It's like kissing my sibling," we both said in unison. The laughter doused the necking.

Later that evening, I dropped Donna off at her new home in Westport. We exchanged a chaste kiss before the door—but a little extra hand squeeze too, just to show we meant it.

I was feeling a little lightheaded as I drove out of her driveway into the street—a little like riding a bike to early morning Mass without breakfast. Suddenly I saw a police car's flashing red lights in my rearview mirror. I was frightened.

What have I done? Is it wrong to be feeling this good? How could the cops tell?

A Westport policeman walked up to my car. He blinded me with his flashlight. He looked suspiciously at me from under the shiny brim of his hat.

"What are you doing driving a junk car like this here?" I told him that I'd just dropped off Donna at her home. The cop wanted to check out the story, so I led him to Donna's doorway. Donna's mother answered the door and was startled to see a police officer standing behind me. She looked annoyed as she assured the cop that I was okay.

The policeman smiled, and as if to apologize, "Just checking."

She shut the door hard in his face.

Donna's mother looked hurt and sympathetic when she said to me, "This is the second time I've had to intervene on your behalf with the guardians of privilege. I'm sorry. You deserve better. You're no crook."

I joked, "I've been called worse," and winked at Donna while looking over her mother's shoulder.

Donna retorted with her own brand of humor, "Maybe the cops didn't like the look of your cowlick."

"You're right. I find it aggravating, myself."

We laughed, then said good night to each other for the second time. Donna and her mother each gave me a kiss on the cheek to assuage any bad feelings I might have while driving away a second time. I was still riled up and walked right over to Donna, and right in front of her mother, gave her another lingering kiss on the lips.

As I drove away, I put the Westport Police into the same box as Dwayne in his speed boat and the lifeguard at the country club. Small sample size, sure, but significant for preoccupations with class prejudice. But then that box got put next to the one with Donna and her mother, high class people anyway you mean the term. They were another variation on the same theme, belonging to the same changes. The unsettlingly wonderful experience of listening to jazz for the first time stayed with me. Jazz was working-class, blue-collar music. The musicians had only each other to listen to and play off against. The four I saw had no music stands or charts. They all knew the same song. The basics of harmony and melody gave backbone and direction to the conversations of men of different races and backgrounds—regardless of handicap. They spoke as equals.

The Longer Story

1962

By the waters of Babylon we sat down.
—Psalm 137:1

A year after the date at the jazz concert, Donna called me right after our high school graduations. She knew I was planning to join the Jesuits in the late summer. She called at the beginning of June, just before the start of summer vacation.

"Before you enter into the Big House, why not sell your car and fly down to spend a week with my mother and me at my uncle and aunt's house in Puerto Rico. You come for a week. Come around the twentieth of June and there'll be a surprise waiting for you."

"Of course, I'll come," I said eagerly. "I love a surprise, and you've never led me astray."

Donna continued, "Good. I'll even tell you the surprise ahead of time. June 24 is the Feast of San Juan Baptiste, the patron saint of San Juan. It's like Mardi Gras, Saturnalia, the Fourth of July, and New Year's Eve rolled into one. Everyone on the island goes to a beach and parties all day, then lights bonfires and continues to party all night. The idea is if you submerge yourself in the water, it's like a baptism, and all your sins are washed clean—and if you do it at night—even the ones you committed during the day get washed away. It's also very Catholic, which you should like. And don't tell anyone I'm telling you this. But . . . it was our mothers' idea. They think the big party on the beach could be the final test you have to pass before going off to become a celibate Jesuit for life. Plus, you can meet my serious boyfriend, Mark, who lives down here."

"Have you been two-timing me?"

Donna answered with a pout I could feel over the phone. "You don't want to live in time at all. You want eternity."

I asked my mother how to fly to Puerto Rico.

"It's simple at the beginning. You take the train to Grand Central like we've done before. There's a bus to the airport. You get a ticket at the counter of an airline that flies to San Juan. The airline takes it from there. I can't tell you what it's like on a plane, since, like you, I've never flown on one before. It'll be good practice for all of us as you fly away and leave the nest."

The plane trip began auspiciously. Initially, I could only buy a coach standby ticket. There was a no-show, and I got bumped up to first class. It came with a big leather seat. The stewardess didn't ask for any ID when she offered a free cocktail.

I had a window seat, and the entire trip stared out the window at the endless vastness of the ocean. The scene was as mesmerizing as the bicycle rides to morning Mass in all the wet of fog and sea.

Donna asked me to go swimming with her and her boyfriend, Mark.

"Sure, I'd be delighted to, so long as you'll stay close to me. This is a whole new body of water for me."

Donna said reassuringly, "No worries. You'll find it feels the same. It's connected wave by wave with the water in East Norwalk."

Once we got offshore (no restraining roped swimming section this time), I was astonished at how effortlessly Donna and Mark swam in the waves. It was like they were walking or jogging without breathing hard. When they swam farther off from the beach, I couldn't keep up and was a little scared. They saw me flinch when a barracuda and then a huge stingray swam under them.

Mark saw my fear. "Life in the sea isn't always about killing and eating—either us or the fish, or the fish us. Sometimes it's just swimming around with everything else that's swimming around—the fish are just like us that way."

"Like us and the porpoises," said Donna, mimicking their roll over and under the surface with her hand. She blew a spray of water and then gave my hand a friendly tug.

On the afternoon of the feast of San Juan we found a spot to put a blanket on the sandy beach that curved endlessly in both directions around the entire island of Puerto Rico.

We swam then had lunch sitting on the beach blanket. Mark spoke cautiously, as if he was taking a chance. "This might seem presumptuous for me to ask—but Donna's told me so much about you, so I feel I already know you. Tell me, why are you going to join the Jesuits? Right now, in your bathing suit, you don't look the type. You don't need to answer my question . . ."

I replied, "That's okay, as long as I can say I'm not completely sure myself. Making a long story short, I feel like I have a vocation."

Mark acted surprised, "You mean you have a *vacation*?"

Donna corrected Mark, laughing, "No—it's voh-cation!" She said to me, "He has a lot of trouble with those kinds of words."

Mark sounded both friendly and curious when he continued, "Either way, I'm not sure what that means. If you're willing, tell me the longer story."

I started out in an almost formal tone of voice.

"I decided to join the Jesuit order of priests and remain celibate, poor, and obedient to the Church to do good on the earth and win a place in heaven."

Donna interjected, "I've heard you say something like that before. My problem with it is you sound like you're reading off a recruitment brochure."

"Give me a break," I said peevishly. "I have to start somewhere. I do have more to say. I had come to feel comfortable around priests as an altar boy. I had admired the way Jesuits handled themselves at their leisure, and I like wearing black. I think it makes me look more distinguished. Don't you think so?" I pointed to his black swimming trunks.

Donna turned to Mark and said with a giggle, "It's not just that. He was impressed at how the Jesuits played basketball while wearing black shorts!"

"She's right. That was a start. But I got to see more of what they were like. I went to a Jesuit high school and found many of them astonishingly smart and happy with each other and students. More and more, the Jesuits seemed to me to live in a bright bubble of their own. They dressed alike. They were always laughing with each other, as if they were all in on some joke. They lived in a wholly different world even while they were teaching us and talking to us in ours."

Mark said, "Sure. But you're well aware their world doesn't have any pretty women in it like our lovely Donna here."

Donna pointed at Mark and said sharply: "Let him go on. He's way beyond any woman like Donna now at this point—as I can attest to from personal experience."

"You need not elaborate."

"Thank you both. What I'm getting at now is more personal. Growing up, I had grown increasingly dismayed at the increasing cultural divide between the working class of my origin and the affluent commuting class from the fancy towns of Darien, New Canaan, Westport, etc., outside the smoky fringes of the working cities of Stamford, Norwalk, and Bridgeport. The way I saw it at first was the division between those who took no vacations and those who could afford to. It didn't help that both sides of the divide also drank too much. Where did a kid like me belong?"

Donna blurted impishly, "For now, don't worry. You belong on the blanket. We have beer."

"There's no place else I'd rather be just now. While in high school, I decided what I wanted to do in life was teach literature. I could not imagine any way better to do it than to become someone like my Jesuit teacher John L'Heureux. He was empty of worldly goods so he could fill the world with wonderful writing. Like Jesus. I know I'll never be the equal of John L'Heureux, but I can try to become a Jesuit who taught and wrote. Writing and reading a poem is more like 'catch and release' than writing advertising copy or legal briefs. Both Jesus and John lived inside the bubble of themselves."

After a pause, Mark asked, "Have you started writing poetry too?"

"Yes, but it's pretty primitive."

Mark asked encouragingly, "Can you recite one?"

"Yes:

> Rain in the city is one song
> in many movements. A crane
> speaks clear steel
> high in the rain,
> rain is pizzicato on the street,
> rain is silver running in a drain
> wheels a song on tar
> puddles bursting in the street.
> The doors of shops have sound
> recorded of a blue guitar.
> Winds in the forest, one song
> in many movements. High trees
> magnificent in benediction
> tangled birch and beech
> of thicket mangle faces turning
> each to each, a stream
> is restless in its dream, one
> song in many movements.
> We on a string of time
> are one song with many movements."

Donna and Mark agreed that the poem was pretty good.

Donna said thoughtfully, "What I liked is that by having one scene in the woods, and the other in the city, you make it seem like you're referring to the whole world. And no matter where you are in the world, you sing one song."

Mark added, "And it's powerful that you use 'string' for the run of time—suggesting a classical musical instrument." Then Mark asked pointedly, and I wondered, with a touch of jealousy? "Is that 'we' at the end you and Donna?"

I answered carefully, "It could be."

"Could it also be me and Donna?"

"When you listen to any poem or read it—it belongs to you."

What I didn't say to Mark was that wherever Mark's romance with Donna might take them, Donna would also always be strung as a bead on my string of memories. One that interwove memories of swimming together, sailing with porpoises, talking together about vacations, hearing jazz, even necking on the beach, watching Jesuits playing basketball, riding a bike in the dark of the early morning to Mass, reciting musical Latin as an altar boy. She was the one who first got me thinking as Miss Sonneberg had encouraged. Stringing reminiscences was improvising second thoughts ceaselessly. Like jazz music.

When it became dark, the Puerto Ricans started lighting fires up and down the beach. There was loud music from portable radios, and I could see down the beach little orchestras setting up. People were singing, dancing, and running around in the sand, in the shallow water, drinking and passing joints with bright red tips.

Fireworks went off. Donna and Mark started snuggling under a large blanket they had bought. I noticed Donna's big feet formed a hill under the blanket and I really didn't mind. I wandered down the beach then walked backward into the water, as I had been told was the local custom. When the water got up to my knees, I found myself abreast of a topless woman with a huge afro who had waded over. She started dancing, holding my hands. A pointless erection became obvious in my bathing suit, to the delight of the woman dancer who nodded to it. I couldn't cover it with my hands because she was holding them.

More than a little uptight, I smiled politely, broke free, walked away, and chastely strolled down the increasingly frenzied beach. After all, Donna had said swimming in the ocean at night only cleansed away the sins of the morning.

After the night on the beach with Donna and Mark, I flew back home. I told my mother everything that had happened, including dancing with a topless girl.

She asked pointedly, "And you still want to go with this Jesuit thing? You still have your early-acceptance two-hundred-dollar deposit down at Georgetown University. You could still go there this fall. Jesuits teach there. You could spend some more time watching them before deciding to join them. But of course, it's up to you. If you're sure you know what you're doing, go with my blessing."

I looked down at my feet and admitted, "Actually I'm not sure I know what I'm doing. But I'm sure I have to try to find out." I dramatically dropped to my knees on the kitchen floor. "But I would be happy to have your blessing."

"Whatever blessing I've got to give, it's yours to take."

Instead of making the sign of the cross, she kissed me on the head.

Later, she would tell me she had to fight to get the two hundred dollar deposit back from Georgetown. "When I called the Jesuit admissions person to ask, he said regretfully, 'I'm sorry. It's not refundable this late.' And so I said to him, 'Look, he's not backing out. He's going to join the Jesuits.' And he replied, 'I'm happy to hear that. But again, I'm sorry. That's our policy. No refunds.' And then I got mad and yelled at him, 'Look, that's two weeks' salary. He's the one who wants to take a vow of poverty, not me.' And then he laughed and gave in. 'Okay, don't tell anyone. We'll send the deposit back.'"

The Ridiculous and the Sublime

1962

Sell all that you have . . .
—Luke 18:22

I stood looking up toward the roof of a red brick building four stories high. Summer clouds moved majestically behind it across a blue sky. The front doors of Shadowbrook shone like gold.

Is this the portal to heaven?

After receiving her blessing on the kitchen floor, in the middle of August 1962, I had ridden with my mother from East Norwalk up to Lenox, Massachusetts, in the Berkshire Mountains of western Massachusetts. That's where Shadowbrook, the Jesuit seminary, was. A Jesuit "boot camp," it was the novitiate building where a young man learned rudimentary Jesuit priestly tools like Latin and Greek, German, and French, history and math, as well as to endure—even treasure— the acetic rigors of praying, singing, worshipping, working in silence, and praising the Good Lord. After two years of apprenticeship, an acceptable young man would take Jesuit vows of poverty, chastity, and obedience. All this and heaven too.

It was a long drive. It was hot. I hung an arm out the window.

"Why are you drumming your fingers on the roof of the car?" my mother chided.

"I didn't know I was doing it. Should I stop?"

"Not if it helps."

"I know what you're thinking: why should I be nervous if joining the Jesuits is what I've said I want to do? I guess it's like joining the army or getting a call-up from the minors to a big-league team. It's natural to worry whether you have what it takes. Who knows if he can be brave until he finds himself in battle?"

"Honey"—she never called me that—"my worry is you're going to love it, and we'll never know who you are again."

We pulled up to the curb before a huge brick building of at least four stories. Several older priests were standing at the base of a long concrete staircase leading up to large glass doors with shining gold trim. A dozen younger men all dressed in the same style of black habits stood with the priests.

Will I ever feel at ease with them?

Everyone was smiling, introducing themselves, and shaking hands with the new arrivals, who were dressed just like me, looking silly in motley, the same coats and ties I had worn attending my Jesuit high school.

We kissed and hugged our families, said goodbye and saw them cry, and watched them drive away. When the coast was clear, a small group of jovial novices picked up our suitcases and led us new recruits up the stairs. The novices would be our guides for the next two weeks. Later they told us they were our "angels." They were wearing black habits—just like the priests we had seen outside—but otherwise the angels looked as young as we did; and certainly, they did not seem to be nervous. Their confidence helped ease my anxiety. It made it seem like the first step I had just taken in getting through the front door was going to be the hardest one. I had one look behind at the grand expanse of the grounds, the sky, the clouds, the hills, and the lake.

"I can live here."

I would learn that many notable people had favored this spectacular setting. Samuel Ward—the brother of Julia Ward Howe, who wrote the "Battle Hymn of the Republic," and a friend of Ralph Waldo

Emerson and the poet Longfellow—built the first grand house he called Oakswood on the site in 1844. In 1892, Anson Phelps Stokes, a banker and railroad owner, tore down most of the original house. He tripled the landholding and built an elaborate home he called Shadowbrook. His daughter suggested the name. She had learned Nathanial Hawthorne, who once lived nearby, had so named the brook that ran through the property while on a picnic with his children.

Stokes sold the house and land to Andrew Carnegie, who lived there from 1917–19. The Jesuits bought the home and grounds in 1922. And in 1923, forty-one novices moved in, with five priests and seven lay brothers. The grand home burned down in March 1956, and four resident Jesuits died. Almost immediately the Jesuits broke ground for the current massive, institutionalized brick building I now stood within, four stories high, with a cavernous basement. It opened again for business in 1958. And here I was in 1962, just as the paint had dried. (A delightfully witty and learned history of Shadowbrook, and the tragic fire, can be found in F. X. Shea's *The Shadowbrook Fire*)

The first thing I noticed inside was polished austerity. The walls and floors were clean, shiny, and bright and reflected cold fluorescent ceiling lights. No place for filth to hide. We walked silently to our assigned rooms, each with a number on the door. Inside the room was an unmade bed, a chair, a kneeler, a desk, a dresser, a sink, a window, and a closet with empty wire hangers on a rod. The one concession to luxury was a foam pad on the kneeler. It was red, the only splash of color in the room with gray walls and flooring. Light tan desk and chair. Gray steel framed bed.

This looks just like Gramps's bedroom, I said silently to myself. *It's not all that strange.*

How quiet it was. The angels told us that, except for the novice master, for the first few weeks we would speak only with them. When we had meals in a separate area of the refectory or attended Mass in the chapel, I looked across the large silent spaces at a crowd of at least a hundred other novices. They were dressed all in black of course. They smiled and looked friendly, if appraisingly. They said not a word to us, nor to each other. A rule of silence prevailed. I liked the quiet. It left me alone within myself, looking out through the window of new surroundings, assessing what I saw. When young men walked by my door, I could hear their shoes squeak. Their treads were purposeful.

The silence broke into laughter and animated conversations during recreation times inside rec rooms, or outside when the already resident novices were doing landscape work or gardening or playing sports. The only time we postulants even talked among ourselves was during walks around the novitiate grounds. We talked about the spectacular view down the hill to a beautiful lake. The angels took us there one day for a swim and to go rowing. Down by the lake, Shadowbrook had bathhouses and large halls for summer meals. I spent a few minutes alone, looking out across the water. Its smooth serenity reminded me of the waters in the Long Island Sound looking out at the sea from *Flotsam*.

I began to feel comfortable with the silence after a few days and didn't have to struggle to find something to say to the twenty postulants in my group—who only a short time earlier had been complete strangers.

Two weeks later, we found our own new black habits laid out on our beds after we came back from a conference with the novice master. The angels went from room to room, showing us the knot for tying the cincture so that the two ends hung down just to the level of the knees. I was fascinated to discover the cincture knot was a clove hitch, one of the knots I'd learned to tie to earn the second class rank in the Boy Scouts. I'd also used it on *Flotsam* to tie down the boom at mooring. It's also mentioned in *Moby-Dick*. The great compendium *The Ashley Book of Knots* traced the knot back to its use in ratlines, horizontal lines in rigging that serve as ladder ties for seamen to climb masts and set sails. It goes back in time to the first quarter of the sixteenth century, which curiously corresponds to the time of Saint Ignatius founding the Jesuits in 1534.

"Was there a causal link?" I asked an angel.

"A clove hitch? That's a question for a higher power than me."

I soon learned by observation that tying a cincture made a Jesuit fashion statement of sorts. More liberally inclined young Jesuits tied it low on the hips. The more traditionally inclined tied it just under the rib cage. Only those with eyes to see ever noticed. And the signifier only reiterated the obvious.

Newly robed, we were invited to an evening ice-cream party, where we met and started to get to know the other class of twenty novices who had already been living there ahead of our group for two weeks. They formed the other half of the forty men in the entering class of 1962. Then of course there was another group of about sixty men that made up those novices who had been in residence for one and two years. The group of one hundred of us novices seemed like a huge crowd in a small room.

Within a few minutes of shaking hands and exchanging names—we started awkwardly getting used to calling each other "Brother"—followed by last names only. The atmosphere became electric when the whole room erupted frequently, uproariously with laughter.

There was genuine happiness in finally meeting each other—the pros and the new apprentices. There were a few cases of the reuniting of old friends, some of whom already knew each other from high school or college.

There was a pair of sibling brothers among them, who, because each had the same last name, were allowed to use the first initial of their first name as part of their titles. Even more bewildering at first was discovering five men had the same last name of Kelly, reflecting the strong presence of Boston Irish Catholics in the New England Province of the Society of Jesus at the time. "No matter child, the name," in the words of the Jesuit poet Gerard Manley Hopkins. They broke from their cocoons of silence in a flutter of black-winged butterflies hovering together.

Some were recent graduates of a Jesuit-run high school; others were from public and parochial high schools throughout New England. At least half were older. Brother LaCasse had sailed on the first nuclear submarine, the USS *Nautilus*. Brother Nelson had graduated from West

Point and been the captain of a military tank company in occupied Germany.

I asked him, "Which did you find tougher? Being a cadet or a novice?"

"A novice by a lot. But both were good."

Brother Madek spoke native Polish. He had been a member of the CIA. Brother Brenekmeier, lanky and tall, over six foot, with thick blond hair, had been born in Holland under Nazi occupation. He remembered using newspaper for toilet paper after the war. Brother Schweiter held a PhD from Princeton in mathematics. Brother Willard had dropped out of Harvard to join the Jesuits. His ancestors came on the Mayflower. Brother Cloke was a fine painter. Brother Orsini's ancestors were royalty in Italy.

How different everyone was. Every other group I'd been a part of—scouts, altar boys, students—had all pretty much been alike. Now ages, talents, looks, and sizes were all in different shapes. None measured square to another.

I wanted to be a Jesuit for personal, almost selfish reasons as an escape hatch from class prejudice—from what seemed at the time a miasma of uppity people who acted holier than thou (or more literally, better off than thou.)

I had no idea until living my first few months as a novice that in 1962, the boil at Shadowbrook was taking heat from the Catholic Church itself. In the early 1960s, church attendance was booming for all denominations. Over 50 percent of Americans attended church on Sunday mornings in 1958. Many Catholics were galvanized by reading Thomas Merton's *The Seven Story Mountain*, his autobiography tracing his dissolute life as a young intellectual as it gradually flowered into his romantic vocation to become a Trappist monk.

There was a widespread fascination among many Catholics for medieval theology (before the messy disruptions of the Protestant Reformation), especially in those Jesuit communities like this one that could mount elaborate medieval-style liturgies, with candle-lit processions of chanting monks entering a chapel at night.

In addition, there was a new, handsome Catholic president in John F. Kennedy after 1960, with an astonishingly glamorous Catholic wife. Pope John XXIII took over the Church in 1958 and began to talk about serious reforms.

In 1962—when the pope instituted the Second Vatican Council—I entered the Jesuits. Every month there were promulgations about welcoming women fully into the life of the Church (meaning even the possibility of ordination?), making ecumenical overtures to Muslims, Jews, and Protestants, and preparing vernacular translations to replace the Latin Mass.

Shadowbrook was buzzing with all this revolutionary atmosphere and change, which was taken up with great enthusiasm and joy by the most amazing men I'd ever met. The Jesuits numbered then around thirty-two thousand throughout the world, eight thousand in the US; my New England Province had almost two thousand men, who ran four universities, four high schools throughout New England, plus high schools in Jamaica and Iraq that were fertile recruiting grounds.

Novices were only allowed to listen to Western classical music, which—like jazz before Brubeck—I had never listened to before.

It played in the background of every recreational hour.

Some brothers were teaching the callow innocents like me how to listen to it. Several could do "air conducting," where they pretended to lead the orchestra using a pencil or a ruler as a baton—but they probably could have done it for real. I was really impressed when I saw one air conductor flub a shift from brass to strings.

"Ah ha! They're using the 1818 edition of the score."

Otherwise, they actually knew the music by heart and just when to urge the horns to cut loose, the drums to pound, or the strings to sing.

Very heady stuff.

I was incredulous to find that classical music included the bawdy and raucous "Carmina Burana" by Carl Orff, featuring gambling abbots, roasting swans, and young shepherds chasing nymphs in the woods. I thought only rock 'n roll music could be raunchy. Orff's cantata was sung in Latin. But you could translate it easily in a Jesuit seminary.

Perhaps a dozen novices had brought guitars with them. They sang early 1960s folk songs by groups like the Kingston Trio ("Charlie on the MTA" was a big hit with the Bostonians among us); Peter, Paul, and Mary; The Weavers; the Limeliters. Even some rock 'n roll. The music of the Beatles and the Rolling Stones slipped over the walls. On quarterly visiting day weekends of novices with their families, familial brothers of the Jesuit brothers would bring their guitars and teach the increasingly revolutionary young music of the day. Brother LaCroix developed a foot-stomping imitation of Mick Jagger singing "I Can't Get No Satisfaction," which became a kind of anthem for young Jesuits blowing off steam at the weekly Thursday night evening recreation.

He'd only play it as the finale; young voluntary celibates relished the double entendre safely—for only the length of a song.

Some of the young Jesuits who had taken vows after two years and lived on the other side of the huge house from us novices were called *juniors*. In their third and fourth years at Shadowbrook, they took the first two years of college courses. One time, the juniors put on an amazing performance of Shakespeare's *Macbeth*. There was some momentary tittering when one of their own, dressed in theatrical drag, first came on stage as Lady Macbeth. But in Shakespeare's time, all his actors were males, and so it was easy to accept the convention. It helped that the acting was great. I can still see Lady Macbeth wringing her large bloody hands.

I'd read *Macbeth* in high school. Now its language in the mouths of fellow young Jesuits was a revelation. Were even Jesuits susceptible to ambition?

There was more.

Famous Jesuits visited from around the world. Daniel Berrigan, SJ, came to Shadowbrook wearing his black beret and black turtleneck, just back from his stint as a worker priest in Paris. He and his Josephine Order priest and brother, Phil, would be arrested as members of the

Catonsville Nine after burning draft office records with homemade napalm in 1968.

Jesuits from England, Japan, Germany, and Spain passed through, always willing to give us a pep talk about what was shaking from Vatican II. Abbot Fox, Thomas Merton's Trappist superior, visited his brother, a Jesuit priest at Shadowbrook. He looked smashing in his white robes with black trim. Like a skipjack. Cardinal Cushing of Boston visited—wearing his full scarlet Cardinal regalia. He told funny stories in the house dining room from a podium.

"The only fasting you young men should be doing is eating as fast as you can."

I befriended another Jesuit passing through for a few days, traveling from the Maryland Province in Baltimore where he worked as a prison chaplain. He said he was born Jewish, then had converted to Catholicism and joined the Jesuits. As a result, he'd been disowned by his family. He opened the trunk of his car to reveal an outboard motor he'd gotten permission to purchase with his earnings (otherwise turned into the Province treasury) as an offering to his father who had called and welcomed him back to the family. We both cried as he told the story. How magical it was to belong to the same group as this wonderful Jewish Jesuit man. And all the others I had befriended in less than a year among them. They lived as one.

Several months later, I was standing in the dark outside the chapel on Easter Eve in the spring of 1963. I had come to think of myself as a blue-collar kid who had been inducted into holy royalty. My hands rested that night on the wheelchair handles of the invalid Father Hennessey since on that night I was his designated attendant. The priest was strapped in, shivering from advanced Parkinson's disease. One task was to wipe away his drool when it began to run. He was rumored to have fought with the White Russians against the Bolsheviks as an idealistic young man before he'd joined the Jesuits.

I had recently turned nineteen years old. I was dressed in a black habit and standing in a large open hallway along with at least a hundred other young Jesuit seminarians. My close friends Brother (Charlie) O'Leary and Brother (Joe) McEttrick stood nearby.

The lights overhead gradually dimmed as we passed around candles and began lighting them. Now the lights were out. We were all holding burning candles and waiting, uneasily, since it was now a few minutes after midnight. Father Healy, the choir director, was supposed to lead the chant we would sing as we processed into the chapel just prior to celebrating Easter Sunday Mass—the most elaborate and most sacred liturgy in the Catholic Church. Healy was a short man with a large head, who smiled widely when we'd sung well. A step stool had been placed next to the doors into the chapel so he could be seen above our heads. He was supposed to blow the pitch pipe and signal the downbeat that would start things off.

However, this Sunday morning he was nowhere to be seen. He was late. One of the more musical among the gathering hesitantly began to hum the beginning note to start the procession moving without him. Otherwise, all stood in silence. For once in this highly orchestrated life, there was nothing on the agenda. I looked around.

Even in the dark I could see what little light there was reflecting off Brother Brenckmeyer's big teeth in his mouth that always opened in a smile.

Suddenly the elevator next to the chapel entrance chimed. The older priests in the community used it to reach the first-floor chapel from their third-floor residence. Two stainless steel doors slid majestically open. Bright fluorescent light spilled into our candle-lit darkness and momentarily blinded our dark-adapted eyes. We gasped.

Father Healy took one step forward, then stopped and stood looking bewildered in the middle of the elevator. He blinked, opening his mouth speechlessly. Before he could make another move, some wag among us improvised and shouted in Latin, "*Ecce Lumen Christi,*" or "Behold the light of Christ," and we all spontaneously burst into laughter at the comic *tableau vivant* of Jesus's resurrection from the tomb.

Our collective laughter blew some of the candles out. The man next to me, Brother McEttrick, dropped his candle and stepped on it, and I heard a faint huff of frustration. Like a porpoise blowing steam. When Brother McEttrick started to kneel down to salvage what was left of his candle, I grabbed him by the arm to hold him up. Somehow, I managed to be holding two candles, so I handed one over. Brother McEttrick smiled and nodded his thanks. We weren't supposed to make any sounds until we began to sing. It took several minutes for the laughter to die down.

Father Healy stepped up on his stool. He looked grim. He blew the opening note, and we began the procession in a sonorous and jolly mood perfectly fitting, after all, for the holiest and happiest of holy days.

None of the young men were nonplussed by the opening moment of levity. They were smart, young, and modern men who'd willingly ordered their lives according to ancient regimens. This sort of abrupt juxtaposition of the ridiculous and the sublime happened all the time. Whatever the appropriate demeanor should be at any given time, we were prone to spontaneous laughter. We couldn't help ourselves. We didn't give it a second thought.

A powerful moment of faith occurred a few weeks later. I guided Father Henri de Lubac on a tour of Shadowbrook to meet Father Hennessey. He was the priest with Parkinson's disease in the wheelchair I'd handled on Easter Eve.

Father Hennessey loomed large in our lives. Each afternoon one novice walked outside with him. It was agonizingly slow. He walked with a gimp; he drooled and shook. It took one hour to walk a hundred yards. Novices dreaded seeing their names assigned to his daily walk for reasons we were too shameful to talk about.

We awoke every morning at 5:30 a.m., and by the afternoon had already spent two and a half hours on our knees for morning meditation, Mass, and chapel visits. We routinely sat through another hour of instruction about expected Jesuit behavior. Surprisingly, that included eating bread at the table only after tearing it into small pieces.

A number of us worked in silence helping prepare, serve, and clean up after breakfast and lunch. Everyone was raring to blow off steam, even if it was three hours of *laborandum* (literally "work that must be done") outside clearing brush, pulling weeds, mowing, digging, gardening, and piling rocks. We would sing and shout and kid each other in the fluid English we were allowed to speak only outdoors. Inside the house, only Latin was allowed.

When it was my turn to be the designated walker on that warm spring day, I got permission to take Father Hennessy rowing out in the lake at the bottom of the large hill upon which the massive Novitiate building perched. Brother McEttrick drove the two of us down in one of the house cars. I sat in the back holding Father Hennessey upright. While Brother McEttrick steadied the boat, I carried Father Hennessy. The priest was very small and could not have walked upright in the sand. The only way to settle the priest in the boat was to hug him close to my chest as I stepped into the boat, and then work him onto my lap as we sat down on the stern thwart. I slid the priest sideways onto the seat and propped him up with two life jackets. Brother McEttrick pushed us off.

As I sat facing the priest, rowing, I saw him almost smile. Later when Brother McEttrick and I got him back into the infirmary, he gasped out a raspy "Thank you."

"When you had him on your lap there in the boat for a moment," Brother McEttrick said wryly, "I thought you two looked like Michelangelo's *Pietà*."

"When I saw you waving at us from the beach, I thought you looked like Jesus signaling the apostles to throw the fishing net overboard."

Brother McEttrick thought for a moment. "I think this place is starting to get to us."

"I think it's supposed to!" I said, pointing upward, as if proclaiming a hidden truth.

One particular morning during the daily conference, the father master of novices told the assembled novices that he had attended a public meeting in the town of Lenox, where Shadowbrook was located. A number of locals had approached him to say how moved and impressed they were when they saw young men taking such wonderful care of an infirm old man. We were all wearing habits and were walking on the roads when they had driven by. We were shocked to hear this and ashamed to admit to ourselves silently how we dreaded taking Father Hennessey for his daily constitutional—even though of course we did it and tried our hardest to keep him upright and to keep up an amiable chatter. We always quietly assumed that, ideally, if we were sincerely religious, we should indifferently find hard and easy tasks equally appealing within the overshadowing duty of "doing God's will." Having embarrassingly vain or impatient feelings hinted at how hypocritical our overtly pious demeanor might be.

My powerful experience with Father Hennessy was when I was assigned to accompany Father de Lubac from France on a tour of the building.

Father de Lubac was the closest thing to a rock star for young Jesuits. He was another one of the great older churchmen cultivating the young. He was visiting during a break from serving as one of the top theological consultants during Pope John XXIII's Second Vatican Council. He had been born into the French aristocracy but had turned toward a life of poverty. During the war, as a priest, he worked in the French Resistance against the Nazis. His early writings called for more democracy in the church and had been banned by earlier, more conservative church authorities. Pope John XXIII recognized him as a leading thinker and elevated him to the rank of cardinal late in his life. He was also imperially slim and had a long, aristocratic face.

I fastened eyes on de Lubac, given the honor of showing the great man the chapel, the refectory, and the library.

I can't believe I'm wearing the same black habit as him, I thought.

The young and the elder Jesuit entered into Shadowbrook's infirmary and the room of Father Hennessy, SJ.

Father Hennessey was the priest, it was rumored, who had, as a youthful volunteer, fought with the White Russian Army against the Bolsheviks. Now two former heroes filled the same small space together while I stood in awe.

Father Hennessey was sitting on his hospital bed, slightly tilted to the side. His body shook. The front of his habit glistened with drool. He could no longer really talk. But you could see his eyes brighten and hear the patter of his grunting sharpen when Father de Lubac entered his room. He knew who de Lubac was—and what he meant to the Jesuits.

Father de Lubac rushed to his bed, embraced him, and cried, "Father, without your prayers my work would be meaningless." Both hugged and wept—as did I. For that instant, three men believed what de Lubac said with soulful certainty. Brilliant, sick, or young, each stood small and equal before God. What more profound revelation could anyone imagine of the power of religious faith? I would never see its equal. A man who could only drool and grunt and stagger was led to believe he was essential to the success of God's will to save the people of the earth for Heaven. As Wordsworth said of the French Revolution, "Bliss was it in that dawn to be alive / But to be young was very heaven!" Or as Jesus said, "What you do for the least among you, you do for me" (Matthew 25:40).

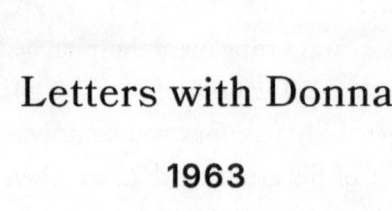

Letters with Donna

1963

> *Write what you see.*
> —Revelation 1:11

During the second year in the Shadowbrook Novitiate, I wrote to Donna for the first time. She had sent a short note asking how I was doing.

I love my fellow novices. Some are already college graduates from places like Princeton, Harvard, West Point, Boston College, and Holy Cross who look to us younger men as brothers they were eager to mentor in music, literature, history, art, and stuff they already knew something about. They're all so different. I'm only 19, but I have friends, brothers, much older.

I also told her about singing folk and rock songs with guitars at recreation, working in the fields and kitchens, swimming and rowing in the lake, and the story of taking Father de Lubec to Father Hennessy in his room after having taken the old priest for a row.

But to give you a sense of the spirit of the place, let me tell you what happened moments before midnight on my first Easter at Shadowbrook last spring.

Donna wrote back.

> I loved the story about your first Easter and the wonderful re-enactment of Jesus rising from the dead. You still can tell a terrific story like you wrote about your first vacation during the rainy week on the island. You still have the touch. Keep writing.
>
> What I once said to you about your Jesuit high school being like the stage set in a Shakespearean play was true. Those funny adult Jesuits having an argument in the hallway of your high school had probably learned their lines at Shadowbrook. I must say it's amazing that you sing the Beatles and the Rolling Stones. Us outsiders imagine monkish places like yours have you singing lachrymose hymns and chanting matins at dusk, your black cowls bent over in reverence. But what about you? You used to write poetry in high school. Are you doing any writing on your own? Besides just your wonderful, long letter to me? Or would that be thought to be immodest, or self-centered?

I responded to her letter.

> I'm still scribbling poetry. And it turns out quite a few of us do. And we have an underground network like the Soviet samizdat where we pass around what we've written. It's interesting how hard it is not to write pious slop when so much of the language we hear has to do with belief and church doctrine. And you're right. It's interesting to explore in writing what remains of your own inner self even while most of your outer life you spend with a group.
>
> Here's one that shook me that I think you'll appreciate.
>
> I'm copying from my notebook now: "Walking alone during our evening half hour free time after dinner. At the

edge of the pasture, over the stone wall, into the trees of the woods, I hear a cacophony of twitters as hundreds of large iridescent green-and-blue-headed grackles, a large migrating flock, come swooping in just about ground level over the golden leaves piled on the ground under the trees, making a loud racket out of what individually would be each a harsh tweet. The sound guides my look. I'm enchanted. The birds slide into the leaves, kicking them up, batting them with their black wings, feeding on something they're finding under the leaves, which I can't see at the distance, but there must be something since they just keep doing it for the quarter hour I watched. Once in a while, the entire flock would rise as a cloud a few feet into the air and change direction, shoveling through the leaves in the other direction, perhaps to disorient whatever edibles they pursued."

After I saw that great scene, I had some free time left.

I went back to my room to write down what I just copied out for you. The next night I read it over. I doodled with the words. I concentrated the scene into:

This sudden flight from fallen leaves . . .

And then, maybe because sometimes I color myself in black and you in gold like the birds and the leaves when I'm reminiscing, and I do think about you a lot, the line came out:

Is all we were . . .

And then, socko! Running through the rhyme file in my mind, I finished the line with the words "and why I grieve" to cobble a rhyme with "leaves," sort of.

This sudden flight from fallen leaves
Is all we were and why I grieve.

This kicked me into questions.

"Do I grieve giving up Donna to become a Jesuit;" *Do* I, *did* I, love her that way? Is how I'm living a big mistake? I spent a couple of days wondering about the meaning of words

I wrote, which apparently came out of nowhere; what I might be feeling; what I don't want to admit, even to myself. And then I decided; no that's not it, although there's *something* to it. I can measure my deep satisfaction at how I live by the high cost of what I had to give up to get it. I decided to leave the poem right there. Not to treat the two as opening lines, since I don't want to know any more than what I say here to you. Instead, leave the questions hanging like those second thoughts we've talked about. Okay?

But I did do one writing project that pushed through to an ending. A few days after I wrote the little poem, I was commissioned to write the annual St. Stanislaus Kostka Day play in honor of the only Jesuit saint who died as a novice—and thus is held up to us as a model of what we could achieve for ourselves even at the entry-level. The whole house attended the performance, the priests and juniors, not just our own cohort of first-and-second-year novices, so some gravitas was expected.

I created a staging that required two circular platforms. On one were enacted key scenes from the vigorous life of the Jesuit founder Saint Ignatius Loyola, who had been wounded in war and then fought hard to convince a suspicious Catholic hierarchy to sanction his new idea for a religious order.

On the second stage were enacted the much more mundane events in the life of a sickly, slight, eighteen-year-old son of the Polish aristocracy, who legend had it once fainted headfirst into a bowl of soup (a variant to the story said it was a bowl of mashed potatoes) when he heard one of his father's friends curse at the dinner table.

Don't laugh. As a young Polish-American man, I felt certain affinities with his upbringing. The idea of my play was to juxtapose scenes and speeches from the lives of these two different kinds of Jesuits to point out how similar they were in bravery and devotion for all their differences to each other, and of course, to all of us in the audience. A little bit like the story I told you about Father de Lubec meeting Father Hennessey. The play had a one-night stand. But it was well received. One brother told me afterward the dialogue reminded him of T. S. Eliot. My immediate reaction to hearing that was to tell him, "You don't know anything about T. S. Eliot."

The early stages of production had been stressful. I cast Brother Antoon in the role of St. Ignatius. Brother Antoon already declared that he's going to work in the theater as a Jesuit. He had put on his own theatrical production a few months previously where he strung all the speeches in Shakespeare having to do with kings into one massive monologue. Brother Antoon performed it himself—and in such a way as to show Shakespeare's covert hatred of kings. It was astonishing. No props. Just a solo actor moving restlessly over the stage, which happened to be a grass lawn.

When Brother Antoon got word of my play, he demanded the role of what he was sure was the main character—Saint Stanislaus. But I cast Brother McEttrick in the role. He was closer to the type of a timid, slightly built but resolute young man that St. Stan apparently was. Brother Antoon kept badgering me for the main role. I wouldn't budge, however. Brother Antoon played St. Ignatius defiantly and way over the top, shouting histrionically and pounding in his boots around his circular stage.

Later that night, during the Sacred Silence observed through the house during our last fifteen minutes before bed, Brother Antoon stood in my doorway and, in defiance of several house rules, with his eyes wide open, anxiously asked me in English how I thought he had done. Ignoring the same house rules, as well as the code of politesse, I said, "You were really good, if a little hammy." He slammed the door and would not speak to me in either Latin or English for several months.

I ended the letter to Donna by saying, "I hope you'll never be like that with me."

Donna wrote back.

> College for me is nothing like yours. The other students are very bright and work hard, and I've made good friends. Mark is near and dear. But even he and I, and certainly the others, are more alone than you. We all see ourselves moving on eventually, getting a job doing what we've learned. At school, we pick and choose like shopping in a grocery store for what we think we need. You and your fellow Jesuits are in a school like those porpoises we sailed with. You're all together with yourselves. You live and eat and swim and sleep in the same place you always make wherever you are together. I wonder if there'll ever be a place for people like me as a friend to fit in even edgewise in the world you're immersed in. I hope so. I'm happy to see you say we should keep writing to each other. I'm not going to say anything more than what you did about that wonderful little poem you wrote about the birds and maybe about the two of us. Let's *leave it* (forgive the pun) right there. It shimmers. I feel a little sad and just as happy in the shimmering. We both did the right thing—ouch! I like the description of the play. And we better leave that right there too, since if I had seen the performance, I don't think I would have understood a word of it.

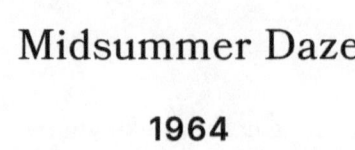

Midsummer Daze

1964

Each day has enough trouble of its own.
—Matthew 6:34

I didn't write to Donna about the darker laughter. The topic was unsettling: when the laughter became uncontrollable—unnerving. In these instances, the sharp breaks in the overlaying tensions of our otherwise silent, celibate lives would approach pathology.

A likely occasion for such an outburst would occur at the end of the day, during a communal ritual in the chapel with all of the novices kneeling side by side. By this time of day, we were tired and, at times, uptight. We all detested the least favorite religious ritual of the day—litanies. Under the prompting of the assigned priest kneeling in front of us at the chapel altar steps, all two hundred would run through a tedious fifteen-minute antiphonal litany. The priest, for example, would intone one by one the names of saints: "Blessed Mary Virgin . . . Saint Ignatius Loyola . . ." and so on. After each name, as a group, the rest would drone a fixed response: "Pray for us . . . Pray for us," which would resonate off the darkened walls.

It was a tricky process, since one pattern would replace another. After a run-through of sixty saints, there'd be a series of petitions such as "Forgive us our sins, O Lord . . ." or "Grant us true repentance . . ."

These calls required the group's response to change, in this case, to repeating in unison: "We beseech thee hear us . . . We beseech thee hear us." The trouble would start with one mischievous novice.

Typically, he'd be kneeling next to another and sense that one was seething with suppressed anxiety. Under the cover of the group response praying, "We beseech thee hear us," this mischievous novice would solemnly intone just loud enough so only the one kneeling next to him could hear it: "Put peaches in baskets . . . put peaches in baskets."

The poor innocent novice would twist his torso trying to suppress an intense giggle—and suddenly burst out barks of uncontrollable laughter. If the group were "tight" with tensions that night, the whole novice section of the chapel would helplessly explode in response, and start laughing hard, even while trying frantically to choke the frenzy back. What would be worse was to have one shaking so hard, he'd slip off the kneeler and his head would suddenly drop down out of the lined-up row of the heads around it—and the laughter would ring out against the walls without any possibility of restraint.

We couldn't help ourselves, like the lighthearted laughing that night when the elevator door opened on Father Healey. But now there was something grim in the air. In the wave of mass hysteria, the priest would give up and stomp off. The novices would subside into a final ritual of ten minutes of meditative silence and shuffle embarrassed down the darkened silent hallways to our rooms for the night.

Sometimes after this happened, and on the way to the chapel for morning prayers, we'd see a notice pinned to the bulletin board—in Latin—that announced today would be a *Dies Ludos,* "a day of games," or a "ludi day," as we happily called it.

That meant, after the essential Mass, meditation, and morning chores, we'd be free from 10 a.m. to 4 p.m. for walks, hikes, swims, skiing, skating, and playing field games with the intent of blowing off steam. Lunch would be sandwiches served in the large beach houses down at the lake, weather permitting, or in the rec room.

We'd play guitars and sing funny satirical songs or play sports. During a softball game on one of these "release" days, an older brother,

Walsh, who was big and robust and had, incongruously, previously worked as a businessman, was trying to stretch a double into a triple. About ten feet from the bag, he leaped into the air horizontally. He flew feet first into the chest of little Brother Eagan who was playing third base—knocking him down hard.

Brother Eagan was outraged and, for good measure, made a tag holding the ball tightly in his hand as he punched Brother Walsh in the face. They fell down, rolling in the dust and shouting and punching each other. The rest of the players were thunderstruck. None of us had ever punched another. We rushed over to pull apart the two of them and immediately the two brothers were falling over each other apologizing. All of them sensed that this brief moment of violence was when the rising tensions of recent days were finally released.

I had my own private "crucifixion of tight." One summer's night, I was having trouble sleeping. I could feel nerves twitching, and that morning had just stopped short of slugging another novice for examining his fingernails too long in chapel.

While I was supposed to be working outside later clearing some fallen brush, I went down to the tool shed to get an axe and snuck off into the woods. I found a large dead tree. I started shouting. I swung the axe and brought the blade down hard and deep into the trunk. I felt better already. As I was raising the axe for another mighty blow, the wasp's nest I hadn't seen hanging from a branch emptied. Down dropped dark undulating streams of angry wasps who stung my exposed skin, even through the thinner parts of my clothing.

I dropped the axe, screamed, and ran back to the house and immediately sought out the brother infirmarian in the house infirmary.

"Stung by bees, were you?" he asked, stating the obvious. "You have hives all over your arms and face that must hurt. Lie down on a bed and I'll give you another kind of sting that might help with the pain. I'll keep an eye on the hives."

The needle, either adrenaline or a muscle relaxer, did help to the point where I began to think what happened was funny. I giggled, which the brother infirmarian noted, was a good sign. He probably knew from long experience what medical care might loosen up a tight, strung out, stung Jesuit novice.

I woke from a long nap on the infirmary bed. Both of us decided my body was back to normal and I was free to go about my duties again. Both of us prayed thanks to Saint Luke—who was a doctor, it is said, and who remains their patron saint.

The bed I had recuperated on that day was the same bed Father Hennessey had occupied permanently when I had ushered Father de Lubac into his infirmary room a few months earlier—shortly before Father Hennessy died.

When I woke up in Father Hennessey's bed and realized this, I felt embarrassed by the trivial reason that had brought me there. Perhaps my humility was part of the healing process too. At the same time, I wondered whether moments like this canceled all the ridiculous behavior of young men under stress, laughing during what were supposed to be solemn rituals.

This time, I initiated a letter exchange with Donna out of a sense of need to confide in a dear friend from outside the world I was living in, to get some perspective. I began referring again to the powerful experience of seeing Father de Lubec embrace Father Hennessey.

> It came out of nowhere. There was no ritual lead-up to it. The only preamble was walking into a sick man's room on an ordinary day. I was "surprised by joy" in C. S. Lewis's notion that rapture was always unanticipated. This kind of thing happens to me here. Like when dawn's light comes through the stained-glass windows in the chapel. I'd been standing among strong smart men in the morning and had just taken a shower and felt utterly light and clean and just myself. The walls were reverberating with Gregorian chants. What's gratifying for me is that, although I have no sense of pitch or how to stay on key, the great wave of my musical brothers' singing sweeps my

meager voice into a heavenly chorus. What's striking to me about these moments is they seem more powerful than the actual experience of the Mass—the ritualized sacrifice of Jesus once again with his blood-the-wine separated from his body-the-bread. Our joint holy meal, which should be the climactic moment of my daily routine, often seems just routine.

I know it's a whole different scene, and I know it might seem a real stretch. But at these moments of absolute serenity, I sometimes find myself having second thoughts—reminiscing about our boat ride together out to the sandbar with the crabs and the Jesuits. By second thoughts I don't mean I should have followed you and "gone with the crabs," but I find I am now—as I was then—completely at peace in both these different places. I love where I've wound up . . .

But what I still can't figure out—and what turns out to be odd about these moments of great peace—is that we are officially warned against seeking them. They were called "consolation," and their danger was you could become mystically addicted to them and then become dissatisfied with the normal humdrum stuff of reading dull holy books or cleaning toilets. I almost think the reason behind this idea is that we're not expected to put any value on anything that happens to us in our life on earth. Bliss is for heaven—something to be avoided in our ordinary lives—because—if we decided we like it here—then there's a danger our ordinary life on earth, staying home, will come to seem sufficient. I even think if I told anyone here about my reminiscing about our sail to the sandbar while singing chants with my fellow Jesuits, there'd be more worry about the idea of having pleasure of any kind than daydreaming about a woman at Mass.

Donna wrote back. We wrote carefully to one another because as I told her, one of the rules of Shadowbrook was that all incoming and outgoing letters were subject to a priest's censorship. You turned in letters you wrote unsealed. Every incoming letter was slit open before it was delivered as a reminder of this possibility.

Donna wrote:

> I wonder whether the house censor read what you wrote, or if one did, he didn't find anything wrong with it. I imagine it's the former since it sounds close to religious heresy to me. If you're so inclined to the pleasures of ordinary, daily, earthly life—even one as mundane as walking with a crippled priest—instead of aspiring to a future everlasting bliss—which is what you seem to be saying the church authorities or the Jesuits want you to believe—and yet you still want to remain an earthly Jesuit, maybe what you're saying is that you find leading a celibate, dedicated life is right for you even if you don't really believe in religious orthodox teachings. You're in it for the giggles and the consolations of chant at dawn—and probably basketball. I'm happy for you either way. And I mean it. You have found your place—your home in the world—as tightly fenced in as it is.

Donna was right, of course. Even wise. About being fenced in. Yet her pointed insight deserved some second thoughts. Was I truly happy as a Jesuit or just in it for the "giggles," for the excitement of joining a group of astonishing young men who considered me one of them?

With her letter lying folded on my desk, next to the Bible, I decided a partial answer to Donna's question—was yes, I did love the Jesuit life for the so-called giggles. But there were prayers laced into the giggles. Some popped out spontaneously.

I was driving Shadowbrook's surplus World War II troop truck with Brother O'Leary and Brother McEttrick in the spring. We took the back road to the shore area and the beach buildings that the rector, Father Langguth, a tall, regal, muscular man, had developed. He had trained as an engineer before he entered the Jesuits. But he surveyed this road to the lake through a small swamp. Water often overflowed the road in spite of the numerous culverts he ordered dug in. On this spring day, we hit a wet patch, and the wheels of the truck sunk in up to the bottom of the hubcaps. I tried rocking between forward and reverse for a few minutes, but the tires just sank more, kicking showers of mud up I could see in the rearview mirror. For a few seconds, we sat in silence. Brother McEttrick said cheerfully, "No problem. There's still an hour left of *laborandum*. Let's one of us run up to the house and get the tractor and a chain to pull us out."

"That'll be fun," I said with a smile.

"No, wait a minute," said Brother O'Leary sharply. "We haven't prayed yet. Let's all calm down and each say a Hail Mary for the Blessed Virgin Mary to help us get out right now." So, we all did, silently. We nodded to each other when finished; I turned the key, slipped the clutch into low gear, and the truck crept out of the muck like it was solid ground. All three of us cheered, "BVM to the rescue!"

Brother McEttrick said sardonically, "You know, I don't think this sort of prayer is supposed to work."

"Oh ye of little faith," laughed Brother O'Leary, who punched him in the upper arm.

The house tractor, an old, huge, 1930s Allis-Chalmers with huge studded rear wheels, evoked another spontaneous eruption of exclamatory prayer. Late on a dark evening, deep in the winter, Brother O'Leary and I were told to go along with Brother Brenikmeyer to take the tractor down to the main road to Stockbridge that ran between the house grounds and the playing fields. A large tree had fallen across the well-traveled public road, Rt. 186, between Lenox and Stockbridge. As we drove down, we could see cars lined up in both directions with their tailpipes smoking and people walking around in front of car headlights. The novices' task was to push the tree off the road. Brother O'Leary and I were given bow saws and limb clippers to use while Brother Brenikmeyer would use a chain or plow to do the heavy work.

Brother Brenikmeyer was native Dutch. His family still lived in Amsterdam where he had been born during World War II. When the family flew over from Holland to visit him on visiting days, the rest of us were struck dumb with awe at his brace of tall, lanky, blond, beautiful sisters. He was big and strong, with large teeth, and always laughed with a *huffa huffa* sound. He always got assigned the jobs that took brains and brawn and usually required a large machine. He drove. Brother O'Leary and I stood on a crossbar between the wheels behind the seat holding hand tools, feeling snug in wool hats, big boots, and heavy gloves.

All the car drivers were happy to see us. Most knew or figured out we were young Jesuits, who rarely got to meet with any local citizens. There was a festive air as Brother Brenikmeyer first chain-sawed the large trunk half broken off its stump. He expertly wrapped a chain about it. With the tractor in low gear, he pulled the tree parallel to the road and then pushed it into a ditch with the front loader. The two other brothers were busy, along with drivers and passengers, clearing away limbs and branches. One person asked me, pointing up at the big house with most of its lights burning brightly through a lightly falling snow, "What do you guys do up there?"

"Pray for drivers to get into trouble so we can get out of the house to help them," I said. We both laughed.

"So," the driver said, "guardian angels are for real."

Everybody thanked the three of us for clearing the road and waved as they drove through in both directions until the road was quiet in the snowy night. We three novices took our time cleaning up the evergreen fronds. Brother Brenikmeyer went back and forth across the empty road, pushing debris and snow into the ditch. Brother O'Leary and I whacked each other with pine branches.

Suddenly, we heard a car horn and screeching tires. A single car came careening out of the dark at high speed. It banged into one of the huge rear rubber tires of the tractor. Brother O'Leary and I watched in great horror as Brother Brenikmeyer catapulted out of the tractor seat. He turned a somersault high in the air, his long arms and legs extended like the wings of a cartwheel. His wool cap fell off. His blond hair swung wild around his head like a halo in the brief flash of the car's headlights as it rebounded into the ditch on the other side of the road.

"Oh dear Jesus!" I cried. Brother O'Leary cried, "Oh, God, no!" Our prayers were answered as quickly as we shouted them. Brother Brenikmeyer had dropped into a soft snowbank. He sprang to his feet laughing. He felt his wild blond hair with one hand and begged, "Have you seen my hat?"

After the three of us shared a tight hug, we ran over to the car with its headlights pointing up into the sky from the ditch. The doors opened; four drunken teenagers climbed out, moaning and giggling.

"My father's going to kill me. Please don't tell anybody."

With the chain and the tractor, we pulled the car out of the ditch. Remarkably, it only had one dented front fender, as if only a glancing blow had been enough to send one man into a snowbank and another four into a ditch.

As we drove back to the house in the dark and the snow, Brother O'Leary said, "I was disappointed the kids in the car weren't as grateful as the people in the traffic jam when we came to help. Not one of them even said thank you."

I answered piously, quoting Matthew 6:1. "Beware of practicing your righteousness before other people in order to be seen by them . . ."

Brother O'Leary completed the verse: ". . . for then you will have no reward from your father who is in heaven."

Brother Brenikmeyer said, twisting around to look first at one, then the other of us, "Amen, Brothers. And you're both right. In answer to your prayers, Brother Glennon promised us hot chocolate when we got back to the house."

It was even better than that. He had made a fresh batch of his special donuts. Brother Glennon had been born in County Cork, in Ireland. He was the kind of older Jesuit who never became a priest. Instead, he usually did manual labor for the support of houses like ours, such as being in charge of the vehicles or the infirmary or the tailor shop. Brother Glennon was both cook and gardener, in charge of the massive vegetable gardens that not only grew most of what we ate at Shadowbrook but, with unpaid novice workers, grew enough potatoes in a huge field near the sports fields to send to every other house in the New England Province. What a treat to be assigned to one of the trucks that made deliveries! Brother Glennon spoke Gallic to the birds while he tended the garden. He delighted in eating live worms whole that he dug up, waving the worm around above his open mouth so his novice helpers could see it.

"Thank you. God, for the food we are about to eat," he'd intone prayerfully, then tipping back his head, and to our disgust, he'd drop the worm straight down his mouth like a robin. He had a heavy brogue and, having never really learned our names, addressed us all indiscriminately as "breather dearie." He was over seventy years old, with a broad face and wispy white hair he never fully combed. Everyone at Shadowbrook loved him.

Another fretful prayer happened on a summer afternoon. A dozen novices were out on the raft, down at the lake sitting around, drying off, chatting, when the house Angelus bell went off. It rang at noon, and for fifteen minutes, wherever you were, you were supposed to drop what you were doing to say some prayers to the Virgin Mary. It's probably a vestige of the habit of monks singing the Office all day and night. The novices would lie down to sunbathe, each silently praying. Suddenly, a speedboat came roaring toward us. Probably because they knew what we were doing, the callow teenagers in it decided to have some fun. They swerved by the raft and sprayed us all with water.

"I'll bet Dwayne's driving," I muttered and looked sideways to see. The novices were sitting there, dripping wet. Nobody moved. Out of the sides of our eye slits, we saw the boat making a wide turn to make another run. The brothers ground their teeth.

One muttered fiercely, "Blessed Lady of the Lake, we beseech thee hear us." The rest grunted with repressed giggles.

I had rowed out to the float. I grabbed an oar with the intent of throwing it at the speedboat if it came back. *Alas*, I thought, *I don't have a horseshoe crab to toss like Donna once did*. The speedboat didn't come back, which was a blessing for us and them, doubtless through the intercession of the Blessed Lady of the Lake.

Okay, it's silly to call Brother Glennon's grace before worms or our expletives on Route 186 *prayers*, as well as attributing petitions to the BVM as resulting in her pushing the truck out of the mud and staving off another speedboat attack. But our lives were saturated in prayer. The hour-long daily meditation; the extended prayer of the Mass; the dreaded ritualistic litanies in the evening; a dining room full of men mumbling in muffled Latin—half the words of which they had forgotten as a group—grace before meals; our recommended twice daily private visits to the chapel, where we used to tell one in other, Jesus, cloaked in the pasty circles of the reserved hosts, would, faster than the speed of light, throw open the tabernacle door to scan with tiny binoculars who was showing up so he could check off his daily list. We had deep prayers and silly ones, loud ones and silent ones, private ones and community ones, in Latin or English, musical and rasping. It was the water we swam in. No one ever put it to us this way, but Ignatius's idea of putting the monastery into the Jesuit finally came to mean, in Blake's phrase, "Everything that is, is holy now."

Which is a nice, spiritual, almost mystic way to put it.

But there was a Hieronymus Bosch turbulence in the spirits of the men and in the air at Shadowbrook. Bright, strong-willed, passionate men saturated with religious images and rituals, repressing our natural youthful sexuality and made to perform empty rituals like litanies and to subscribe to pieties like the worship of the Sacred Heart, images of which were everywhere on the walls—a simpering Jesus pointing a delicate finger to a heart hung on his clothing.

We were, to our astonishment, required to flog ourselves only partially symbolically, with a small whip to be lashed over the shoulders three times on designated nights. Some men walloped the pillows with exaggerated moans ringing down the otherwise silent hallways.

At least a nod of culpability to the legend of Saint Benedict skinning his genitals on a thorn bush, the story of which was taken from the preposterous *Roman Martyrology*, which was actually read from a pulpit in the refectory at the beginning of meals. The young men would be dishing out potatoes as they listened to descriptions of the temptations of Saint Anthony, who spent thirteen years starving in the desert, bedeviled by images of naked women riding on elephants.

I had such a temptation.

One sunny summer afternoon, I was rowing with Brother McEttrick. We came ashore at an island and as I stepped out of the boat, an underwater jagged branch of a sunken log tore a hole in the bottom of my bare right foot. I shouted in pain, fell back into the boat, looked at the profusely bleeding foot, and passed out, swooning into a beautiful dream of a shore full of handsome young men and women angels wearing khakis and blue shirts and singing folk songs. When I came to lying in the bottom of the boat, Brother McEttrick was furiously rowing us back to the Shadowbrook beach. I looked at my throbbing foot, wrapped in my own bloody T-shirt. I swooned again.

I awoke lying in a hospital bed in a Catholic hospital in Pittsfield, Massachusetts, with the now cleanly bandaged foot elevated by a sling. Several medical people were slowly unwrapping the bandage. They peered with interest at the foot, as if intrigued by the challenge of a rare wound to heal. I stayed for a week while swabbed and stitched and given antibiotic drips. One delightful moment was an evening visit from my friends, Brothers O'Leary, McEttrick, and LaCroix. We joshed and told stories.

At one point, laughing boisterously and shouting each other's names, we were startled as the night nun on duty broke through the door with an angry look on her face. She looked like Big Nurse in *One Flew Over the Cuckoo's Nest*.

"Think of the patients trying to sleep," she hissed as if we were rowdy children. Sheepishly, we suppressed our revelry into whispers and giggles.

The climactic moment occurred later that evening. I lay alone in a darkening room watching the evening settling into the shadows beneath the Berkshire hills. Marion, a beautiful, slender, dark-haired nurse who was not a nun, appeared by my bedside. She usually brought meals and meds.

"This time, I'm here just to chat. I see your foot's out of the sling. Roll over onto your stomach. You need a massage. Doctor's orders."

I complied. Without either of us saying another word—of either command or question—she untied my hospital gown from the back. I heard her rubbing her hands together. She started slowly kneading warmed oil into my back. I slipped back into something like the swoon that followed stepping out of the rowboat. Her oiled hands slid to my buttocks. As I tried to muster resistance to my reluctance, I slipped into a groan, then a sigh.

Marion whispered sweetly in my ear, "There, that's good; that'll help. My shift's at night this week. I'll be back."

"Marion, that was wonderful, thank you." But then, making a quick, painful assessment, I realized that if I had known what was coming, the unexpected pleasure would have not been strictly "on the house." Speaking with considerable artificial deliberation to her, mustering the iron determination of Saint Anthony—as well as speaking heroically to myself in the privacy of my religiously obligated soul—I insisted sadly, "But Marion, please don't come again."

After these reflections, I decided the answer to Donna's question in her letter—that I was not in the Jesuit life just for the "giggles," as deranged as they sometimes were, prayers shouted in dismay or panic. I could pray properly on my own. It was not just being a member of a group that I loved. It was finding myself comfortable within my soul. Gospels to the rescue.

Learning how to pray as a Jesuit was often the subject of the daily group conferences with the master of novices, which was integral to his directing us into learning about the history of the order—into which, the hope was, we would entwine ourselves.

The master of novices emphasized again and again that what's unique about the Jesuit life was that it was sacramental, the definition of which is an outward sign of inward grace. That is, outward emotional affections for each other: de Lubac embracing Hennessey; the verve with which they worked together, played together, and worshipped together. Yet, the outward signs must be moored to the inward conviction nurtured in prayer. Prayer brought us to the bottom of it all, where we needed daily to touch down from our dives and our surfacing.

Prayer was the foundation established by the founder of the Jesuits, Saint Ignatius, a fifteenth-century Spanish chivalric nobleman who had a Saint Paul-like sudden conversion that he should renounce the world and found a radically new religious order.

Instead of praying and singing in a cloister, these holy men would learn to pray privately while they took action to resist the Reformation; the first Jesuits founded missions, like Francis Xavier baptizing millions of Hindus who probably didn't understand a word he was saying. They set up schools, like Edmund Campion who, some scholars think, secretly tutored William Shakespeare as a Catholic child—before Campion was drawn and quartered by the English Protestant Roundheads.

Jesuits learned obtuse languages, like Matteo Ricci who almost convinced China's Mandarins to convert the Chinese to Catholicism. The pope refused their request to have the Mass said in Chinese, and so the Mandarins refused to convert. Ignatius himself had to overcome the suspicions his idea evoked from traditional church figures with their fingers ready on the trigger of the Inquisition. His radical idea was to take the man out of the monastery and put the monastery into the man—"on the run," as the Beatles sang. "Contemplation in action" were the watchwords.

The portable meditative technique I favored Ignatius called the "composition of place." The idea was to imagine yourself inside a scene taken from the Bible.

On my cushioned kneeler one morning, I opened the Bible and

flipped to a favorite Gospel story from my earliest days of reading after Father Finnegan's awful sermon. Jesus is preaching to a crowd of five thousand people sitting down next to a lake. I thought, *That fits. Here I am kneeling in a house on a hill above a lake.*

The disciples ask Jesus to send the crowd home so they can get something to eat. Jesus asks how much food they have. They answer two fishes and five loaves. Jesus tells them to start passing them around. They do, and the narrator then notes with, it seems, some astonishment that there were "twelve large baskets of food left over after everyone got enough to eat." (Matthew:14).

Mediation by this method *composition of place* was what you did next. You walked into the scene. With your mind's eye you begin looking around at the people, the scene by the lake, the figures of Jesus and his followers, without wondering about how the miracle of the multiplication worked, or what it might portend about, say, the doctrine of the eucharist.

When the master of novices explained this technique, he suggested imagining yourselves inside the scene, walking around for different points of view, even asking characters questions and imagining their answer.

I never wanted to go that far. What would all those enraptured people at the lake make of a young man suddenly walking among them wearing a black habit and shiny black shoes? I would not understand a word of the Aramaic Jesus was using—and couldn't even ask intelligible questions of the crowd.

My idea instead was to 'look on from the outside.' As a spectator. What was important to me and what made it a meditation, was not to come to any conclusions. I remained a curious spectator to the drama on the literary page.

On this particular morning, my attention wandered from contemplating the scene by the lake. The prayer hour began at 6 a.m., and I was drowsing on the kneeler—my adjacent bed looked forbiddingly enticing. This time, I read the story immediately adjacent to the story of Jesus and the five thousand at the lake. Gospel narratives invite such browsing since they are only loosely chronological. One episode leads to another usually on a vague temporal hinge like "After this happened, the following happened . . ." or "Sometime later . . ." In this instance, the multiplication of the loaves and fishes story follows after the story of the beheading of John the Baptist at King Herod's birthday party. The daughter, Salome, of his illegitimate wife, Herodias, danced and so delighted Herod that he made the classic mistake many ancient storied male divine or earthly despots made to fetching females: "I'll give you anything you want," he tells her.

As usual, Salome asks for the worst thing imaginable.

Herodias had told her daughter to ask for the head of John the Baptist. He had annoyed her by making a public claim that her marriage to Herod was illegitimate. Not long after, the severed head is brought to the girl on a platter. In this instance, the temporal link between the court scene and the lake scene is a little more consequent: "When he had heard about what had happened, Jesus withdrew privately by boat to a lonely place." (Matthew 14:13)—to bail out the bilge water?

I was galvanized. Now the story of Jesus at the lake that begins with his withdrawing to privately nurse his thoughts looks to recount his arranging another event where, instead of a closed-door party of aristocrats featuring a grisly dish, imagine a gathering in an open space of poor people eating healthy food. It's a kind of open-air tent revival meeting that ends with a picnic. With leftover food in baskets, not a head on a bloody plate.

Jesus spontaneously arranges a ritual event contrasting the horrors of political power in the hands of the rich to the nourishing kindness of the open-hearted—and open-minded—poor. What seemed astonishing to me at the time was that only me, the lonely reader looking in from the outside, was privy to what the stories came to mean in the depths of implications deriving from their juxtaposition one to the other. There's no indication anyone in the crowd has heard about the beheading of John the Baptist.

Just as I was kneeling in a quiet room in a distant time and land, I was on my own. I had to look at—and into—what was on the page in order to reach this level of meaning and to speculate that perhaps Jesus himself was creating a kind of theatrical event to present as devastating a juxtaposition of the rich and poor as he could muster. I thought, *This ties in with my mother's revulsion for rich people.*

Later, during a regular conference with the master of novices, I described the meditation. "I've always thought about things this way since I was a child, seeing one picture and then next to it another picture and then allowing the juxtaposition to start prompting thoughts. Do you think it's okay to pray this way too? I thought about changing the name from 'composition' to 'contiguity,' but that sounds awkward."

The master chucked. "You're right; I'd drop the term. But your method has promise. My concern is your comparison of praying to thinking. Thinking is part of it, of course, puzzling things out. But prayer weaves in worship, marveling, making promises, assertions of belief, as well as asking questions. Make sure of that. And I think you shouldn't go beyond juxtaposing two scenes at a time. Meditation's only for an hour, after all. You've got plenty of time ahead of you to work the whole Bible in."

"I hope so," I said earnestly, pleased with the go-ahead.

Back in my room, I thought about what the master had said about worship and assertions and making promises; I probably should have brought up my concerns about these concepts. They seemed contrived. You turned away from what you were meditating on to make some silent offerings to an invisible God or resurrected Jesus who wasn't really there at the moment. In other words, you stopped the free flow of the images in the mind. You abandoned literature for theology. Which didn't seem right. The Bible *was* literature, not illustrated doctrine. A forest of trees, not the lumber yard.

Weighing these second thoughts, a pop and bright light went off in my mind. Thinking second thoughts, by way of juxtaposing images, was very much like telling the Jesus story by juxtaposing scenes showing contrasts between what he was doing and what Herod was doing. Or say, between the passage in Father Finnegan's sermon about a stern Jesus's puzzling story of a man clearing out his house so that devils could move in—and a more lighthearted Jesus brightening up a party by turning barrels of water into wine. You could read them together, however far apart they appeared in the narrative—because each episode already was disconnected from the others around it. One could shuffle the cards and deal a new hand.

I learned from reading rudimentary studies of the Gospels available in the Novitiate Library that the four Gospels themselves were "compositions" even in their earliest forms—written down 70 to 140 years after the events they reimagine. To reach the printed page, stories about Jesus passed through the memories and imaginations of a few generations. Four different versions of the scene of Jesus at the lake occur in the four canonical Gospels, each different, as the processes of composition of the original episodes were different.

So, bringing scenes together by the process of second thoughts imitated the way the Gospel writers arranged their stories. To pray like the Gospels were written! Like jazz improvising. I had to be on to something.

I didn't bring this up with the master because I realized even at this early stage as a Jesuit novice—that my way of having second thoughts did not turn away from scenes. It continued the interplay between them. It did not stop for any affirmations of faith. And, after all, how could I honestly change my way of having second thoughts in order to conform to what, after all, was only a suggestion of how to pray? I wouldn't be the same person anymore—that person who was eager to join his life to the Jesuit enterprise. I thought of Donna's comment about relishing the earthly pleasures of a Jesuit life and decided perhaps *that* was what I was doing praying this way. The scene printed on the page was itself an earthly thing, representing earthly people and actions down to earth.

In short, the Gospel story was "earthly," written by humans on paper and printed in books. And it was about Jesus while he was living as a human on the earth. He is not ethereal. He's not sitting on a cloud.

So then, what's the need for praying by making references away from the story toward such an abstract location?

It was as deep as I could go. My place was at the side of the lake with Jesus's crowd. And I just sat there. The space between adjacent scenes was the hinge, the swing point, the pivot from which unsolicited, unanticipated insights flashed.

Learning to meditate this way was a great gift I still enjoy many years after leaving the Jesuit order to live another life. I could continue to read the Scriptures this way for sure. When I became a professor, I taught academic—not sectarian—courses in the Bible as literature. I encouraged students to trust themselves to read *any* literature this way. Read a novel or a poem or a story aware of how one scene or section bears on the one before or after. Artistry shimmers in the back and forth. Read to its conclusion so you get the satisfaction of finding out who did what to whom. Then go back. Reread any section by itself to experience how it compares with the final scene toward which it is inclined. Go back again. Reread anything you find beautiful, or arresting, and then let it rest—read it adjacently to other arresting passages, and begin to see, to wonder, to understand what the passages say to each other without any of the guidance the plot or narrative directions would sententiously provide. What depths of aesthetic and ruminative pleasure are to be had if your meditation never really has to reach bottom?

Yet . . . yet . . . even then, in those happy, heady novice days, I sometimes wondered if I was drifting away from the real anchor beneath the surface mooring ball. Maybe authentic prayer was supposed to end with a cold-headed prostration of the will before God, or a personal affirmation of a Catholic doctrine that would cap the meditation.

Would resisting this final step that the master of novices urged eventually cause me to lose my mooring as a Jesuit? To leave for another life altogether that I had no desire to have during my wonderful early years at Shadowbrook? But the real value of the gift was in discovering I could find the meaning of the life I was living this way.

If a modern man compares his own recollections of his life with the ancient writers' compositions about Jesus, he could be said to harken to Jesus's own invitation to "come, follow me, and I will make you fishers of men." (Matthew 16:24). Even when in so doing, he would walk right out of the Jesuit Order, the Catholic Church, and even the practice of organized religion over all.

What I also eventually took with me were lifelong friends. On the day Charlie O'Leary first arrived at Shadowbrook in the summer of 1963, this time I was one of the jovial novices who met Charlie and the other incoming postulants at the door. This time, I was an angel, and as the appointed head of the team, the *archangel*.

One of my duties was to pass out mimeograph sheets for them to fill out, asking routine questions and then instructing the postulants to write an essay that was supposed to be titled "The History of my Vocation." I made a fateful typo. I wrote "The History of my Vacation," and then compounding the error, and I'll admit, being a bit pompous, I translated the assignment into Latin—and doubled down on the typo—"*Historia Vacationis*."

Charlie O'Leary was the first one to get the assignment sheet. The two of us were both standing in my cell doorway as Charlie read it over. He pointed to the words *History of Vacation*.

"Are we really supposed to write about our vacations?"

I looked dumbly at Charlie and then at the sheet. At the same time, it hit both of us; it was just a dumb mistake. And we both started laughing. It got so bad, tears started running down our faces. It would be salacious for Jesuits wanting to know how postulants had spent their final worldly days up and till their embrace of celibacy.

Later, sitting at my own desk in my cell, I wondered if I'd made the mistake because of some deep Freudian recovery of the terror the word *vacation* had held for me in the third grade. Well, maybe, yes, but provocatively so. As I came to think about it, *vacation* was a pretty good contrast to *vocation*, as I had come to understand the words. *Vacations* were grounded. You left home, went some place, and then refreshed, returned home. *Vocations* had a person cocking an ear to a silent heaven, "troubling deaf heaven with my bootless cries," as Shakespeare writes in Sonnet 29, "when in disgrace with fortune and in men's eyes . . ." *Looking to* heaven for a beckoning call to a life lived *looking away* from the world.

Furthermore, looking back now years later, I understand that when Charlie O'Leary (several weeks later, Brother O'Leary) caught me at the vocation/vacation mistake, that was the moment that caused the two of us to become friends for life. We discovered we had the same sense of humor, which created a profound bond. The friendship then solidified when we were assigned to clean the Shadowbrook septic beds.

The Fellowship of the Pits

1963

Go down quick into the pit.
—Numbers 16:30

Brother O'Leary and I stood before the bulletin board looking for our names and afternoon work assignments. We read with dread we'd been assigned to clean the house's septic beds. Up to this point, we had not even known they existed. Human waste just disappeared, effervesced into heaven or dropped through a hole into hell. But now more practically: where to go? What to do? How bad was it?

Brother O'Leary spoke in the crude house Latin: "*Hoc non sonat bonum*"—"That doesn't sound good."

I responded in a pious tone: "*Ad majoriam dei gloriam*"—the official Jesuit motto—"For the greater glory of God."

During the first two years of Jesuit bootcamp, we were required to speak Latin with each other if we were inside the building but were allowed to speak English if we were outside the house. If there was something complicated to say, two of us would step outside briefly to speak in English. For example, should one need to tell another, "If you find the power to the big soup kettle has gone dead, try crawling underneath to find the socket with the GFCI red button. If the button's bulged out, you push it back in."

It's hard to imagine Cicero ever having to deal with anything like this. Since Brother O'Leary and I were inside the house at the moment, we both became uneasily silent. We'd have to wait to share anxious thoughts until going outside.

An older brother who had been a sanitary engineer in his previous life, met us outside the tool room. He had told us to get rakes and a shovel and a wheelbarrow. On the way down the hill from the house, he explained how the system worked.

"All the wastewater from the house flows out in pipes into a great holding tank buried underground. There it ferments into a gooey black liquid. A timer spews the liquid out periodically into four large sand beds each framed with thick wooden planks. The liquid goo then dries in the sunshine and air until it breaks into little black curlicues—the residue of holy men's fecal matter."

Brother O'Leary and I laughed for the first time since reading the assignment.

"The separated liquid then drains down into the sand for final purification before being pumped into the lake. Your job is to rake the curlicues into piles."

Brother O'Leary interrupted at this point. "They look like black corn flakes."

"While you're down here," he replied, "you can call them anything you want. Your job is to shovel the pile into the wheelbarrow; and using a single dedicated thick plank." He pointed to one. "Wheel the pile up and out of the bed and dump it onto a larger pile some distance away.

"Whenever you think it gets too high, sign up for the house tractor. Come down with its front loader and bury the bigger pile. In conclusion, yours is a critical task. If this system gets clogged up, our whole holy way of life will have to be abandoned."

Brother O'Leary and I thought this was funny too.

Left to our own devices, we started raking the sand beds. We relaxed. None of this was hard to do. There was no smell, nothing even disgusting looking. A thick barrier of pine trees surrounded everything, providing a sense of seclusion and privacy from the monastic way of living up the hill. We said to each other this might be the best *manualia*—"manual labor job"—ever. Much nicer than cleaning the toilets at the upper end of the system.

After a few assignments, we let it be known we wanted to be assigned there permanently, and not only once a month as had been the previous schedule but weekly, making the argument that it was what was needed to keep the beds really clean. Our volunteering apparently solved a scheduling problem—by taking on the most distasteful-sounding job that no one else wanted to undertake. The request was quickly granted. Our other brothers enthusiastically congratulated our generosity.

We told a few close friends about our real deal.

"We want in," Brother McEttrick demanded.

So, we went to the novice work foreman and made the further case that we needed the Brothers McEttrick and LaCroix, who said they were also willing volunteers. By getting the crew up to the strength, we could do a first-class job cleaning the septic beds of the dried waste—using its Latin name "*exaruit stercore*"—"dried shit." The shock effect of the phrase helped clear the way. Anything we said in Latin had gravitas.

Again, the request was happily granted. Nobody ever cared to look closely into what we were doing down there.

With more workers the work was even easier to do, and frankly, it never really required the amount of manualia time scheduled for it.

Brother O'Leary put it succinctly: "It's amazing what you can get away with if you're willing to do what other people think is disgusting."

To stretch out the time to fit the schedule, we improvised elaborate rituals. Running the wheelbarrow up the plank and up out of the bed became like an Olympic event. Scoring would begin the moment the wheeler grasped the handles of the wheelbarrow. He would be judged on his serious demeanor. No cockiness or histrionics. Points would be gained for the coolness of approach, gracefulness of ascent, and the quick snap of the dumping. Scoring continued until the wheeler brought the wheelbarrow back into the bed, adjacent to the next pile to be removed, and lifted up his arms in hopeful triumph. You could lose points for complaining about the score the judges were sworn to be fully objective about. Scores were kept secret by the scorekeeper—lest any judge be influenced by how a new high score might jeopardize his own standing.

Once a bed was raked clean of the "corn flakes," we'd use a wooden rake to create a version of a Zen-garden, with furrows in the sand formed to look like ocean waves, and various rocks positioned to look like islands. It usually took an afternoon just for that. Then followed a dedicatory program of speeches and songs. As some corn flakes would begin to accumulate on the Zen-ocean, birds continually descended to hop around and feed.

"There's no accounting for taste," Brother LaCroix said.

So too schools of butterflies. They appeared on the sand like a flotilla of sailboats seen from a plane. Chipmunks dug tunnels in the pliable sand to nest; small weasels went in after them, pulling them by their teeth out of the tunnels going backward.

We were puzzled at first to find many small tomato plants growing in the beds, until we asked the brother who had been a civil engineer about it.

"Tomato seeds are very tough, able to survive time in the human gut, the fermentation tank, and then to sprout in the richly fertilized water to take root in the sand."

The crew selected good-looking tomatoes and staked them with branches from the pine trees. Occasionally, ritually, they shared eating together as a group bonding communion.

We called the septic beds affectionately "the Pits" and kept its pleasures a secret among ourselves, lest others horn in, or worse, find out that working in the Pits really didn't need the care we provided.

We christened the Pits with an ecclesiastical title too—like naming holy places and buildings after saints. The saint was Peter Claver, a seventeenth-century Spanish Jesuit missionary to Colombia who came to call himself "the slave of the slaves."

He would climb into the filthy holds of arriving slave ships, bringing with him medicine, soap, bandages, and food. So, our official title for the place was: "The Pits of Saint Peter Claver."

Peter Claver became my favorite Jesuit saint for real. When I took perpetual vows at the end of my second year at Shadowbrook, I inserted Claver's name into the middle of the recitation of my own name in the formula of commitment.

Taking Vows. Reading Books. A Jesuit Education.

1964–1965

In my Father's house there are many mansions.
—John 14:2

I stood inside the door of a classroom on the other wing of the huge house of Shadowbrook. The first "mansion" in my Jesuit life just one hundred yards away, down the corridor in the middle between the Novice and Juniorate Wings.

A friend who crossed over before had set me up. There was a chair with a view out to the lake. Next to it hung an Impressionist picture by Monet of a lily pond. My friend gestured for me to sit, and without a word, turned on a phonograph cued with the Modern Jazz Quartet playing "Softly as a Morning Sunrise."

"My gift to you is a ritual of introduction to your new and promised land," he said, and quietly left the room.

From now on I could listen to jazz. At least once a week I listened for an hour. Often to the Dave Brubeck Quartet. I became enamored of the chordal changes in the twelve-bar blues. You could even hear it in classical music.

The Novitiate had lasted two years. Now I was twenty, having graduated to a different world, located on the other wing of Shadowbrook, with the Jesuit elders in the middle in between. It was called the Juniorate.

The key to entry was saying one word in Latin: "*Voveo*"—"I vow" After running the gauntlet of the first two years of monastic-like (lite) life, on the precise two-year anniversary of my entrance day, I knelt on the bottom step of the chapel sanctuary and vowed to be a Jesuit for life—promising to be poor, obedient, and chaste all the while.

By reciting the key word "vow," instantly our formal prefix changed from Brother to Mister. We were now called "juniors" in the juniorate. We could call each other by first names. At first it almost seemed impertinent: *Charlie* O'Leary, *Joe* McEttric, *Dennie* Lacroix.

Having said the ritual words, we qualified to wear a black suit with a roman collar that ran around the neck. A white checker poked out of a slot in the black overcollar of either a specialized shirt or a bib-like vest fastened by a hidden cord behind the neck. Unlike most other preordination seminarians, Jesuit scholastics were entitled to wear the regalia of a suit with a roman collar usually associated with priests. In public, they looked like young priests years before they officially became one. One advantage was to publicly signal by a kind of large white letter *C* hung around our necks a commitment to celibacy. The underlying meaning was "women beware!" Another was to gain us awkward public respect—or abhorrence—something we did not deserve.

As an example, the first time I boarded a trolley in Boston several years later, I started to put the fare in the collection box. The conductor put his hand over the top to stop me. I thought, *Great, maybe priests ride free.*

"Oh, thank you."

"You pay when you get off," the conductor growled.

Safe and Isolated: The Traditional Schooling for Jesuits 1534–1968

Though I walk through a valley dark as death . . . your staff and your crook are my comfort.
—Psalm 23

For those who hadn't attended college yet like erstwhile Brothers O'Leary, McEttrick, LaCroix, and me—the second block of two years at Shadowbrook was similar to studying humanities in college—Greek, Latin, German, French, math, history, music. The Jesuit Trivium and Quadrivium. They were taught by priests who lived permanently at Shadowbrook.

By this stage, I was reading and praying with the Gospels in Greek. It was pretty simple Greek, with the same words used over and over, and many present participial phrases such as "After Jesus was walking on the water, he . . ." It was easy because by this time I knew the Gospels almost by heart in English. So, I could look at the Greek version and know what it said, *see* how it said it. I used the same trick brushing up Latin, and reading the Gospels in different languages kept them fresh. And it worked too, studying German. I got a copy of *Die Heilge Schrift* from the library. And read how the German said it. Later I used the same trick learning old English, having discovered a translation in the stacks of the Harvard Library. My tricks brought me close to the Gospels as they were written and as I could read them. I stopped reading the Epistles by Paul and others. No stories there. Just worthless moralizing.

These translation tricks did not work with classical Latin and Greek authors, especially the succinct concentrations of rhythmic poetry in the *Iliad* or the *Aeneid*. Which we were drilled on intensely.

McEttrick joked, "We're getting a medieval education to prepare us to live in the twentieth century."

O'Leary responded morosely, "What's unfair about it is they give us poor grades to make sure we stay humble. Like those medieval flagellants banging their heads against blocks of wood."

"I'm excited to find out how the *Aeneid* turns out, now that Aeneus has finally gotten to Italy!"

"Spoiler alert," said Dennie to me sardonically. "He founds the Roman Catholic Church."

The resident teacher priest, Father Sullivan, taught advanced Latin. He kept referring to the hero of the *Aeneid*, Aeneus, as "pious" Aeneus, an attributive adjective that is used often in the *Aeneid*. There it means "loyal or persevering." When the priest used the word in class, he would look out at us as if to insinuate we should be *pious* too. Among ourselves, we took to calling the character "Pissus Aeneus," a nickname we also gave to a mischievous, imaginary imp we blamed for a flat tire on the house truck or for ripping up underwear before it came back from the laundry. Our language became more vulgar now that we could speak English to each other all day long, in or out.

There were other glorious benefits to taking vows: no more manualia working in the kitchen or cleaning toilets. Instead, a scholarly paradise.

There were about forty of us who still remained at Shadowbrook in that stage of the game for two more years—with a full library at our disposal of more than forty thousand volumes. It was heavenly. I did the required work, plus read all of Hemingway, Fitzgerald, Mann, Tolkien, Wolfe, Cather, Camus, Emerson, Thoreau, Melville. A delicious hodgepodge. One after the other. No need for any theories. Now I became a spectator for sure. I got to look in on the sex, war, and deaths of people out there beyond the walls in the real world, so to speak, while I was sitting smug in a silent carrel in the library of a religious house. I felt both safe and isolated. I meditated on Gospel scenes in Greek every morning, which also provided a protective fence between me and the raucous outside world my imagination roamed in.

One night, walking by myself on one of the driveways around Shadowbrook, the moon was bright and cast my shadow before me. I was musing about all the wonders that had poured around me since taking vows. Abruptly I felt a chill.

"No sons," a voice said.

I stood dead still in the darkness. The leaves on the trees stopped rustling. I had never thought about having children until this moment I realized that I'd given up having any. *Is this what I wanted?* was the obstreperous tone. It was no angel asking this. The question came from a resolve in my soul I hadn't known I had. The moment passed. If there had been a question implied, I did not answer it. I went back to my cell and read Psalms before going to bed. By the next morning, after I got up, the voice and the question were gone. I was eager to finish Hemingway's novel *The Sun also Rises* in the novitiate library.

As wonderful as all this was, I feared I was living in a fool's paradise, intimidated by what appeared to loom ahead of us. Traditionally, after Shadowbrook and the novitiate and juniorate, young New England Province Jesuits moved to another huge house in a tony suburb of Boston called Weston College.

Our rank and title would change again: promotions from novice to junior to philosopher. But that meant the young Jesuit studied Thomastic philosophy—in Latin. But what already intimidated us as juniors was knowing Jesuit philosophy professors lectured in Latin— students spoke Latin in class and wrote exams and papers in Latin. To us it looked like a long slog ahead. The Latin most of us spoke in the house at Shadowbrook was crude—almost pidgin—*hoc non sonat bonum* ("that not sound good"). Cicero would have gagged. I had real fears the Jesuits would finally find me out. Tongue-tied in Latin. Unable to use the right words in which to pray and think. After three years of that, having had seven full years and summer school courses tucked in between, we would receive a bachelor's degree in a secular subject and a master's degree in philosophy (actually, a licentiate, a license to teach Catholic sanctioned philosophy).

Three years of Regency followed Philosophy. Most young Jesuits, like John L'Heureux, taught in a Jesuit high school like Fairfield Prep.

Some famous examples of New England Jesuit academic superstars are Robert Drinan, who became dean of the Boston College Law School and served as a representative from Massachusetts in Congress where he became a member of Richard Nixon's impeachment committee. James Sheehan established a world-renowned seismology station on the campus of Weston College. John W. O'Malley wrote elegant and esteemed books on the history of the Church and the Jesuits. Joseph Appleyard published his doctoral dissertation on Samuel Coleridge with Harvard University Press and a second book years later with Cambridge University Press. John L'Heureux, after only one year of teaching high school, attended Harvard, then taught writing at Stanford University for many years and worked as editor at the *Atlantic* and the *New Yorker*. He published many novels, essays, and short stories. There were always Jesuits like that.

However, the rank and file—or those of us thought to be that caliber—taught secular subjects in high school as regents. The New England Province of the Society of Jesus in the 1960s conducted four high schools in New England—in Boston, Massachusetts; Portland, Maine; Fairfield, Connecticut (where John L'Heureux taught); and Lenox, Massachusetts. The last, with the tony name Cranwell Prep, was housed in another old Berkshire mansion-cottage and run as a high-end boarding school for rich Catholic kids.

In addition, the New England Province ran two more high schools under missionary conditions in Baghdad, Iraq and Kingston, Jamaica. Regent bodies were always needed in all these classrooms. We would become something like shock-troops. Enlisted into the money-making enterprises to begin to pay back some of our keep—since any salary money we earned was garnished into the Province treasury.

A four-year period called Theology followed Regency. The Jesuit Scholastic moved back to live in another wing of Weston College from where he'd had his cell during Philosophy. Four more years learning about God in Latin.

Because, again, much of the classwork was taught to theologians in latin; although now there were advanced courses available in all the ancient languages whose writings influenced the writing of the Bible. There were a lot of different kinds of theology—moral theology, historical theology, biblical theology, canon law, systematic theology (Catholic doctrine), natural theology (where you learned why fornication, masturbation, adultery, divorce, birth control, and abortion were forbidden), and finally, eschatology—the theology of "last things." At the same time, during summer school classes, the scholastic would work toward getting a master's degree in some secular subject. After ordination, and as a full-fledged Jesuit priest, he'd be prepared to teach both Catholic religion and some secular subject in any high school to which he'd be assigned. And say Mass and perform sacraments as relief priests in parishes near the school. Monitor retreats. Say daily Mass for nuns.

So, anyone like me entering the Jesuits right after high school faced a minimum of fifteen years of training—in addition to any secular graduate studies. Into the gauntlet at eighteen, out at thirty-three—the same age as Jesus. We heard rumors that after finishing this rigorous and lengthy curriculum many Jesuits would feel deflated. For the first time in almost half his lifetime, there wouldn't be a structure to dictate tasks and overall direction. A Jesuit could be early middle aged—and just starting a career. And too often, the only advanced degrees he held were in either philosophy or theology. A complete Jesuit education was lengthy, intense, and parochial—as lengthy and as narrow as that of a neurosurgeon.

I was not daunted. Who, young, worries about middle age? The life of mind and soul and body and purpose and friendship was wondrous, as it was to rivet me in the *now*, with all its promise. And perhaps, subconsciously, we had the sense that if so much was changing in the Church and Jesuits and even at Shadowbrook, any institutional unpleasantness would stand corrected before it got to us. Well, it would, but it proved very damaging.

In 1965, the traditional foundation of Jesuit education quaked. The Jesuit authorities far away in Rome and Boston abruptly decided the next generation needed secular undergraduate and graduate degrees. Young Jesuits would still matriculate after Shadowbrook to Weston College, located just outside Boston. Now its huge building would serve as a large, remote dorm. Philosophers would take daily school buses to Boston College ten miles away to take regular undergraduate courses with nearly ten thousand mostly Catholic lay students. They should strive to qualify for higher degrees in subjects beyond philosophy and theology.

Their superiors had to do something different with the kinds of men now entering the order. Many already had advanced degrees. They breathed the spirit of what Pope John dubbed *aggiornamento*—literally "to bring up to date," but which he himself improvised the translation "to throw open the windows." What now?

My personal premonition of such a future was during an interview with the jolly, elderly, rotund Father Fancy, whom the New England Province dispatched to Shadowbrook.

Father Fancy was director of higher education. His task was to annotate dreams. He called me into a private room and asked for my opinion, which was itself a startling experience for me to be sitting face to face with an unknown Jesuit priest who asked *me* a question.

"And so, mister, looking at your grades, you've done well so far. What would you like to study?"

"Literature, I guess—novels and poetry, I suppose."

"That's just fine," he said with a chuckle. "Declare yourself an English major. It's a great department at BC. If you apply yourself as you have, you could be on the faculty there yourself someday. Some BC graduates get into Harvard afterward."

This was as exhilarating as taking vows.

The plan was that scholastics would take regularly scheduled yellow school buses thence to attend all their remaining required undergraduate classes at the main Boston College campus in Chestnut Hill. They would sit shoulder to shoulder in classrooms with "ordinary people," even those who were bright—and often very beautiful—young women.

Individually young Jesuits could declare majors in other fields in addition to philosophy and—by taking overloads during the regular semesters and summer school courses—earn two bachelor's degrees simultaneously. After that loomed the possibility of choosing to be a regent teaching in a Jesuit high school. Or better yet, to attend graduate school for anyone who qualified. Think: the possibilities of theology studies and the rest of it to follow after that and become both a Dr. (PhD) and an Fr.!

In 1965, the juniors at Shadowbrook were told to pack their trunks! The message was clear: the future was now. We'd be leaving Shadowbrook early, after only three years, to become philosophers a year earlier than was traditional and then to enroll as sophomores at Boston College. We were ecstatic.

Then the authorities flinched. They inexplicably delayed the start for another year to begin in 1966 instead. The Shadowbrook rector, Father Lannon, SJ, called the juniors into a large classroom. There was no way for him to break the news gently. Our shocked cries faded to grim silence and tears.

Father Lannon had been trained as a concert pianist and tried sincerely to convince us he felt our pain and was deeply sympathetic. He declared a week's holiday from classes. We filed out to unpack the trunks and to dig in for what loomed as a grim and gritty year. The vow of obedience became as ornery as the vow of celibacy for the first time. We had always treated the vow of poverty as a joke. Who needed anything else anyway than what we had in our rooms, our food, our work and play and books, and what we could find in the bins of clothing in the laundry room? Until now the vow of obedience had only required us to do what we zealously wanted to do: living with each other as brothers with a mission. But now we learned it could pack a wallop.

Dennie LaCroix coined a mantra—attributing the phrase to the anonymous, execrable, authorities: "We want you to be where the action is NOT!"

To ease our collective pain, Father Lannon once offered a course in the history of music. He often allowed us to attend art openings and concerts in the tony Berkshire Hills or to attend classical concerts during the summer at Tanglewood just down the road. I attended a magical performance of the medieval and Renaissance ensemble New York Pro Musica Antiqua in Pittsfield. Enamored of the recorder player Bernard Karinis, I took up the instrument and got to the point where I could play a credible "Greensleeves." And I could even appropriate playing something close to a melodic run of the twelve-bar blues.

The rec-room hootenannies darkened. We fervently sang Dylan's "Maggie's Farm" and "The Times They Are a-Changing;" Country Joe and the Fish's "The Fish Cheer" (we whispered the F word); Phil Och's "I Ain't Marching Any More;" and Aretha Franklin's "Respect." The finale was still LaCroix's cover of Mick Jagger's "I Can't Get No Satisfaction."

This much could be said about the dark mood: we endured. Charlie, Joe, Dennie, and I stuck it out. In 1965, not a single one left the Society of Jesus during this year-long test of obedience to Jesuit authority. We stayed in the game we thought still held true.

At the same time, the Jesuits as a group became uncertain about what was happening among them. The Province hired the consulting firm Anderson Little for guidance in planning its future. Superiors of various houses met in Boston to brainstorm. The juniors were miffed no scholastics were invited.

Dennie said, "What is needed is for there to be at least one scholastic invited. He would be allowed to say only one word—but whenever he thought it appropriate: *Bullshit*; he'd transform the New England Province in six months."

In the summer of 1966, the authorities did come through with the original promise. (Otherwise, the scholastics might have stormed their Boston offices with pikes.) The juniors would leave Shadowbrook for Weston and commute to the Boston College campus for the remainder of their undergraduate classes. We packed trunks again and slammed the lids shut. With each other's help, we hauled them to the house garage, where the trunks were loaded onto a large panel truck and strapped down. I was on the crew that tightened the cinches.

Joe solemnly blessed the straps. "Thou shalt not come undone till you reach the promised land."

Once the truck turned down the driveway and out of sight, we young Jesuits knew the Yellow Brick Road had its trail of crumbs we would follow to the ends of the earth. Sure enough, a few days later, we took new yellow school buses from Shadowbrook to Weston College.

When I looked out the window of the bus as it crossed the town line, I saw many astonishingly beautiful mansions on both sides of the road. Jesus himself had promised as much, I thought, with those many mansions of his father's house. *This place looks even richer than Westport, Connecticut. The Jesuits sure know how to leaven the vow of poverty with a flair for buying upscale real estate.*

Then the bus pulled into the circular driveway of the huge, but ugly, Italianate building that was Weston College. My second thoughts flew up from Shakespeare's trusty 29th Sonnet.

Like to lark at break of day arising.

From sullen earth [to] sing hymns at heaven's gate.

When I got inside, the interior was dark and gloomy. The mood quickly dissipated when the young Jesuits already in residence grabbed the trunks and suitcases with boisterous, mutual happiness.

Each room had a huge window and a view of lovely green grounds. Mine looked out over the New England Jesuit Province cemetery. Jesuit gravestones never looked somber. Heaven was just another place they'd all get together again.

Our friends pointed out where the toilets were and then brought us newbies into the rec room for a special celebratory dinner of lobster and steak. We stayed up much too late singing songs and gossiping, all traces of what now seemed our pint-sized agonies at Shadowbrook fading into laughter.

Father Shine, SJ, introduced himself at the beginning of the dinner as our new father superior for philosophy. He asked whether we wanted to spend a few days in the new building, getting oriented, before taking the new buses to visit the Boston College Campus. By acclamation, we chose to ride to BC the next day. I didn't unpack my trunk for a week.

The next day that same fleet of yellow school buses took us the seven miles to the Boston College campus in Chestnut Hill where classes would start in a few weeks. From this date forward, the buses would leave on a regular schedule several times a day, every day of the year—so we could attend classes, meet with professors, visit the library, even sometimes have a meal in the large Jesuit residence house, St. Mary's, on the campus. When the bus crossed over the town line of Chestnut Hill where Boston College was located, I saw out the window many more beautifully built and landscaped homes on a par with those of Weston—more evidence of the Jesuit flair for buying high-value real estate.

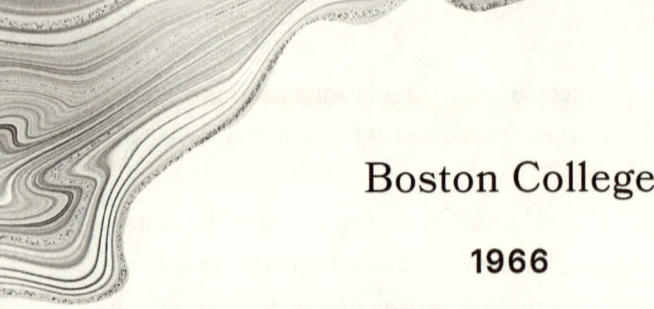

Boston College

1966

... descending like a dove upon him.
—Matthew 3:14

I stood just outside the door of the bus while the other young Jesuits piled happily down the steps onto the solid ground of Boston College, gleaming in the sun on the first day of the rest of their lovely lives. Regular students walking past the bus looked over with smiles and curiosity at the file of young men in black robes. The huge BC campus, with its maze of paths and buildings, looked intimidating but that impression faded just as quickly as it does for all young students attending a college campus for the first time.

When I stepped off the bus every day that first semester, I felt like Superman. He had lived his early life on the planet Krypton, where the atmospheric density was seventeen times greater than on Earth. Like Shadowbrook. Here my lightness of being hovered high over the ground. Wearing, black habits (fluttering like windswept superhero capes) the young Jesuits dispersed to attend daily classes in chosen subjects with ten thousand other students, including women—all of whom looked beautiful to start.

Many regular students would tell us that they found our presence ominous in their classrooms. We did our homework and wrote papers religiously, sharply upping the ante of the professors' expectations.

It's not clear how far our Jesuit superiors had thought this radical change through, whether they worried that releasing us into the excitement of the secular college marketplace of ideas might shake our faith, or whether they were confident we'd be so intoxicated by what we could think and do we'd become a vanguard for a renaissance of religious living that had truly been the intent of Vatican II to unleash. Theirs was almost like a huge experiment in Einstein's "combinatory play" between faith and knowledge.

It turned out to be a tragic choice the authorities had to make to remain faithful to the promises of Vatican II. As an infamous paradoxical aphorism that arose out of the Vietnam War put it—"They had to destroy the village (the Jesuit Order) in order to save it."

At any rate, at the start, our young Jesuit lives became so intensely exciting there didn't seem to be any time to waste questioning what any ultimate motives were—or any future crisis of commitments might be.

The Jesuit superiors were cautious about allowing us to get involved in extracurricular activities. They probably feared the young men would neglect our studies or start to lose touch with our own community—or more probably—get involved with women.

There was no stopping the tide, and many got involved anyway. The superiors had released the flood gates. Young Jesuit scholastics played intramural sports; we joined language clubs, such as a small group learning Arabic, to prepare ourselves to teach at the Jesuit high school and university in Baghdad. Some scholastics became interns in the Boston College student ministry; one became a Jazz DJ at the college radio station. Musicians played in the college orchestra and sang in choral groups. I acted in plays. I wrote topical skits for performances in the college coffeehouse. I wrote movie and theater reviews for the college newspaper. I also published stories and poems in, as well as edited, the college literary magazine *Stylus*. And therein lies a tale.

It was something like the Barbara Fritchie scandal. Richard Sawaya (to be clear, decidedly *not* a Jesuit) at the time was, by campus consensus, its most brilliant undergraduate. He finished his coursework in three years and took the fourth to write a novel, prior to matriculating into the Harvard English PhD program. He was also the editor of the Boston College literary magazine *Stylus*. He was imposing to look at. Dark curly hair, a robust black mustache, and a wrestler's build. He carried the air of a man who brooked no nonsense. Almost every issue of the magazine for his four years on campus carried one of his short stories. He had been its editor for three.

In my senior year, I became assistant editor. That lay the groundwork of the crisis. I joined the other staff to agree to publish a chapter of Sawaya's unfinished novel in the *Stylus*. In one scene, an unmarried male and female character roll around in bed and "have pleasure from each other." That was it. No more explicit than that. Yet that was too much sex to suit the faculty adviser of *Stylus*. He was sweet Father Sweeney, SJ, whom everybody liked. He was the campus Mr. Chips. He was short, with unruly hair, always smiling. He called everyone he knew *carissime* or "most dear one," in both Latin and Italian. He spoke fluent Italian and spent any free time in Rome. He had become a personal friend of the great American-English writer T. S. Eliot, whom he brought to campus several times for readings. He corresponded with Jack Kerouac. He was notorious for picking up bums on the streets of Boston and inviting them to join him for a meal at a fancy restaurant nearby—which almost always led to both of them being denied service and to which he would say something caustic about Jesus and the poor to the management.

Father Sweeney used his authority to block the publication of the offending chapter. He was quoted in the campus newspaper the *BC Heights*: "We are a Catholic University, after all. How can I condone any depiction of what the Church declares to be a mortal sin?" In response, the *Heights* published several articles and editorials condemning his "silly prudishness," even asking, "Where does the good Father think babies come from?" Richard Sawaya resigned as editor. The rest of the staff of the magazine, including me, voted to override Sweeney's veto. Sweeney threatened to resign. Sawaya remained adamant. He would not take out the offending phrase. Poor Father Sweeney was distraught about a *Heights* poll that showed most student respondents sided against him. He had always been considered one of the more popular, loveable Jesuits on campus.

Much tempest in the teapot. Both an undergraduate and a Jesuit, albeit a very junior one, I now by default became editor of the *Stylus*. I pleaded with Father Sweeney to change his mind, and although he still smiled and called me *carissime*, he said he could not, in conscience. The *Stylus* staff decided to poll other editors of other college literary magazines in the Boston area for their policies about this kind of impasse. The only editor to respond was from the Harvard University undergraduate literary magazine the *Advocate*. His message was sarcastic and condescending, to the effect that at Harvard there were no such things as faculty advisers. And students were trusted to be adults. (No help from Elysium for us proletarians.)

So, with staff approval, I wrote guidelines about how the *Stylus* would handle such matters in the future. Basically, if a faculty adviser vetoed a submission that was acceptable to the staff, the staff had the right to publish but under the proviso that the staff itself would hold itself legally responsible for any consequences on whether the piece broke laws against publishing pornography or libel. When he read the guidelines, Sweeney said he still could not agree to remain faculty adviser under any such constraints.

Playing my apprentice Jesuit card for what it was worth, I asked the president of Boston College, Father Walsh, SJ, for an audience. For the first time I walked into a power office, with lots of space, large windows with stained glass filigrees, dark shiny paneling, a huge desk, and photographs of important politicians on the walls. There was Tip O'Neill, then Speaker of the House, with his arm around Father Walsh and both of them beaming. Second-generation Boston Irish men who had made it to the top. In his office, Father Walsh tipped back his head, as he did when he spoke to anyone.

He smiled. "Yes?"

I started to describe the impasse.

Father Walsh interrupted. "I read the *Heights*," he said softly. And then, encouragingly, "What's next?"

I showed him a copy of the guidelines. "They look reasonable to me," the priest said with a smile. "We teach students to use their minds and take responsibilities."

"Thanks," I said in relief. But looking at him frankly, Jesuit to Jesuit, I ventured with some trepidation. "The problem still is with sweet Father Sweeney, who really finds himself in a pickle with this. None of us want to hurt him. Could you somehow persuade him to go along, maybe helping him save face with some joint statement with you accepting the guidelines? I know it's not something you usually get involved with."

Father Walsh stood up, bent over his desk to shake my hand, and still smiling, said, "I'll think about it. Thanks for your efforts." And he did, and they did. Years later the guidelines came into play in a similar impasse—and they worked! Even Jesuits could adapt—*improvise*.

The two years at Boston College were the most exciting in my life. I kept telling myself while it was happening, *Look, all you do here is Mickey Mouse. None of it means anything in the larger world.* Nonetheless, I felt like another cartoon character leaping and bounding over buildings.

I formed a small ensemble of actors called the Uncle Marvin Players, covertly named after my neighborhood elementary school. We regularly performed politically (and religiously) satirical skits in a Boston College coffeehouse called Middle Earth, and at other college venues around Boston.

Richard Bruno, the star actor, over the course of several years played a crab, an ant, a cigarette, and an elephant. One audience member said after his performance as a cigarette, "When his butt burned out, I was close to tears." Richard provided the voiceover in one skit, alluding to the oft-told stories about dolls and puppets coming to life after everyone goes to sleep: "It was midnight at the college, and the students were all snuggled in bed. This was when all the test tubes and pencils got together for their enchanted mixers." Richard brought the house down with his snide innuendo.

Charlie remained musical, mostly. He sang and played beautiful music all over Boston in two groups of young Jesuits who called themselves The Celibate Six, and later, The Good News Singers.

AJ Antoon was all over the place. He refused to have anything to do with the established drama on the BC campus. In the Middle Earth coffeehouse he staged short avant-garde plays by Jarri, Albee, and Cocteau. In open spaces on campus, he performed comic revivals of medieval miracle and mystery plays off the back of a garishly painted pickup truck that he used in place of the original horse-drawn carts. No one who knew him was surprised when, eight years later, he won a Tony for his direction of the Broadway hit *That Championship Season*. At one time he would have his name as director on the marquees of two Broadway theaters—for a revival of Shakespeare's *Much Ado About Nothing* and Neil Simon's *The Good Doctor*.

In the play he staged at BC by Cocteau, he cast a Black student as the one-eyed man leading five blind White actors through the world. As part of the presentation, he invited the audience and the actors to sit around after the play and discuss American racial strife. I was part of that audience; I commented that it was powerful that a one-eyed Black character led the blind White ones around, remembering how Eugene Wright had led Joe Morello to his drum set.

The cast was happy to hear that. "Yes, yes," the Black actor agreed happily, "that's what we had in mind."

Later, I told AJ privately it was equally amazing to me that he could even find a Black student on the BC campus to cast in the role. AJ would do things like this throughout his professional career. He cast all Black members of a benign voodoo cult as the magical figures of the woodsy world outside the palace gates in his *Midsummer Night's Dream*. He directed the show for Joe Papp at his revolutionary New Theater in New York City in the early

1970s. Later, one of the actors who had played one of the "rude mechanicals" in the play (he played "Wall"), a life-long actor, claimed that the production was the greatest theater he had ever been a part of in his career.

Looking back, I can see now we reveled and learned in a parochial fantasy world just starting to fray. Boston College between my undergraduate years there of 1966–1968 featured a very large empty space in the middle of its cluster of buildings—the site of a projected future building. Students nicknamed it "The Swamp." It was trampled flat and rendered grassless by student shoes and got muddy after rains. It was BC's Hyde Park. The first protests against the Vietnam War happened there, only at first a dozen students standing behind signs saying, "Get Out." There were a few instances where bumptious Boston Irish students roughed them up that were only reported in the student newspaper *BC Heights*. Here was held in 1967 a protest against the Massachusetts standing legal prohibitions against birth control—amazing to think of it now—even in that day and age. Boston was the big population center of the state, and doctrinaire Catholics and the charismatic Cardinal Cushing dominated its politics.

Ed Cripps was the first among us to catch the fever of the times. He'd complain bitterly about the living conditions in Roxbury, where he tutored poor Black children in the Boston ghetto. "King is right," he'd insist. "The Vietnam War was racist against both Asians and the Blacks the government recruits to kill them." He was prescient and correct. But at the time the literary man and editor in me found the logic murky. The logic itself wasn't murky. My mind was just too preoccupied to follow it.

Jesuit Solidarity Cracks

1968

A house divided against itself cannot stand.
—Matthew 12:22

Saint Mary's, a giant Gothic building, served as Jesuit residence at Boston College. It housed thirty to forty priests who taught required courses in Catholic philosophy and theology to all regularly enrolled students.

In addition to Boston College, the New England Province ran Holy Cross College in Worchester, Massachusetts, Fairfield University in Fairfield, Connecticut, and Sophia University in Baghdad, Iraq. All Jesuit universities at the time required their regular students to take a philosophy or a theology course every semester. This practice required a stock of Jesuit bodies to fill out the faculty rosters for these courses. Most of them held only master's degrees in Thomistic scholastic philosophy and theology they had earned as a matter of course in their long, traditional education.

Most of the students hated the requirements. My good friend Richard Bruno with great frustration asked me once, "Why don't you young Jesuits have to take these shit courses? If you did, you'd make such a stink, BC would drop the requirements, and we'd all rejoice."

Sitting with the two of us in a student cafeteria, Carol Frank, a wonderful comic actor who was also a part of the Uncle Marvin troupe spoke. "What's awful about them for women," she said with real bitterness, "is that Catholic philosophy and theology circle around the idea women are necessary embarrassments. We should just shut up and have babies."

For the next performance, I got ready laughs out of the Middle Earth crowd, as Carol, beautiful and buxom, playing a Thomistic cat howling on a fence, got hit in the head by a brick, which "severed her prime form from her substantial matter," a voice-over said, alluding to a tagline in Thomistic philosophy, borrowed from Aristotle. Before she collapsed the floor, she fixed a stare at the audience as a brilliant, long slow burn. They howled in response.

The Jesuit authorities wanted to hypereducate us young ones so that we could join the regular faculties. The handwriting was on the wall. Regular student anger at required courses in doctrinaire philosophy and theology they hated would push them out of the curriculum. But what would become of the cadre of older Jesuits teaching the dreaded required courses? Their only credentials were only parochial degrees like the licentiate. They could only teach courses like these in a Catholic university. As if trained to be farriers as the age of the automobile dawned, this cadre of priests began to see what was coming.

The first thing they became was bitter. They used the derogatory term "New Breed" to sneer at the young Jesuits given privileges and freedoms they'd never had. The phrase was coined in an article in *America*, the reputable Jesuit opinion magazine which, ironically, praised the phenomenon.

In the spring of 1968, Charlie and I came up with a scheme to try to raise, at least, a flag of internal generational truce. We arranged reciprocal dinner engagements. Once a month, the Weston scholastics would invite the older priests at Saint Mary's to have dinner with them at our Weston College residence hall. We created a ribald, covert acronym: MORASS (more older reverends at supper Saturday). Also, once a month, the scholastics would be invited to dine at the Boston College residence hall Saint Mary's. We dubbed that one—SCOFF (scholastics call on fathers Friday). The two acronyms were playful. But, sadly, predictive.

Both efforts cultivating collegiality flopped. The only Jesuit priests who came to dinners at Weston were the hipper ones whom we knew from our classes and with whom we were already friendly. When we tried to sit at a table for dinner at St. Mary's, we were met with silence, or several priests would pick up their plates and leave.

It was out of our hands. The Jesuits were undergoing a widespread cultural disruption. The Greatest Generation who had fought through the Second World War with a finely frenzied patriotic fervor became perplexed when the very children they thought they'd fought for to secure their freedom, now freely chose to reject war of any kind, for any purpose whatsoever. In other words, what if human communities prospered only by the reference all its members had to what was in reality a nebulous, ambiguous, fraught set of common values? Pull out that stool and "all fall down," as the nursery rhyme said.

More pernicious doubts crept in. Eventually, I came to the conclusion that of all the Jesuits I had met at Shadowbrook, Father Hennessey was the reigning superhero. Not just because of his great act of faith—since who can ever measure the strength of spiritual faith in a person? But because of Father Hennessy's palpable physical courage. He lived a full and pleasurable life for as long as possible given the enormous practical price to be paid for the dignity of endurance.

Hennessey rose higher in my estimation after de Lubac fell. In his later years, de Lubac founded a journal, *Consilio*, dedicated to attacking what he considered the dangerous liberalism of the post-Vatican II Church—the very Church that set the souls of young Jesuits on fire. Father Hennessy did not resent youth. He never betrayed them.

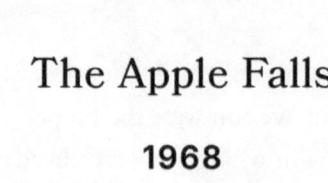

The Apple Falls

1968

Why do you speak to the people in parables?
—Matthew 13: 11

I stood, troubled, just outside the door to the room of my spiritual father as I quietly turned the handle closed.

Scholastics at Weston selected a spiritual father from the older priests living in the house. They were expected to set up regular times to meet with the priest in his room to say what was on their minds about their Jesuit lives. Each session usually ended with a private, personal confession. One walked out light and clean and clear.

Some of these priests were holdovers from the days when the faculty and student body at Weston College lived together and took classes together in the same building. Many were retired or commuted daily to their jobs as teachers or counselors or even parish priest assistants.

I chose Father O'Donnell because he was funny and smart. Every evening as the priests filed out of the dining hall ahead of the scholastics, Father O'Donnell would be the last in line. When he got to one of the pillars holding up the ceiling, he'd circle around it three or four times—until he had to hold his hand out to steady his dizziness. The rest of us, of course, couldn't begin to file out until he, the last priest, preceded us. Pure, goofy slapstick. Always good for a laugh.

He attended recreation with the young Jesuits and told hilarious stories about his time in England at a house where he lived with a Jesuit priest nicknamed "the dropper and the breaker." He routinely dropped cups of tea and plates of food. Once, he broke off the spigot on the coffee urn and the entire contents spilled out on the floor. He walked bent over and sometimes stepped on his own hands walking up stairs. It was hard to believe such a person existed, but no one could be sure he didn't.

Father O'Donnell looked funny too. He was short with a big head on a thick neck like a bullfrog. He was very smart and good to talk to. Once a week I'd stop by the priest's room and the conversation would flow freely about what I was thinking, what was bothering me, etc. Rarely did we touch on matters of faith or any sense of vocation, perhaps because I didn't bring the matters up. Perhaps because we both assumed the other was comfortable with how we were both living.

The priest took me to AA meetings, which I found very moving. At the meetings, wearing clerical clothing, Father O'Donnell would tell his story about depression and drinking fueled by the always open bars in every Jesuit rec room. Others in attendance looked to be working people without much education. They, of course, listened sympathetically to his stories as we did to theirs. I thought bringing me to listen was him opening his own soul to mine. We were comfortable with each other. A spiritual father in the Jesuits was usually fatherly, as he was. Father O'Donnell had the added cache of having overcome his alcoholism, as my own natural father never could.

But alas, eventually as with my own natural father, we became estranged.

In one fateful visit, on my birthday as it turned out, I told the priest about a philosophy course I was taking at BC from a non-Jesuit. Students read Mircea Eliade and Paul Ricoeur—two scholars of the power and role of mythmaking. Eliade developed the notion that myths were stories about actions that happened outside of the limits of time and space—in order to probe the essential truths of human experience. All myths revolved around an eternal return to the beginnings of life to provide orientation for the minds of people living in the present.

Ricoeur coined the phrase that these myths "gave rise to thought." They were not themselves the products of either history or of human perceptions. There was no core of meaning in them. Instead, contradictions would be left provocatively juxtaposed as a stimulus to thought—not its resolution.

I told Father O'Donnell I found this idea to reiterate my practice in daily meditation of allowing Gospel stories to give rise to forward-inclining speculation—not looking backward toward history or doctrine. To give rise to thought.

He smiled. "That sounds a sound way to pray. Keep at it. And Happy Birthday. And Happy Groundhog and Candlemas Day."

"Thanks. My totem animal is a woodchuck holding a candle in his paw."

The priest laughed. I went on.

"In Ricoeur's reading, the story of Adam and Even in the garden with the fruit tree and the snake was a myth about a god who had to allow human characters to discover on their own how to defy God. God needed them to have that freedom in order that afterward, if they freely chose to worship him, the god could be sure that worship was sincere, i.e., not instinctual or motivated by blind fear. In other words, even an all-powerful god initially faced a logical problem. His created humans had to discover disobedience on their own. Otherwise, God's creating the power of choice in them would have made whatever humans did or said about God to be nothing but ventriloquism.

"So, God went about preparing humans to improvise their own self-discovery. He provided the initial prohibition about eating the fruit but also the cunning of the speaking snake to tempt the humans to ignore the prohibition. That cunning included playing on sexual politics of the female taking a bite and assuring the male nothing bad happened—despite what the god had threatened. The humans took the bait by biting down on the fruit and getting hooked by the consciousness hidden inside. Their first awareness of this was that they were naked, as no animal or fish ever was. Naked meant there was the choice of getting dressed. The upshot was the myth gave rise to thinking about God's initial dilemma while also being entertaining.

"This is my understanding of Eliade's and Ricoeur's writings, anyway, influenced doubtless by my own practice of having 'second thoughts' arising out of the incongruous juxtaposition of memories.

"What it boils down to is, for one example, the Adam and Eve story is mythic. There is no core of history in it."

I paused for breath. We smiled at each other.

"Go on, it's a nice lecture," he said.

"I was particularly galvanized by these lines of thinking because I know you are considered to be the Catholic Church's authority for the doctrine that the Adam and Eve story is in fact, historical."

(It was called the doctrine of *primogeniture*. All humans were the heirs of this first couple. This was critical to the orthodox teaching that the rest of us inherited from our parents the stain of sinful disobedience to God, that in Saint Paul's simplistic theology, required the Son of God to sacrifice himself to the Father in expiation. This in turn required every legitimate follower of Jesus to acknowledge his or her own inherent, original sinfulness and to look to the Church for its doctrines and rituals of repentance and reconciliation.)

"What do you think of that? How does that sound to you?" I asked him. "Don't take my word for it. Here's my copy of Ricoeur's book *The Symbolism of Evil*. Why don't you read it and see if I got it right, and what you think of it. I'm asking you to do this because I know that your scholarly work has been in support of the Church's doctrine of primogeniture."

It was appropriate to challenge any priest. After all, I was having an unsettling experience up against an apparent contradiction between Church doctrine and unfettered human philosophizing as in Eliade and Ricoeur. What else was a spiritual father for but to hear such thoughts out?

Father O'Donnell smiled encouragingly. "Hand over the book.

I've heard of it. And now's my chance to read it. Give me a week, and then we'll talk about it."

And alas, a week later, sweet, funny Father O'Donnell admitted with a chuckle, "I read the *Symbolism of Evil,* and your account of it is fair, and I agree with you that Ricoeur's ideas were compelling. Genesis is a compilation of myths that work as Eliade and Ricoeur say."

I persisted with genuine curiosity, "Well, does that mean you'll give up writing in defense of primogeniture?"

"I can't do that," he said with a wink. "It's the only thing I'm known for. That's what I've written about for my whole career. I'm considered to be the Church's leading authority on the subject. I can't stop now. It's all just theater anyway."

That was an incredible comment to hear from an ordained priest. The shock of hearing him say this reduced me to silence. So much so, it didn't register at the time.

I do not remember what I said next. But after leaving the room, I felt very uneasy standing outside the door, until I was able to get my feet moving. I went right to the room of Charlie O'Leary to ask about my misgivings. He more or less agreed that nothing could be done about doctrines like primogeniture except to ignore them until they just faded away—like the belief that the world was flat, or Noah rode out the flood in a gigantic boat filled with animals. But questions still nagged me. What if my faith finally rested on a false understanding of myth—even perhaps the central story of a man-god who dies and then returns to life as a promise of his own 'eternal return'?

I called up Donna in her first year of medical school at Harvard. "Can we get together for lunch and to talk about something?" I pleaded.

"Take the T and meet me at Harvard Square and I'll pay for lunch," she said promptly.

"It's great to see you," I noted as we sat down. "Your hair is messy, and you look pale. You're studying too hard."

Donna responded curtly, "Mind your own business. And what's up? It's your business you wanted to talk about."

I told her about the conversations with Father O'Donnell and with Charlie. "But I still feel funny about this. Can I stay with a spiritual father like this?"

Donna smiled. "Look, it seems to me, you like doing what you're doing as a Jesuit, regardless of what anyone else says about what the Church says about anything. It's almost like the Jesuits have separated and gone their own way, especially with people like you and Charlie and Ed and AJ running all over the place. So, if you like talking to the man and he calms your soul, what's the problem?"

I hesitated before saying, "As always, your advice is sound. But I must say what's still nagging me is I think this primogeniture thing gets to the heart of all Christian belief. It's critical to believe humans inherit sin from a woman's deed. And that then most of the sins men commit are with women. And that keeps Christians feeling guilty about sex and women. And the only remedy to avoid final death, is to keep putting money in the collection box."

I don't remember what else Donna and I talked about. We saw each other regularly enough, so we never had to spend much time catching up. But I did stop going to see Father O'Donnell because I felt uncomfortable talking to a man who thought one way but wrote another.

Now I see this specific episode in the spiritual father's office as indicative for the way I was living then. The crisis of soul was over a genuine contradiction between doctrinaire religious belief and my delight in unfettered improvisational thinking. It brought back to mind my rejection of doctrinal interpretations of Jesus feeding the five thousand as prefiguring the Eucharist—and my fascinating discovery of the theater the Gospel writer has Jesus improvise at the edge of the lake. Every rereading convinced me the writer could never have envisioned anything doctrinal. The story was about the harsh divide between Jesus of nurture and Herod of horror. The Eucharist wasn't even established as a sacrament of the Church until the middle of the first century, fifty years after the speculated dates for the writing of Mark's Gospel—the first one to record the story. It was even more far-fetched to treat the Adam and Eve story this way. St Augustine (AD 354–430) declared that Eve's original sin of disobedience was passed down to all her descendants through the concupiscence of sexual intercourse. More than one thousand years later the Council of Trent declared this to be Catholic Doctrine in 1563—twenty centuries after the estimated composition of the Genesis story between 600–500 BCE.

You can't cram doctrine into any story improvised out of a writer's imagination. It's dropping a rock into a glass of water.

I went so far as to apply this thinking to the Gospels. Jesus was a picaresque hero in the literary jargon in my college literature classes. That is, an outlaw whose story can only be a collection of episodes—and epic like the *Odyssey* and the *Aeneid* and the *Adventures of Robin Hood*. Like these stories, the Gospels did not need to be literally or historically true to be true to life as a reader would find them. In fact, it occurred to me that doctrinal readings of the Gospels all believed Jesus did what the Gospels said he did in real history. That was the only way the doctrinalists could base their claims that any other human being in his or her own real life had to behave like the doctrinalists claimed Jesus said or did in fact.

My beloved Gospels, like Genesis, belonged to no canon. They were stories to give rise to thoughts that I found could be as profound as my mind could muster the gumption to reach.

But I did not choose to allow doctrinal rigidity to trouble my sense that to remain a Jesuit, following the informal council of my two dear friends, I could ignore church doctrine as so much idle chattering—while remaining enthusiastically alive in the fellowship of remarkable religious men.

But the question nagged me.

Was I fooling myself to gloss over my discomfort as Charlie and Donna had urged? Was I close to standing with Luther before the locked doors of a church declaring, "Here I stand"? At issue, ultimately, was how to remain true to my professed vow of obedience.

As it had been presented in the novitiate, the mechanics of this vow were straightforward. You did what you were told. Most of that was by inscription: what was written on the bulletin board about the daily schedule and our assigned tasks within. But this made things appear simple that were in fact spiritually complex. By following the daily order, we were obedient to our priestly superiors who ordered them. And they were interpreting for us the underlying regulations about the chain of command in the Jesuit order. Standing at the top of that was the Jesuit father general who lived in Rome. His mandates came from the pope. What the pope said translated the divine will into the mundane. So, by scrubbing toilets, we were obedient to God's will, *toute suite*. We were required to ask our immediate superior several times a year for "general permissions." They were always granted. This covered the need to get dressed, brush our teeth, make our beds, even go to the toilet. Because we had been given permission to do these things from down the chain of divine command, we got credit for the faithful, minute obedience to God's will. You could imagine the pope's sigh of relief when he received reports we faithfully brushed our teeth.

What had never been spoken of directly, but was widely implied, was that we were to remain obedient to the doctrines of the Holy Church as they had been promulgated and reiterated and refined through two millennia. Most of this sat lightly on our shoulders. We enjoyed taking communion with our fellow Jesuits and Catholics in a solemn ritual celebrating our sense of family. I can safely say, I never gave a thought to the doctrine of transubstantiation by which the Church taught, using the legerdemain of scholastic logic, that Jesus's body lay "under" the substance of the bread. That the separate consumption of the bread as body, and the wine as blood, repeated the bloody separation of Jesus's body and blood during his execution. The act of which earned the redemption of our original sins inherited from the disobedience of our foreparents in the Garden who gullibly listened to a serpent persuading them to eat a piece of fruit.

If communicants shuffling back to their pews didn't think about any of this, the fact remained that at the bottom, I came to be convinced, lay a doctrine of the Church called *primogeniture*. And that doctrine rested on a bad interpretation of a simple, provocative story, such as articulated by scholars like Father O'Donnell, my erstwhile spiritual father.

What if having second thoughts let cognitive dissonance ride until something precious got broken?

Another Flight From Fallen Leaves

1968

I have become a stranger in a strange land.
—Exodus 2:22

I stood clear headed, having stepped down off a train at the Hauptbahnh of München. The almost unbearable lightness of being like getting out of the car at Shadowbrook and off the bus at Boston College. I had graduated with a double major in English and philosophy and a minor in classics. I was accepted into the comparative literature program at Yale. I received a grant to support studying conversational German while attending the University of Munich and living in a nearby retirement house for German Jesuits.

No one met me at the train. I had to wander with a map and very poor German for several hours to find it. Nobody met me at the door to grab a suitcase this time.

The German Jesuits in residence were an older generation just like at Saint Mary's. They looked grim in their dark habits inside the house that had small windows and looked dark. To my dismay, all of them refused to speak to me in German. When I sat down at their table for a meal, they would gather their food, stand up together, and leave me sitting alone—just like the older priests had done at Boston College. I heard them say several times, almost out of my hearing range, the phrase "New Breed" in English. Apparently, it had by now become a universal and international slur by the most embittered of the older generation. Added to their disgust was that the German Jesuits still didn't like Americans, who had apparently dropped a bomb on their house during the war. Luckily for them, it was a dud that came to rest without further damage than to the intervening ceilings and floors in the basement. Several of the older German Jesuits still living in the house had survived that impact. That too, perhaps, fed their animosity toward me as a "New Breeder" because I could've been the same age as the American pilot who'd dropped the bomb.

Once, sitting alone at the table, finishing a meal in silence, I wondered whether I and other young Jesuits of my generation, during our early days of great enthusiasm, along with all the great Jesuit heroes of the world coming to knock on our doors, had all gotten caught up with the older ones in what I now would call a religious Ponzi scheme—whereby different Jesuit generations invested their own faith in what they were doing after being inspired by what the other cohort was doing. Again, I'd think, if this reciprocal reinforcement was all vice versa—where was the capital in the middle? Shouldn't that be a belief that whatever changes were in the air, however unsettling, there remained the dedication to following God's will? The old guys should just grin and bear it? Like we young guys had at Shadowbrook when the authorities yanked back their original offer to send us to Weston College early? Callow thoughts.

After one month in Munich, I felt at home alone. After breakfast, I'd walk several blocks to classes. I didn't come back until late at night. The sound only I could hear of the key turning in the lock of the door to the Jesuit house was intimate—like Miss Sonneberg turning the latch on the classroom door. I had enough money to buy steeply discounted meals at the university's cafeteria. I ate alone there too. I tried sitting at tables with other German students and striking up conversations. But they either looked at me and my miserable German with silent incomprehension or got up and walked away. I only tried sitting with male students, not daring to risk looking like a foreigner on the make for female students. Maybe the men thought I was gay.

For the first time in my life, there was no one to talk with, no group to which I belonged, no set of spelled out expectations for reference. Maybe this was what the desert had been like for Saint Anthony. It didn't matter much. After all, I was here for one thing alone—to learn to speak a foreign language without thinking about it. I sat and studied and attended classes and spoke German when I could. I kept asking directions in the streets, even when I knew where I was going, and feigned confusion just to keep the conversation going. I walked and walked, talking to *myself* in German as if I were a child babbling back at adults, striving for comprehension.

Meine Uhr ist krank—"My clock is sick"—was my first triumph. I had taken the alarm clock that didn't work that came with my room to a clock repair shop I had noticed on my walks. The people at the shop were friendly and delighted with my rough effort, even if *hoc non sonat bonum*.

The city was elegant with a wonderful park called the English Gardens to wander in. I listened to German on the radio and on TV and went to German movies. It was fun to hear cowboys speaking in a Prussian accent, and Indians in a Bavarian accent. I translated everything written in advertising on the sides of buses. I practiced phrases over and over. I read and read. I listened in on conversations on sidewalks and pretended to join in silently. I loved the beer and the food. I stopped wearing clerical garb outside the Jesuit house and even bought a tightly tailored shirt like I saw other students wearing so as not to look like a tourist. I even took to walking like Germans, with sharp mincing steps that looked like exercises in being precise. My great delight was to be asked for directions that I could give with great sprinklings of *recht, links,* and *gerade aus*—"right, left, straight ahead."

My favorite class was Shakespeare, taught in German, where I at least had a head start knowing the underlying English. I was puzzled at how bad the professor's English accent was when he read an original passage from Hamlet aloud: "Der's da divinity dat shaapes zour minnds." I probably sounded that bad in German.

I tried striking up conversations with students sitting next to me before or after the class period. Every time, they just looked away. The women would get up, looking a little frightened like I was a literal *Auslander* ("outlander," i.e., foreigner) making a pass. When I'd sit down at a table in the student cafeteria and try to strike up a conversation with a student, the student usually looked startled, and immediately got up and left the table. Maybe they didn't like foreigners, or maybe just wanted to be left alone to brood over their liter-size glasses of milk and buttered *broetchen* (little bread buns with an *X* slashed on the top.)

I had no success finding conversational partners until I stood outside the door to the English department and waited for the first friendly looking student who emerged. I figured one of these students might be willing to trade conversations in German and English. The first student-aged person walking out of the departmental office did look friendly, and even smiled patiently as I made a spiel in the best broken German I could muster. Afterward he—Erhard—told me he thought I was speaking with a Polish accent because I overdid the guttural sounds.

Erhard smiled, and we began to meet for bilingual meals and walks. I came to know other students in his circle of friends who were also happy to lead a hesitant speaker along—perhaps out of fascination with any foreigner eager to learn their language when in 1968 a taint of suspicion about Germany's war history still hung in the air. There was a building on Leopoldstrasse—a main drag—that still had bolt holes in the outline of a swastika where the original had been yanked off.

My first linguistic triumph was at a party at a new friend's parents' house where late in the evening someone told the group of my newfound delight in a German drinking game. The guests pressed me to preside. When everyone within ear shot had a full glass in hand, I shouted, "*Was sagt der Zahnarzt?*" (What does a dentist say?), and everyone shouted back, "*Spulen!*" (Rinse!). Everyone then took a deep swallow, and some even gargled their beer. Next, I shouted, "*Was sagt der Lerher?*" (What does a teacher say?). The response—"*Wiederholen!*"

(Repeat!). Everyone took another slug. The third question was usually "*Was sagt der Pharrer?*" (What does the pastor say?). The usual response was "*Weg von den Weibern!*" (Stay away from women!). Then everyone would take a very big slug of beer, applaud, and laugh.

I improvised. Munich is in Bavaria, where many Germans are Catholic. Pope Paul VI had just issued his infamous encyclical reaffirming the Church's prohibition against birth control. My third question was "*Was sagt der Papst?*" (What does the pope say?). I could hear a gasp. Then I paused; breaths were held. I shouted, "*Weg von der Pille!*" (Stay away from the pill!). That brought the house down. Some older people were doubled over and laughing so hard they almost fell down. They shed tears. It turned out to be not only my earliest triumph as a German speaker, but my only true triumph as a stand-up comic in any language.

So, I had moments, like anyone learning to speak a foreign language, but they were few and far between. Day by day it was very hard and humiliating to puzzle small children who could not understand why any adult would speak wretchedly ungrammatical German. Worse, it was impossible to ever win—or even score points—with other students arguing with them in German about the miserable American politics of the Vietnam War.

Perhaps I should have espoused my grandfather's strategy. Gramps was illiterate in English and only looked at the tabloid *New York Daily News* that was mostly photographs, always one of which was a scantily clad woman on page three. Thus, Gramps was free to believe only his strong American prejudice. He thought all the pictures of riots and demonstrations against the war had behind them the evil machinations of the Republicans.

My sense of cultural or class alienation was kid stuff compared to Gramps—and indeed for my parents. Only then did I understand what it must have been like for Gramps to become an outsider in a strange land. My uncomfortable feelings as a blue-collar kid dipping his toe in a wealthy world of privilege didn't even come close. I should have recognized Gramps when we lived together as my first great hero.

I never told my grandfather I studied and learned to speak German. Gramps hated Germans, with a hatred as deep as the history of German evil toward the Poles was long.

A Jolt

1968

Look! Here Comes Helena.
—A Midsummer Night's Dream 1.1

During a lunch break between conversational German language classes, I walked by a table with three young women speaking French, a language in which I had no speaking skills. One in particular was radiant and smiling, and I took notice because she dressed like Donna did—mostly in brown and yellow. She was beautiful. I thought she was French.

"*Bon jour*," I said to her several days later when we met at a coffee machine.

"That sounds like an American accent," she said in English with a smile. We both laughed and introduced ourselves.

"I'm Helen. I just finished a year as an exchange student in Nice, France. I'm studying German in Munich before heading back for my senior year at the University of Kansas."

"I'm Jan. I just graduated from Boston College. This fall I start comparative literature at Yale."

"That sounds impressive."

"Well, yes, it does. But right now, I'm more scared than excited. I hope this summer helps my German."

I didn't tell her I was a Jesuit. I wasn't wearing clerical garb. We started having lunch together, trying to speak to each other in rough German, which was painful. Lonely, with no one to talk with at the Jesuit house on Karlbach Strasse, one day, during a pleasant chat between classes, I asked her, "Would you like to hear some jazz? There's a club I know. A quartet's piano player is Jan Hammer. He is a refugee from Czechoslovakia after its brief, brutal revolt against the Soviet Union. We could talk English there."

"I love jazz, and the piano player sounds interesting just for his name even without hearing him."

During an intermission, we sat on a bench outside and kissed, which gave me a jolt. I had not touched a woman like that since fondling Donna's breast seven years earlier. Helen was surprised by my ardor, she told me later.

We started dating several times a week at the club.

On Midsummer's Eve, we took a train to Venice for a long weekend, which was a lovely place to lose one's virginity. We spent enough intimate time together that I began to get the basics right. Helen was sweetly helpful and patient.

I told no one either in Germany or back home about any of this. I got back to the Jesuit house so late at night that nobody else was up, so nobody noticed my absence, especially since I had stopped eating in the dining room. At the end of the summer, Helen moved back to Kansas for her senior year. We promised to write. I still hadn't told her I was a Jesuit.

Another Splendid Hill

1968

The day is coming, and it is now here.
—John 4:28

On Labor Day, I stood outside the arrivals door of Kennedy airport, waiting for a bus. I took the train from New York City to New Haven, where I had already forwarded a truck of my belongings from Weston. I moved into the Jesuit residence at Yale, Virgil Barber House. I wore a tailored German shirt.

The accommodations at Virgil Barber house were splendid. I lived with eight other Jesuits at the top of Prospect Street on Prospect Hill, probably the most elegant address in New Haven. Other homes in the neighborhood housed Mayflower descendants like Yale's president, Kingman Brewster, and its eloquent university chaplain, William Sloan Coffin. Another Jesuit mansion, Virgil Barber House had its own cook, and the chef was a student at the Culinary Institute of America. Their students proudly wore hoodies with *CIA* embroidered on the front.

After a week of being excited about moving into this new and splendid home, I felt uneasy. Despite all my efforts, and almost in defiance of my official vow of poverty, I wound up living on the top of another splendid hill, like Donna's house on Pine Hill Ridge Road and the houses at Shadowbrook and Weston and Chestnut Hill. It would be hard to imagine Jesus—or Peter Claver—showing up at Virgil Barber

House—even staying overnight. I was disturbed when reading Walter Harding's biography of Thoreau. I calculated that the square footage of my elegant, wallpapered, wall-to-wall-carpeted bedroom matched that of the entire austere interior of Thoreau's self-made cabin, where he cooked his dinner on a wood stove or on rocks outside his door. The kitchen had restaurant-quality appliances. Thoreau would not feel at home here. Certainly not Peter Claver.

Putting aside the images of the liaison with Helen developing at the same time—I felt caught between second thoughts—a blue-collar, working-class kid, living a life of luxury, albeit under the veil of a vow of poverty. And all the while the New England Province was funding my housing in order that my future garnished wages would pay the investment back into the treasury while I lived in some other splendid Jesuit house. Republican economics?

I had to sit for a qualifying exam required of incoming comparative literature students. We had been told before applying for admission that we'd be required to adequately translate three long passages from literature in three languages: French, German, and Latin. Probably to winnow down the number of applications even willing to try. French and German were easy. I wondered if it might qualify as a miracle that the French passages came from a novel by Proust I was reading at the time.

The Latin was laughable: the text of the medieval church hymn "Stabat Mater Dolorosa." It depicts Jesus's mother standing next to his cross, weeping. The hymn contains at least a dozen different words for *weeping* necessary for the sing-song rhyming. During various Jesuit liturgies, I had already sung it in Latin, and after Vatican II's mandated shift to vernacular languages, in English. I had enough time left over during the exam after rendering a rhyming English translation to write out the Gregorian chant musical notation. A triumphant initiation. An archaic Jesuit education had prepared me for success in the real world.

It helped boost spirits that two close Jesuit friends, AJ and Charlie, moved in at the same time—the core of an affectionate community.

AJ Antoon was admitted to the Yale Drama School provisionally, probably because his résumé only covered homemade theatrics. After six months, he received official acceptance as a regular student at the Drama School. He'd bullied his way in. But then, what else is drama but dramatic? In the two years we'd live together at Virgil Barber House, he directed showcases and plays with future stars, Meryl Streep and Henry Winkler, and became a disciple of Paul Sills, an innovator of what was called "story theater." Tagging along with AJ, I would get to meet people like Paul Newman, Mike Nichols, Robert Brustein, Richard Gilman, and Joanne Woodward.

AJ frequently took the train to New York City and haunted the theatrical scene there, catching the eye of Joe Papp, the great theatrical entrepreneur of the day. AJ would begin his career directing plays at Papp's renowned Public Theater.

Charlie O'Leary began work on a PhD in clinical psychological counseling. Even before his coursework started, Charlie worked overtime assisting drug addicts and homeless youth. Sister Jill, who still lived in Norwalk, about an hour's drive away, gave me an old Chevy sedan she was getting rid of. Since I biked everywhere, I gave the car to Charlie, who was often on the road and in and out of town.

For recreational relief as graduate students, Charlie and I formed the New Haven Picnic Club. In the fall, after classes began, when it was still warm and the trees that covered the hills were colorful woven mats of red, orange, purple, and green, Donna would take the train down from Boston. We'd drive Jill's Chevy I had given to Charlie. We'd spend an afternoon at a beach, having lunch, taking a hike or a swim. Another undergraduate, Martha, would later join the New Haven Picnic Club. She'd become Charlie's friend after doing inter city social work together.

Before any inkling of our futures together, Charlie and I improvised a ritual like we had done at the Pits. While Charlie drove Martha back to her dorm, and Donna to the train, we passed around a book of Robert Frost's poems. Each one took turns reciting. We always ended with stanzas of Robert Frost's 1912 poem, "Reluctance."

> Out through the fields and the woods
> And over the walls I have wended;
> I have climbed the hills of view
> And looked at the world and descended.
> I have come by the highway home,
> And lo, it is ended.
> The leaves are all dead on the ground,
> Save those that the oak is keeping
> To ravel them one by one
> And let them go scraping and creeping
> Out over the crusted snow,
> When others are sleeping.
> And the dead leaves lie huddled and still,
> No longer blown hither and thither;
> The last lone aster is gone;
> The flowers of the witch hazel wither;
> The heart is still aching to seek,
> But the feet question "Whither?"
> Ah, when to the heart of man
> Was it ever less than a treason
> To go with the drift of things,
> To yield with a grace to reason,
> And bow and accept the end
> Of a love or a season.

I said, "It's the perfect poem for ending a fall day trip vacation—and the ending is about fall and about love and about things ending for good. Frost wrote it in despair after his eventual wife Elinor turned him down when he proposed the first time. But he decided to 'go with the drift of things,' until they could turn out right. Maybe that's what all of us are doing now—drifting toward our futures."

"It also looks backward. It's a poem about reminiscing," Donna added. She looked at me directly. "I particularly liked the line in the poem about 'scraping and creeping' since it reminds me of what you said to me on that sandbar about my acceptance of 'creepy' things. At the time we were holding our hands pressed down into the body of the horseshoe crab we eventually brought back to my mother from the sandbar."

Fifty years later (November 2019)—almost five years ago as I write this—and two weeks before he died young in his middle seventies unexpectedly of a stroke, Charlie called me. We agreed that whoever died first, the other would recite "Reluctance" at the memorial service, which I did. A year later I recited it again when Donna died.

It's probably not a universal truth. However, I found that the people I became close to had poetry between them. To read it, even write it, was to share the power of its words to create an inner space outside the world of earnest, harsh words.

By this time, Helen had returned to the University of Kansas for her senior year. We corresponded frequently. I no longer needed to hand in letters for review by the authorities. After her graduation in the spring of 1969, she moved to New York City. It was the summer between my two years of required graduate classes. She shared an apartment with several other young women and got a good job as an executive assistant in a large financial firm, where she used her French in overseas correspondence for the company. One reason for taking the job was to get within a train's ride of where I was living in New Haven. We saw each other clandestinely. She still didn't know I was a Jesuit.

Several times, Helen took a train up from New York City to visit a mutual friend also living in New Haven. Hers was a friendship I now got to the point of being open about, as a friendship. "We met in Munich," I told people.

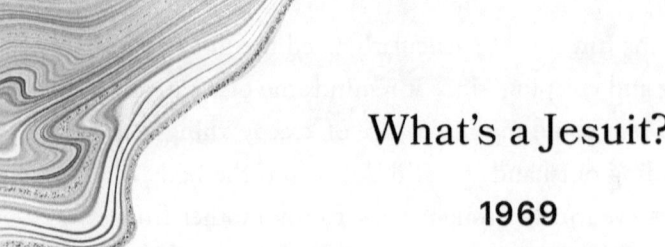

What's a Jesuit?
1969

Who told you that you were naked?
—Genesis 3:11

I stood before her door. Knocked. It was New Year's Eve 1969, in the middle of my second and final year of graduate school coursework. I came on the train from New Haven to spend the weekend with Helen at her apartment in Manhattan. She looked radiant opening the door. Our kiss was awkward, shy. The apartment was quiet.

"The place is ours. My roommates are away for the holiday."

She took my hand and led me into her bedroom. Later, lying in each other's arms, I took a deep breath.

"I have a confession to make."

"You mean I'm not the only woman in your life? That's okay for now. We're still just getting to know each other."

"The thing is, there is no other woman. Believe me, there never has been. It's that I'm a Jesuit, and I shouldn't be seeing you, or any woman like this."

"What's a Jesuit?"

Helen looked thoughtful, then confused. She had been raised a Protestant in the Midwest without an inkling about Catholicism and its various mutations. We had spent some time telling each other about what it was like growing up on a Midwestern farm and a seaside village on Long Island Sound. Both places hardly seemed to belong to the same earth from what we remembered of them. But we both were genuinely fascinated with each other's backgrounds, as if we each had met an alien getting out of a spaceship. But until this point, I hadn't said anything about starting a pilgrimage many years before, following in the steps of the Jesuits I had first seen playing basketball on an island. Now, I cut to the chase.

I told her what Jesuit meant. What an order of priests was. What kind of an order Jesuits where. What kind of vows I had taken to get this far. One of them was celibacy and what that was.

"Does that mean you can't get married?" she asked thoughtfully.

"Alas, it's more than that." I gave her a squeeze and waved my hand over our adjacent naked bodies. "What it should mean is 'none of this.'"

"This is going to take some getting used to," Helen said. "There's certainly nothing wrong about what we're doing."

But her tone was thoughtful. As if to imply all we needed was more time to work this out, and we both had plenty of that.

"It's only the first day of your weekend visit."

She got up and walked toward her bedroom door unclothed. I had never seen anything so beautiful as an unclothed woman walking. She opened the door and took a step into the living room of her apartment. All her roommates were away, so it was for the moment "our place."

A second image popped to mind while I watched her walking, mesmerized. A priest in solemn gait in a religious ceremony, always massively dressed in robes and scarves and hats which completely enclosed the body and hid any traces of its build or gender.

She knocked *that* image flat, as she turned to me with a shy smile and said, "Don't go away. I'll be right back."

After she went through the door, some part of me got out of bed and walked over to her desk chair, sat down, and looked over carefully at the rest of my body still lying in the bed. What was I thinking, lying there? Sinning? Well, no. I was shifting between two phrases: "What's a Jesuit?" and a beautiful woman who'd just left the room but said, "Don't go away." At the moment, it seemed to the me sitting in the chair that the me lying in the bed was comfortable with both the question and the request. "What am I doing?" the spectator took the trouble to wonder for himself and the other. Being a Jesuit and a lover were both plausible?

The spectator quickly got off the chair and put himself back into the body of the man on the bed as the beautiful Helen, full frontal this time, pushed over the door with her bare foot. She walked toward me, holding two glasses in one hand, and a bottle of wine and a corkscrew in the other. Eve with fruit in her hands?

As if she'd heard my silent "Eve," she said cheerfully, "Let's celebrate your confession on New Year's Eve. It'll be a new year for both of us!" She put the glasses down on the table next to her desk and handed me the corkscrew.

I opened a blade on the corkscrew to cut away the seal on the bottle and, for extra leverage while inserting the cork, kept it flat in my palm. With a twist, I cut my hand deeply with the blade. Helen didn't flinch. She ran and got a clean dish towel to wrap my hand against the bleeding. We both took a long look at the cut.

"My first stigmata."

"I don't know what that means. But you better get this looked at," she said as a matter of fact, as if a naked man cutting open his hand in her bedroom was only an occasion for an assessment and decision.

She had grown up on a farm with lots of animal blood. She helped me dress while I held the hand wrapped in the towel like Veronica's veil over my head. I took the elevator to the street. Outside there was a police car parked with its blue light flashing. A policeman stood on the sidewalk writing in a notebook, standing over a man's body.

"Could I get a ride to a hospital?"

"Just walk," the policeman said curtly, not looking up. "It's three blocks down and one to the right."

I carried the toweled hand over my head, down the streets, and then into the emergency room. Four people in white jackets were eating pizza, sitting at a table and chatting. They paid no mind to the bodies of people that lay all around them, stretched out on gurneys and tables, and side by side on the floor, some moaning and twitching, as if recovering from overdoses and benders.

"What's up, bud?" asked one of the white coats as he pointed to my bloody toweled hand held over my head. "Pardon the pun."

I lowered the bloodied, toweled hand in silent answer.

The young man in white didn't ask for an explanation. He said briskly, "Let's have a look." And after he did, he said with no trace of emotion, "No problem. Just lay your hand down here," pointing to a small table. He swathed the hand with disinfectant. "This might sting," he said with a smile while he stuck a needle in my hand to numb any pain. "But you look tough enough."

In a few minutes, with a deft almost ceremonial blessing of my hands with a needle and thread, the wound was closed. Immediately another white coat handed me some pills.

"One a day for a week," she said without making eye-contact as she wrapped my hand in real bandages this time, like the ones I'd seen on my foot when I woke up in the hospital once before.

"How should I pay for this?"

I didn't have any insurance cards. The Jesuits paid my medical bills usually. What little money I had was in a wallet back at the apartment. Was the pain in my hand and the panic in my brain punishment for the sin that had started all this?

"Fuggetabotit. It's on the house." John L'Heureux had said as much.

I thanked them profusely. As I walked back to the apartment, I admired how tidy the injured hand looked. The Jesuit life had little prepared me for all this excitement. I buzzed myself in to the apartment building where Helen lived.

She'd had some time to process what I'd said and now had questions.

"Where do I fit into this, for you? I like you a lot. I think I've fallen in love with you. I think you might love me too. I'm eager to find out if we do really love each other, getting to know each other more and more. But I'm worried. No, I'm upset. Are you just playing at this with me? You're like a married man—to somebody else? *I* vowed a long time ago I wasn't going to get involved with anyone like that. Maybe you need to go home and decide what you want to do. I need some time off from you for this."

"You are right. I don't really know what I'm doing here. I think I love you too. It's wrong for me to use you and do what we are doing without making a decision. Which I promise I will make."

"Good," she said, and shook the hand of mine she had been holding. "Now let's eat before you take the train back."

She had prepared a hearty stew for dinner in the middle of the first night of 1970—which, at the moment neither of us could anticipate, would become an *annus mirabilis* for us both. We would be married in the spring while tear gas still hung in the air over the New Haven Green from the demonstrations mounted in defense of Bobby Seale, the Black Panther who'd been indicted for murder.

Charlie would be my best man. During his studies at Yale, he had been working with strung-out young people in the street, cleaning them up, finding them housing, getting them dressed. He did his most heroic work during that May Day unrest in the spring of 1970, when the Black Panther Bobby Seale was tried for murder in a New Haven courtroom and hippies and yippies and agitators of all stripes arrived from all over the country, including Jerry Rubin, Abbie Hoffman, and Allan Ginsburg, to harangue, march, and willingly inhale tear gas.

During that time, before my scheduled marriage day, I worked at a soup kitchen and ladled soup into the bowls of Allan Ginsburg and Norman Mailer, who were next in line to each other but apparently were not speaking.

After we finished her New Year's Day midnight stew, we exchanged a chaste kiss at the door.

"Now go. Call me when you have something to say."

I left the apartment to walk to Grand Central Station to take the early milk train back home. In the train window, I saw a reflection of myself as an unshaven, self-styled hypocritical celibate Jesuit. Then in my mind I put up next to that a picture of the kind and beautiful Helen alone in her apartment, probably washing dishes and maybe wiping off some of my blood on the floor.

I arrived at Virgil Barber House in time for lunch, looking ragged from lack of sleep and from anxiety about what I was doing and thinking. Charlie kept looking at me. At the bandaged hand. After lunch, Charlie pulled me into his room and said pointedly, "Okay Brother, what's up? Tell me everything." And with a wry smile he added, "What did you do on your New Year's vacation?"

I told Charlie everything.

"Do the right thing. It'll be all right with me," Charlie said simply.

I didn't have any real time to think just then. I had been invited to give a second semester commencement talk the next week at Albertus Magnus College, an all-women's Catholic school several blocks away from Virgil Barber House on Prospect Street in New Haven. The title was "Women Talk Back to Jesus," a feminist account of the encounters Jesus has with women in Saint John's Gospel. His mother Mary pesters him to do something about the empty wine barrels at the wedding feast at Cana. The Jewish Samaritan woman he meets at a well questions him closely about his Judean Jewish religious prejudice. Martha and her sister Mary ask him why he didn't do anything to prevent the death of their brother Lazarus. Mary mistakes the risen Jesus for a gardener, accusing him of having stolen Jesus's body from the tomb. The gist of the talk was—it was time for women to talk back to the Church. The talk was well-received, to my great relief. Because of the topic, and the venue, I had worn full priestly regalia of a black suit and a Roman collar probably for dramatic emphasis. It was the last time I would ever appear that way.

Afterward, at a reception, I walked into a large hall filled with

Catholic women of all ages, and I was the only male, and dressed like a priest with a Roman collar. The women swooned. I could hear sighs and irregular inhalations of breath as they beheld the pure ideal Catholic male—celibate and therefore unavailable to any women like them except by fantasy. I hated it. It was all wrong. I could not go on like this.

I walked back to Virgil Barber House muttering. I got to my room and closed the door. I thought about the women at Albertus Magnus College. My visit to Helen. The evening I'd brought down the house at a party with my German drinking toast about *Der Pille* the day after Pope Paul VI (John the XXIII's reactionary successor as Pope) had issued his encyclical *Humanae Vitae* where it says birth control is "intrinsically evil."

I got out a copy of the encyclical and read it again.

I spoke out loud to myself: "What century does the pope think we're living in? And despite all the promise of Vatican II that the Church would begin to recognize the equality of women among the faithful, to the point of ordaining them priests—instead the Congregation for the Doctrine of the Faith issued the Declaration on the Question of the Admission of Women to the Ministerial Priesthood which pontificated that 'for doctrinal, theological, and historical reasons, (the church) does not consider herself authorized to admit women to priestly ordination.'"

It was all wrong. I continued in silence, talking to myself. But to show you how naive I had been, and as many of my fellow younger Jesuits had been, right up until the day that *Humanae Vitae* came out, we were confident it was going to say just the opposite—that birth control made sense for Catholics—that women needed to be able to rely on choice if they were going to prosper in the modern world. Instead, in its pretense to wisdom, the Church had said just the opposite!

I went back to speaking out loud: "How naive we were! We fully expected the Church would finally improvise on its traditions. Instead, it doubled down on them—reprising the previous movements note for note."

The shock of reading the encyclical was just as sharp as Dwyane's unexpected attack on *Flotsam*. Or Father Finnigan's sermon attacking rock and roll. Or the reception at Albertus Magnus. Or hearing Father O'Donnell say his fervent defense of reading literally a myth to make it appear as a story about the origin of evil in the conviction of a woman. Each thought a shard of the ice poking holes in the hull of the *Titanic*.

I thought, *If the Church is wrong about women—what can it (or "she" as she ironically calls herself) be right about?* Jesus said nothing about abortion or birth control or divorce or even setting up the priesthood and popes. He was much more interested in fishing. He had his deepest and warmest conversations with women in John's Gospel. It now became clear that all this bad thinking began with Paul, who wrote to men condescendingly about marriage as an alternative to damnable lust—"It is better to marry than to burn"—and to women that they needed to wear their hair long under hats to Church to acknowledge their subordination to men. It's Paul who gets the bad balls of Catholic doctrine rolling. And believe me, Paul of Tarsus was no Jesus of Nazareth. The Four Gospels were written after Paul's Epistles—I believe as a failed effort to try to correct Paul's damage, which continues causing harm to this very day. I no longer wanted to be a part of a Church Paul's ideas subverted. This, by the way, had been the subject of my talk at Albertus Magnus College. I wondered if it had given "rise to thought" in any of the Catholic women present.

I sat on the bed and kept going. Pouring ingredients into the stew of thinking. Even all three of the Abrahamic religions exist solely and purposefully to repress women. Clerical Penis Power. Michelangelo's God and Adam reaching out to touch phallic fingers. None of the three religions, for all their vast structures of buildings and hierarchies and history and orthodoxy can withstand the full-bodied humanity of women and their rightful demands about the whole of life. The vow of celibacy the Church imposes on its male clergy and female nuns is elitist and aristocratic. "These people are holier than you are" is the message, *you!* mired in the earthly pleasures of the body. The worst of those is sex. It's enough to turn your look for paradise toward the person you're with, not to gods far away. Most humans experience anxieties about sex, just as all sensate creatures do seeking mates and reproductive sex. By smearing sex with the slime of shame, the Church tied the person to itself with bands of guilt that then it claimed could only be loosened by prayer, alms, repentance. As the anxiety always returned, the remedies always required would catch the faithful in a continuous loop. The three *monotheistics* keep the loop moving.

On second thought, maybe it isn't really the fault of the Church. Its conservatives are right. The Church is hierarchical, male-dominated, entangled with Pauline unearthly ideas and an unfortunate style of biblical interpretation that denigrated the Hebrew Bible by turning it into a footpath to his abstract idea of Christianity. For Paul, little of what Jesus said or did (as reported in the Gospels written much later) impinged on his smooth rhetorical swoop from original sin to the difficulties of redemption to the unearthly rapture at the end. To reform the Church beyond its traditional boundaries, as we young Jesuits had hoped, was like trying to make early twentieth-century transportation better by breeding faster horses.

I fell back on the pillow and took a long nap.

There was still a week to go before courses started. I took the train to Boston to visit John L'Heureux and seek his counsel. John was studying at Harvard then. At the time he was still a Jesuit priest; but he would leave the order himself several years later to marry a beautiful red-headed schoolteacher named Joan. He continued publishing poems and novels. He taught for many years at Stanford University and mentored such wonderful writers as Thomas Wolff, Henry David Hwang, and Harriet Doerr.

We sat in a café in Harvard Square.

"What worries me the most is what my close Jesuit friends would say if I left the Jesuits. That I had betrayed their trust. That I selfishly got an education and then left to go off on my own. This sounds silly. But I find it harder to think about leaving the Jesuits than I do leaving the Church. Part of it is practical—since I can't figure out what I'd do next. I mean, I don't know if I left the Jesuits whether the Jesuits at Boston College would still honor their offer of a teaching job. If BC rescinds the offer, I'd have to find someplace to stay, and figure out how to support myself. But a greater part of it is leaving my friends behind. And I have a hard time imagining who I would be if I no longer had the identity of being a Jesuit."

John listened closely and then said curtly, "You sound like a convert to pacifism who still wants to remain in the Marine Corps. Look, let me be blunt. On the day you leave, how many of your fellow Jesuits will miss lunch?"

After our lunch, I took the T from Cambridge to Government Center near the Boston Commons. I walked to the New England Province Headquarters on Commonwealth Avenue and asked for a meeting with the Provincial. I had to wait for several hours.

I told the Provincial simply, "I need to sign my papers. I want to leave the Jesuits." I ended the statement with a sob. The Provincial handed me a tissue and a glass of water. He asked questions in a kindly way. He appeared undisturbed, as if he was accustomed at this point to receiving lots of requests like this. He told me how to file the necessary paperwork. He said I should continue to live at Virgil Barber House until I signed the dismissal form.

Finally, the Provincial stood up, extended his hand and said, "We would have liked to have you with us longer, but are grateful for the time we had."

I called Helen from a payphone at Union Station to tell her what I had done. "Let's not talk anymore about this until I come up to New Haven and we're face to face. We're still open-ended, you and I, you understand."

"Name the date and the time. Tomorrow? If I can get off work?"

"Make it the next day. I need to get back home first."

She arrived on the train late in the morning. She dropped her suitcase off at our friend Mary's apartment. While we walked together, hand in hand, we just made small talk, but affectionately. We heard mewing. Helen looked up and cried, "There's a kitty cat caught up in a tree!" Sure enough, there was a small, thin orange cat looking down at us from a branch with round eyes. "How can we get it down?" she pleaded.

"It'll probably get itself down by itself. It's not that high up."

I could tell she wanted us to do more. Then she startled me by saying, "Okay, we'll let it be. But with the cat as witness, now's the time to tell me what you asked me here to tell me."

"You know I love you. I'm not sure what you think about my being such a mental mess about all of this. I've decided to leave the Jesuits. Which means I could marry you. Of course, that doesn't mean you'll marry me. I'll leave the Jesuits. I'm not sure how to do that just yet, or what time it takes."

"I love you too. Yes, I will. Take your time. That's what you've been doing all along anyway."

So, there it was. I spoke an emphatic, "Yes, me too. Satisfied?"

"Yes. And thank you, kitty, for being our witness."

We smooched on the street. A woman walked around us on the sidewalk and said, "That looks promising," which broke the spell.

"I really need to get to work. Let's talk about this after lunch at Mary's," I said.

When we walked back under the tree later, the kitty cat was still there. It looked down at us with its big eyes and mewed.

"Cats only mew at people when they need something," Helen said authoritatively. "We've got to do something."

"Well, there's a fire department right around the corner. I'll go see if I can borrow a ladder."

"You do that. I'll stay here and keep an eye on the proposal-cat." She was enjoying every minute of the crisis. After all, the cat had already become a witness to a turning point in human history as the two of us knew it.

I ran down the street to the corner. The large overhead doors to the fire department were open in the front. I walked right in. A fireman in uniform looked up from doing paperwork on a high desk.

"How can I help you?"

"There is a cat caught in a tree just down the street. Could I borrow a ladder to get it down?" I asked.

The man replied gruffly, "Kid, we don't lend out equipment."

I pleaded, "But the cat's been there all day. It doesn't look like it can get down."

The man said with a sigh, "Are you making a formal request we come take the cat down?"

I thought for a moment about the absurdity of the situation. Then I decided I was a patriotic citizen with rights.

"Yes, I'm making a formal request that you come take the cat down out of the tree."

The man sighed again and pushed a button. A large ringing filled the station. I could hear footsteps pounding on the floor from the second story, and men actually started shimmying down a thick brass pole into the big garage-like space. They started pulling on official firefighting hats and coats.

"What is it?" one of the firemen shouted over the roar.

"A cat caught in a tree."

"Oh shit."

"Okay, kid, where's your cat?"

"It's not my cat. It's not far, just around the corner from here. All someone needs to do is bring a ladder."

"Kid, we can only send out a truck on calls. So, tell me again, where is the cat?"

While he was asking, I could hear other firemen cursing and the huge roar of a fire engine starting up.

"It's just around the corner. Look, let me ride on the truck and I'll show the driver where to go."

"Kid, we don't allow nobody else to ride on the trucks."

I ran over to the driver's window of the fire truck. "Just follow me."

I started running down the street, with the fire truck going slowly behind. When I looked back, the driver was scowling. He didn't even bother to turn the siren on, which was disappointing. This was a big moment for me—and Helen and the cat—anyway.

We all arrived at the same time at the tree with the cat. A small crowd had gathered, people looking out of windows. Several burly firemen started detaching a ladder.

"My kind of hullabaloo," Helen cried happily.

A fireman got a ladder off the truck, climbed up and retrieved the cat. When he got down, he handed the cat to Helen, bowed, and said formally, "Here's your cat back, lady."

I was about to say again, "It's not her cat," but decided to keep quiet.

We didn't want the fireman as they drove off to see us just leaving the cat on the sidewalk. We waited until the truck turned the corner back to the station. She put the cat down, gave it a pet, and said, "There you go kitty. The world's your oyster."

The next morning, Helen and I walked to the library. We went under the same tree. The same cat sat on the same branch mewing with its big eyes. Donna looked at the cat and then me.

She said, "This cat thinks it likes going out on a limb. You're not sure you do, really, deep down yet, I don't think. So, if you mean what you said to me yesterday, get the cat down from the limb."

I told her defiantly, "I know what you're thinking. I'm not going back to the fire department again." She looked worried. I caved in.

"Okay, I'll go try to find a ladder, and I'll be the fireman this time and take the cat down."

"I'll stand guard here."

As I walked away, looking hopefully into open garage doors, I noticed an unattended ladder leaning against a house. I checked to see if anyone had used the ladder to get to the roof and saw no one. I knocked on the door. No one was home. I assumed permission to borrow the ladder. I brought it back and climbed and got the cat who cuddled in my arm as I came down the ladder. I handed it to Helen with a flourish and quoted the fireman, "Here's your cat back, lady."

Helen cuddled the cat. Annoyed, she noted, "This cat's thin; and look at this." She brushed the fur back against its belly and pointed to little black flecks. "She's crawling with fleas. Dear me, no one's taking care of her. Go put the ladder back where you found it. I'm taking her back to New York with me. We're not supposed to have them in the apartment, but I can fake it. Consider it our first offspring. I'm naming her 'DeeDee' short for 'DDecisions.'"

"Why two Ds?"

"Two decisions rolled into one. You decided to leave the Jesuits; and you decided to marry me."

Standing there with her and the cat on the sidewalk, I felt I had just stepped out of my entire life to this point, without any real clear sense where to turn next.

"It feels funny not to have any ring in hand to give to you, which you're supposed to do while kneeling on one knee. You know that right now I don't have a penny I can call my own. The poverty thing I told you about."

"That's okay. You did all that climbing down the ladder."

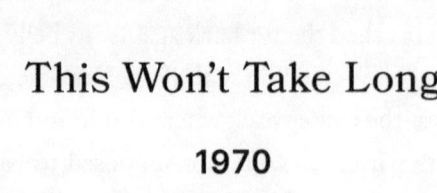

This Won't Take Long

1970

I will be with you always, even unto the end of the world.
—Matthew 28:20

I stood hesitantly in the doorway of the room of the new superior of Virgil Barber House. Father Charles Bent was working on his doctorate in Theology at the Yale Divinity School. Father Bent looked up from his desk.

"Come in. Sit down. This won't take long."

Father Bent handed me a document in Latin with the official words I needed to endorse to formally leave the Jesuits.

It was February 2, my birthday. Now twenty-six, I had thus officially aged out of the draft into the Army, although asthma would have deferred me. My status would slide from 4-D (divinity student) to 4-F (futility).

As I started to read, slowly, to make sure I understood the words correctly, I stood up and began to cry—as I had next to Donna in the third grade. This time not in dismay—but more with a sense of how beautiful the Jesuit life had been and what profound friends I had made who were Jesuits.

I looked at Father Bent, wearing shorts and a T-shirt, who for the moment was looking back at me—perhaps to see if I would go through with it. He had a blond butch cut, was built like a bulldog, drank a six-pack of beer a day, and lifted weights. He had already published a book on theology that had been translated into three languages. Father L'Heureux—dark and slim as an otter—was at the same time working on a PhD in English at Harvard and had published a book of poetry and a memoir when both of them were barely thirty years old!

Through blurry eyes, I imagined standing next to my dear friends Charlie, Joe, Dennie, Ed, and AJ—and dozens of other young men we had lived with and loved during parts of the decade when we remained Jesuits.

All these men had called me "Brother." Who could match these friends, these men? And how generous the Order had been in allowing me to pursue a career as a graduate student and providing the promise of eventually becoming a professor in a Jesuit university.

What prompted me to dry the tears and sign the paper was realizing that the rough noise I was hearing was Father Bent rummaging around in his closet. "My hockey skates are in here somewhere," he complained. When he found them, he waved them my way and concluded, "After lunch, I'm taking the rest of the afternoon off." L'Heureux had been prophetic about lunch the day I would leave; Father Bent wouldn't be missing lunch—or his hockey game—on account of little old me.

As I signed the dismissal document, now dry-eyed, I realized I had reached nirvana in a long preoccupation with the meaning of *vacation* versus *vocation*. No home to vacate. No place to go. "No promises to keep," in the words of Paul Simon's 1964 hit "The Sound of Silence." "No direction known," in Dylan's words. The ultimate response to the call from heaven of the vocation I thought I had harkened to came down to the sound of a pen scratching on a sheet of paper.

Charlie Bent handed me a check from the New England Province for five hundred dollars.

"It's standard. It's for you to use to pay the rent wherever you find to go next." In exchange, he took the dismissal document and waved the ink dry.

Helen and I later used the Jesuit money to buy a good sound system.

The House Broom

1970

. . . there was a wedding . . .
—John 2:1

I stood in the sanctuary of the Catholic Center at Yale University on June 6, 1970, the twenty-sixth anniversary of D-Day. John L'Heureux officiated. Helen wore a traditional white dress she had sewn herself. Charlie and Martha stood beside us—*best persons*, Martha had insisted we call the two of them. A dedicated feminist, she said, "Not only the male is going to be designated 'best,' and besides, I'm not a 'maid.'" My mother and Donna's mother attended radiantly. Donna's mom cuddled a clean, now plump DeeDee, who slept quietly in her lap. Donna came with her new husband, Mark.

Mark gave a toast during our potluck reception in the basement of the Yale Catholic Center. He recited a poem with the line "We on a string of time, are one song with many movements" and told the story about how for him the identity of the couple inside the word *we* had shifted over time.

Before we drove away, Helen threw the bouquet at the unmarried women and the garter at the unmarried men over her shoulder. Charlie told me beforehand to throw a broom at the many Jesuits who attended. Between February, when I had signed the papers and moved out of Virgil Barber House, and June, I'd let myself back into the house and presumed permission to borrow a broom to sweep the apartment floor. I always brought it right back. It was a silly thing to do. I could have just bought a new broom. Finally, Father Bent accosted me one day and said the other people in the house wanted me to stop borrowing the broom. Charlie was still living at Virgil Barber House. He whispered during the reception he had brought the house broom with him.

"I'll get it if you promise to throw it to the Jesuits."

"You'll get in trouble too if they find you took it without permission."

We had purchased a late 1950s Triumph TR-3 sports car cheap. We drove it to a honeymoon at the summer home in Waldoboro, Maine on loan from a BC professor. I learned to dig steamer clams in the mudflats of the tidal river that ran in front of the house. When we took walks, we broke off fronds of leaves from tree branches to bat away the clouds of black flies on their honeymoons too, and out for blood.

We were very happy young marrieds doing well during the final two years of my graduate study and Helen's beginning of her graduate studies in clinical psychology.

Into the Pit of the Bible as Lit

1970

Devote yourself to the public reading of Scripture.
—Timothy 4:13

I stood before the office door of my graduate adviser Rene Wellek, a world-famous scholar of literature who had, perhaps conveniently for me, received an honorary degree from Boston College the year before I applied. I raised the knuckles on my now healed right hand to knock.

Under the rubric of the comparative literature department, a student needed to sit for a comprehensive oral examination, usually scheduled six months after courses were over and before the student began working on a topic for a dissertation. The student was responsible for recruiting members of the examination committee from faculty whose courses he had taken, one of whom was likely to become his dissertation adviser.

Because of the potentially huge range of subject matter for a field like comparative lit, the student and a faculty adviser worked out a list of ten topics, such as, say, the works of Shakespeare, or the novel as a genre, or Romantic poetry in Germany and France, or the theater of Bertolt Brecht. The list was supposed to reflect the courses they had already taken, but also lay the groundwork for the eventual dissertation topic.

I knocked, and Professor Wellek himself opened the door to his office, as if he considered a graduate student worthy of the honor.

"Come in. Sitz down." (Traces of his bilingual German-Czech mother speech remained. He had emigrated to the USA from Vienna in 1939 to escape the Nazi's hatred for intellectuals. He was the wisest literary critic alive.)

"Zo, have you been thinking about the questions for your oral? The idea might seem intimidating to cover too much. But if you stick to what you know and like, the six-month run-up could be like taking a warm bath."

"I have taken a course on Brecht's plays, and another on the history of theater. And with my background in amateur theatrics, had casually entertained the idea of writing about Brecht, whose plays I love. Brecht had many witty and biting things to say about the rich. A professor from the German department agreed to join my oral exam committee and said we could talk after that about my writing a dissertation under him."

"That's a good start. I love Brecht too. He hated Nazis as much as I did."

"Okay. I have also been entertaining thoughts about writing a dissertation on medieval miracle and mystery plays. I loved seeing them staged outdoors at Boston College from the back of a pickup truck. I could compare the French, German, and English traditions. So, it would qualify as a legitimate comparative literature topic."

"Tell me more about these miracle and mystery plays. I've heard of them, but I don't think I've ever seen a performance. There do seem to be a lot of manuscripts around that have been published."

"You'd like them. I have always been intrigued by them. Mystery plays were a form of medieval folk art. Local people acted out stories and scenes from the Old Testament and New, such as Noah and the flood, the creation of the world, the fall of Adam and Eve, the crucifixion and resurrection of Jesus. They originated in European villages where almost no one could read or write—even in the vernacular of the place, English or French, to say nothing of clerical Latin. It's speculated the origin was a short vignette titled 'Whom Seek Ye?' that was incorporated into a Christmas mass to dramatize the arrival of the shepherds at Jesus's birthplace. The popular practice soon spread outdoors. Troops of actors organized and like troubadours, began taking the show on the road to be staged on horse-drawn carts. Initially, Church authorities approved. The staging did allow the illiterate congregations to visualize stories otherwise available only in written Latin or encapsulated in sermons or chants. But by 1210, Pope Innocent III banned them. Church authorities feared performances were taking dangerous liberties with the biblical originals and playing for jokes with ribald satire to please the crowds. This was easy to do with stories like the flood. Noah rode it out with a boat full of animals that was close to comic in the original anyway. Literature tends toward the subversive by the nature of its impish, free-flowing, and imaginative energy. Apparently, actors took liberties with the originals in that spirit.

"What I find fascinating about the plays is that they are actually critical readings of the Bible—but reading the Bible as it was written as stories, stories that could be retold by dressing up and acting out. Church interpretations ignored literature to boil it down to dogma."

"That would be a topic right up your alley, since you came here as a priest yourself."

"Well, not really. I was never ordained. And you know, now I'm married."

"Congratulations. Go on. That's two of ten."

"What about adding a question of the Gospels in Greek as literature. I loved to read them. I know them well. A 'question' might provide a chance to look into more traditional ways of reading the Gospels to see how and why they differed. Maybe add in a historical study of other strategies for breaking through the church's censorship of the idea that scripture was literature. Maybe this topic would ramify to addressing the larger questions of literary interpretation, now a hot topic in lit crit circles. Surely there must have been breaks in the heavy chains of dogma hung on scripture."

"Whoa. That might be an intriguing topic for you, but I'm not sure it's literary."

"I know what you mean. And I haven't told anyone else about this idea. But how about this? I've been kicking the question around for much of my life, in one way or another. I'm starting to think I want to go into it as deep as I can. Erich Auerbach's *Memesis* reads both the Abraham sacrifice of Issac story, and the Gospel story of Peter's denial very powerfully. I want to think about doing something like that too. Or at least to explore how far his ways of reading scripture could be carried."

Wellek smiled. "That's interesting. Both those parts of *Mimesis* are interesting. We were colleagues in this department, you know. We both got jobs after the war. I used to tell him I thought his readings were brilliant. But there was no method. I'd ask him, 'How many people like you can read almost all the ancient and modern western languages?' He would shrug his shoulders and laugh. 'I just can't help it,' he'd say.

"Auerbach's brilliance was one-off. Hard for mere mortals to imitate. Another thing to think is what job would this kind of dissertation lead to? Biblical scholars won't like it; and there's no space in literature departments for this sort of thing. You don't want to be Van Gogh. He never sold a painting. My advice—if you want a job, you should be able to at least talk about the modern methods of deconstruction our department is becoming famous for. It's not my cup of tea. But a lot of people, literature professors, take it for gospel. So you need to be able to stay in their conversations, whatever you think personally."

I was shocked he'd said this. In the pause before I responded, my mind raced. The pause must have lasted a little longer than I realized.

Professor Wellek's expression changed to concern. "Perhaps I am harsh?"

"That's wise counsel, but I'm willing to take the risk. The deconstructionists didn't really like the body of literature, only its dissected guts on the table. I think they drained pleasure out of anything they fed upon.

"Many specialists in literature are turning to film studies. Film for some reason was more pure or didn't dissolve so quickly into a pile of meanings. In the introduction to a book on the deconstruction of Yale, your distinguished colleague Professor Hartman wrote that literature existed in order to provide deconstruction with the fodder to masticate philosophy with. I stopped browsing the book at that point and left it on the bookstore shelf. Please don't tell him that. He is a great teacher. But, where was the thrill of lying in the Spanish woods in Hemingway's *For Whom the Bell Tolls* with Robert Jordan waiting to take a final shot at an officer in Franco's army on horseback? Or better, sitting alone at Shadowbrook reading about Jordan snuggling with Rabbit in his sleeping bag?"

"Shadowbrook?"

"That's a long story. It's where Jesuits start their studies."

"Go on. Do you have any literary theory you like? Something like a rudder while you read?"

I leaned forward, as if once again telling a secret to the Marvin School principal, Miss Ferguson.

"Don't tell Hartman or anyone else in the department about this, or they'll probably run me out of comp lit on a log. I read Susan Sontag's brilliant essay 'Against Interpretation,' in which she compared any work of art, especially literary art, to a movie. It made its peculiar sense through the movement of its many parts from one to the other like a movie does, by providing the eye with twenty-four frames to view per second. At this rate the human eye sends images the brain reads as sequential movement. Interpretation stops the movement to analyze a frame and thereby destroys the art. What art does is flood the brain with an ensemble of images that convey an artistic experience that ultimately cannot survive dissection. Her insight reinforced my own way of looking at the world as a rolling review of second thoughts, one fading to the next, for an experience of understanding that never really has to pause."

"I won't tell anyone," said Professor Wellek with a chuckle. "But you better not either, if you want to become a professor. She's the great heretic, the Wicked Witch of the West, with that essay. On the other hand, to go back to Van Gogh; he sold well after he died. See what kind of a proposal you come up with, with more questions."

I shook hands with another great scholar a few days later—Hans Frei, another émigré from the war, this time from the same area of Poland my grandfather had come from. Professor Frei agreed to serve on my Questions Committee on the Gospels as literature.

We stood by a barbeque grill at Virgil Barber House. Father Charles Bent was hosting a back-to-school party and had graciously invited Helen and me to attend. Helen was happily talking with Charlie and meeting the other Virgil Barber House Jesuits who were eager to show her she was now part of their family.

Father Bent had invited Divinity School colleagues and introduced me to Hans Frei, one of his professors of biblical studies. By way of a conversation starter, Charlie Bent said of me, "He's got some funny ideas about the Gospels."

The professor gave me a big smile and said, "I'm always good for a laugh." He was a world-renowned scholar of what was called "hermeneutics." The name was derived from Hermes, the Greek god of messages sent by the other Olympians to humans on Earth. I had read and admired his scholarship during my first year in graduate school.

"I'd like to ask you a literary question. I'm in the comp lit department."

"Ho, ho," he said with a jolly tone, "you're going to ask me how to deconstruct something. I know what's going on over there. Not that I understand it much, so go easy on me. But now that I've met someone from that department, give me a quick review of what the new crazy business is. In return, I'll pour you another drink."

"Well, you've probably heard of its most influential proponents in the department, Geoffrey Hartman and Paul de Man. They're disciples of the French philosopher Jacque Derrida, who came up with a complexly intricate way of interpreting literature. The critic deconstructed the inner workings of a literary text by isolating what its words say and what its words cryptically mean, whereby the second undercuts the first. Or something like that. Many of my fellow students were excited by it. I spent several months reading about its techniques, thinking I could finally figure it out."

"Oh, good," said the jolly professor. "Now, while you finish that drink, let me in on the secrets."

"Sorry to disappoint you. To me, Derrida wrote in riddles. I decided, 'That's okay. I'm just not smart enough to get it.' When you go to a graduate school, especially one as exalted as Yale, you meet professors and other students so vastly smarter than you, you can relax. They're impossible to match, the realization of which frees you—or me, anyway—from the anxiety of trying. Which was a relief on several levels. The intricacies of its language and methods of deconstruction, later called simply Theory, reminded me of scholastic philosophy in the sense that they required a terrific commitment to master. You've probably heard of that. And then, once you did, you were trapped by a system that left no room to think any other way. You were doomed to sail or sink with that ship."

The jolly professor laughed again. "Great, you're neither a deconstructionist nor a scholastic theologian. So, we can talk turkey. Ask away."

"Tell me if I get this right: the idea behind hermeneutics is to treat the writer of a biblical text as a messenger, speaking directly to the reader. To properly understand the text requires becoming saturated in the language, the politics, and the history of the time of the composition of any biblical story, 'so that one knows the text better even than the writer did,' someone said. To read a biblical story properly, one needs to imagine a mind behind the story and then to try to get the story. It's something like 'getting' a joke, where you don't have to believe as literally true what any given rabbi and priest would say in a bar—but just catch the different ways each might order a beer."

"That's roughly correct, although you have to admit it's a stretch to compare anything in the Gospels to a joke. In fact, I think someone once noted there is a lot of crying reported in the scriptures. But never laughter."

He paused with a little laugh to let me know he was not scandalized by what could be called my blasphemy. "Let me add, as I'm sure you also know, there's a lot of wine drinking in the Gospels, but no beer that I can remember, or anything like this good Jesuit Scotch," he said, holding up his glass with a grin. "Furthermore, I like those kinds of jokes. Want to hear some of mine?"

"Yes," I said at once. "But while I've got my steam up, let me keep going."

"Proceed," he said with a wave of his glass.

"Okay. And even—to go further, critically—whatever the writer intended did not include any divine inspiration. Instead of imagining a Holy Spirit inspiring the Scripture, we could only talk about the zeitgeist of the author's time and place. This theory demanded the writer had to be aware of what inspired him. The buck of biblical interpretation stopped with the imagination of the writer."

He thought for a moment, then said, "You're basically correct. German biblical scholars developed what they considered a humane way of looking at the scriptures in the nineteenth century. Now there's a revival of interest in this method, under the heading of 'The Search for the Historical Jesus.' What was the author telling us he understood about Jesus? I'm interested in it too."

This time, we clinked our glasses. I told him, "I read and admired your book about biblical interpretation. So, I'm bold to ask, have you ever read Erich Auerbach's great study of the history of literary realism titled *Mimesis*? He devotes a chapter to the realistic scene in the Gospels where Peter weeps when in a flash he remembers Jesus's prediction that he would deny Jesus three times before a cock crowed."

"I've heard the name, Auerbach," he said. "I'm pretty sure he taught literature at Yale in the 1940s and '50s. Go on."

"He did, along with many of my professors whose families had been forced into exile by the Nazis before the war. Many of them still speak of him with reverence. Initially, because of the precipitous danger he found himself in, Auerbach escaped into exile in Turkey. From his own library, he could only take a box he quickly packed with literature books in Spanish, Latin, Greek, Hebrew, French, Russian, German, and English—languages he could read. While in exile, he had no access to libraries. So, while he was there, he wrote a big book about what he had on hand. Only the primary stuff. From the juxtaposition of many classical texts, he extrapolated what he considered to be the evolution of realistic storytelling with the Gospels as a pivot point.

"And your point is?" he asked with some earnestness but still sociably (it was a party after all). "Why are you telling me about this?"

"Okay, to get to my point—with his vast knowledge of world literature, Auerbach claims this scene is the first time in any literary history that a poor, working-class man like Peter is shown to be a *tragic* figure, not comic. Before this time, and for long after, only kings and generals or gods could have tragic experiences or emotions. In most literary traditions, like in Shakespeare's plays, all the working-class people are buffoons. Auerbach's idea was that the Gospel's narrative perspective represented Jesus's teachings that even a poor person's feelings could be profound."

"And it shows that ancient Jews raised chickens," the professor wittily responded with a chuckle. I looked him in the eye with a steady gaze and a smile, a rare experience for a graduate student with a full professor. He had a pleasant German face, his wavy hair combed back.

"But that sounds interesting. Could you write down that reference? I'd like to take a look at it."

"I can do better than that. Wait right here, and I'll go and get my copy of *Mimesis* for you to read."

Professor Frei called me up a few days later.

"Thanks for the lend," he said cheerfully. "Could you come by my office so I can give the book back and we can talk about it?"

"Yes, I'd be honored," I said sincerely. None of the professors in my own area of study had ever expressed any interest in my humble opinions before.

In his office, Professor Frei said, "I never thought before that something like the way a biblical story was narrated could have something to say about what it meant. Would you be interested in taking the course I'm offering this semester—The Search for the Historical Jesus—in the Divinity School? I'd be interested in what you have to say, and I think the other students would welcome a different perspective. It's graduate level. I'd sign off on any transfer credits. And if you want, you can just audit."

"I'll audit," I said, flattered. "I've finished my coursework and am preparing for orals. But I'd be tickled to take you up on the invitation."

Rene Wellek was happy to add Professor Frei to the orals committee to examine me on the Greek Gospels as literature. Wellek's notion of the rubric of comparative literature went that far.

"You can compare literature to anything," he'd tell us with a chuckle, "From bird sounds to firetrucks."

Doing the reading for Professor's Frei's course, I discovered the huge volume of nineteenth-century liberal German biblical scholarship—thousands of published books and essays—all by people no one ever read anymore. I assumed this from the evidence of the bare circulation record cards inside the back covers. It was humbling to see how much earnest scholarship from the past—that probably won tenure for the writers—soon sunk into obscurity. *Pretty much like mine will*, I thought ruefully.

I translated from German two seminal but enigmatic lecture notes of the great nineteenth-century German biblical scholar Friedrich Schleiermacher. He's the one who'd said, "We have to understand what the author wrote better than the author himself." Several years later, at the urging of the scholar of hermeneutics, I published the translations in two different scholarly journals.

Professor Frei had flattered me, commenting on the translations, "Until now, I didn't understand what Schleiermacher was saying, even in German."

Professor Frei asked if I would give a seminar presentation on Auerbach's ideas about literary realism. Then he asked me to condense the notes into a discursive outline to share with him and the other students. To my astonishment, Professor Frei called on the phone afterward to thank me and to say he considered the outline, along with the translations together, a qualification for the required research paper—if I had been taking his course for credit.

The most stunning moment I had with him was when, after the course was over, he picked me up in his car for dinner with his wife and him.

Frei asked, deliberately looking through the windshield and not directly at me, "From your literary studies, do you think it's possible to read back through the language of a text—to get at the real history, what really happened in time and place, as you decipher the storytelling? I mean, to a fact like Jesus did rise from the dead—not that his disciples stole his body from the tomb?"

"No," I said firmly. "It's my opinion that literature of any kind, whether considered sacred or not, remains opaque." I was speaking carefully, amazed that such a man would apparently truly value my humble opinion, and because I was being asked a critical question about any literary interpretation—let alone sacred literature.

"It only reflects forward—to the reader—like the painted surface of a painting to a viewer. It's art. Made-up. You can't get any further into what it says than by looking at what the author saw in his mind's imaginative eye. Only the way the author chose to use words—and even then—you can't tell for sure whether the real author was choosing to be ironic or sincere."

There was a quiet moment between the two of us in the front seat. Then Professor Frei said, "Hmmm," noncommittally but with a disappointed tone. He changed the subject to the weather.

It was a moment like my spiritual consultation with Father O' Donnell at Weston— a distinguished authority of religion fundamentally misunderstanding literature. That even biblical literature was at root, literature, not just clumsy theology. You could not shake facts out of it like pebbles from a box.

At one point during the course together, Professor Frei told me to talk with a colleague, a New Testament scholar. That led to an invitation to address a current class on the composition of the Gospels. I put together several examples.

I began pointing out the suggestive juxtaposition of the scene of Jesus feeding bread and fishes to a crowd of poor people listening to him by a lake, to the horrid scene of Herod feeding the revenge of an aristocrat with the head of John the Baptist on a plate.

"Does this suggest the meaning of the story is the great moral dangers of wealth? And not only that, but that Jesus himself appears to stage a theatrical event of contrast that the narrator alone can produce in a connected narrative? Only if you read the two stories narratively, sequentially. You miss this point if you read or analyze the two episodes independently. In fact, I think you can only read any Gospel authentically—narratively—as *literature*. Not disguised theology."

When I looked around the classroom, I saw impassive faces.

To bring this point home, I added in other narrative tricks—like the Gospel narrator giving the reader a superior perspective over a character in the story.

"At the end of the Gospel of John, the narrator sets the scene of Mary Magdalene weeping at Jesus's empty tomb by telling the reader that she is unaware that Jesus is actually standing behind her.

> ... she turned around and saw Jesus standing there but did not recognize him. Jesus said to her, "Why are you weeping? Who is it you are looking for?" Thinking it was the gardener, she said, "If it is you who have removed him, tell me where you have laid him, and I will take him away." Jesus said, "Mary!" She turned to him and said "Rabbuni," which is Hebrew for "My Master." (John 20: 14-17).

"At the moment of the miraculous reveal, the reader's initial superior point of view dissolves as Mary sees what the reader has already been told. Thereby the reader is enticed to also share her recognition that indeed, Jesus has risen from the dead, based on her assertion of what she sees—even though, of course, the reader can only see the shadows of words on a page.

"Later in the same chapter, the narrator of John's Gospel sets a scene in a closed room, when most of the disciples are hiding behind locked doors, fearfully discussing the rumors of the resurrection. This time Jesus materializes, stands among them, and tells them the story is true. Another disciple, Thomas, shows up late, after Jesus has disappeared. When he's told what happened, he's incredulous: 'Unless I see the marks of the nails on his hands and put my finger into the place where the nails were . . . I will not believe it.' In this episode the narrator's set-up is more overt. A few moments later, Jesus does appear miraculously again and tells Thomas to put his finger into his wounds. Thomas exclaims, 'My Lord and my God.' Then Jesus looks first at Thomas, and then in almost a Brechtian aside, looks through the narrative scene directly at the reader. 'Because you have seen me, you have found faith. Happy are they who never saw me and yet have found faith.' Thereby the narrator dissolves the reader's initially superior point of view into Thomas's corrected point of view to entice the reader's faith."

Again, I canvassed the room for a response. There was none. "This *leger de main* is a Gospel narrative literary conceit. Consider another episode only found in Luke's Gospel. The narrator once again tells the reader that Jesus joins two disciples walking toward the village of Emmaus. But again, the disciples are kept momentarily in the dark. The disguised Jesus asks them what they are talking about. They explain to their new companion their confusion about whether the rumors might be true that they've heard that Jesus rose from the dead. Then, after the three of them stop for a meal, the two disciples recognize that they've been talking to Jesus himself when he breaks bread with them apparently in his usual style. Then Jesus magically disappears at the moment of the reveal.

"Aren't these benign, even forgivable literary tricks the author plays on the readers? The narrator allows the readers to feel themselves superior to the characters in the story. Readers know before the inner characters do. But then the twist. The inner characters 'see' the Jesus the reader, of course, can never see. This puts the readers and characters on the same plane. Inviting the reader to now 'see' from without what the characters now 'see' from within. The miracle happened truly.

"Therefore, you cannot use any of these episodes to prove Jesus did rise from the dead. Only that an author using sophisticated narrative techniques once tried to beguile readers into believing that he did."

The presentation met hostile silence. I asked the students if they thought this kind of reading would be of any use to them as students of the Gospels. They emphatically shook their heads. One female student in the class sat looking at the floor. Then she looked up to say, "If what you are calling the assessment of narrative technique might be feasible in reading an English translation—as you just did—it could never come to any valid conclusion about any facts to be found in deciphering the original Greek."

"It works in Greek, too," I replied. "That's one of the beauties of this kind of reading. The juxtaposition of scenes, or the narrative structure, remains unaltered by any accurate translation of the Gospels from Greek to English. The reader can *see* what's on the page as what the story means."

Neither she nor I had anything further to say.

My "extracurricular" experience at the Divinity School went better. The university had posted notices asking people who spoke a foreign language to put their names in a pool from which to draw a match-up with incoming students from various countries around the world. Someone to answer questions and give practical guidance. Helen put her name in for French. I put mine in for German. We were assigned to Roman Yablonski from Poland, who spoke German as a second language. I drove to New York City to pick Roman up at the airport, holding a sign at the departure gate "Roman Yablonhski," which Roman said was very funny, as he pointed at the card. He was tall and formally dressed, with a loose, shaggy blond head of hair.

He said, "*Es haette dein Name sein sollen*"—"It should have been your name." He laughed, holding out his hand to shake.

Aldo Parisot, a world renowned cellist and professor at the Yale School of Music, had recruited Roman for a scholarship to the music school, having heard him play the cello once on a visit to Poland. After Helen and I settled Roman into our apartment, I called up the music school to find out where to take Roman next. There was a snag. The scholarship had been offered to Roman three years earlier. It had taken Roman three years to fight through the "red" tape (literally) of then Communist Poland's paranoia to grant an exit visa. During those three years, the School of Music had assumed Roman couldn't leave Poland and had forgotten about him. But apparently the university admissions office had received notice that he was finally matriculating. Whatever the source for the snafu, here he was, at the hands of a young couple, one of whom was a lowly graduate student. We gave him our couch to sleep on and all the food he could eat.

I started making phone calls. No one I talked with knew what to do. Classes and housing were full. The term had begun. I reached Professor Parisot, who was delighted to hear Roman had arrived, and promised to get him officially enrolled in the music school. But the hang-up was housing. There was no open place for Roman to stay.

Finally, I found myself in some office of the university, agitated and speaking with some heat: "Look, the university brought him here. You've got to find someplace to put him! Either that or give my wife and me a stipend to find him an apartment."

The university's solution was to offer Roman a dorm room in the Divinity School's complex of housing—elegant ivy-covered brick buildings in imitation of the quad Thomas Jefferson had designed at the University of Virginia. Roman was alarmed. He had been raised a good atheist Communist. How would he ever fit in with Christian believers?

The answer turned out to be—wonderfully. The other Divinity School students were delighted to hear they had a genuine atheist to talk with. They welcomed him. Found a TV for his room. Started inviting him to dinners and parties and teaching him, at his request, how to speak American slang. He loved the word *bullshit*.

It was as if, deep in its own soul, the Divinity School was the kind of home that would take in a stranger at the door as if—in line with the old legend—he might just be Jesus in disguise.

However, my own classroom experiences in the Divinity School confirmed what I had assumed for a long time. Any kind of formalized religious interpretation of the scriptures *stopped* at reading a text to affirm an extraliterary assumption—if not about *truth*, at least about some fact. Religious interpreters had no interest in the imagination of the author or the reader. They threw up smoke screens by insisting that only privileged styles of interpretation could be valid and often hid their bias by insisting the Gospels in particular were very poorly written and thus needed clerical correction. Of course, my evidence for this bias was anecdotal, with a small sample size. But I had no interest in any polemics with any traditional scholars. When it came to the serious business of reading the literature of the Bible by oneself, all anyone can honestly do is read according to his or her own lights.

Finally, Professor Wellek approved my writing of what turned out to be a preposterous dissertation, barely acceptable to the rest of the department's professors. The dissertation surveyed the tenuous, sinuous tradition of recognizing the Bible as literature. It began discussing some of the ancient Greek church fathers. A favorite was John Cassian, who recommended dreaming about Bible stories in order to discover their hidden meanings that obviously were not "literal."

The study touched on Jerome's rationales for how he translated the original Hebrew and Greek of the Scriptures into his Latin translation called the *Vulgate*, meaning "vulgar," since it was supposed to make Bible readings more available to lowly learned clerics, not just specialists. Jerome claimed he needed to use some imaginative flair to catch the original meaning when his translation varied from the literal. Which implied the "literal" sense of Scripture was not an impenetrable treasure chest but, instead, an invitation for digging out meaning.

It included a section on mystery play elaborations as a popular and effective strategy for liberating the Bible from its dogmatic reductions. There was a chapter on Erasmus trying to interpret biblical stories as having humanistic values—not just doctrinal ones. And with a few other stops along the way, coming to a crescendo with Schleiermacher's hermeneutics.

I was granted a degree after submitting two bound copies to the comparative literature department. One was supposed to be returned for me to keep. The other was to be put on a shelf in the comparative literature department that held other dissertations, like a trophy case. But the department sent me back both copies, either because of a clerical error, or maybe because of faculty embarrassment at having to put my work on the same level with others whose work was far weightier.

Professor Wellek's counsel proved prescient when I began the job hunt to become a professor of literature. Most university literature hiring committees had not the slightest interest in hiring *anyone* to teach *anything*—from Shakespeare to the modern novel to Old Norse to mid-twentieth-century German theater—who hadn't learned how to deconstruct the subject matter. In one interview with the chair of the English department at the University of Iowa, when I was asked to talk about Derrida, I said that for me, Derrida's writing amounted to incomprehensive puzzles. The interviewer smiled, stood up, shook my hand and said, "That will be enough." So that ship sank.

I qualified for only one academic position being offered throughout the United States: to teach the Bible as literature at Purdue University, a land-grant university specializing in teaching engineering and agriculture in Indiana.

The on-campus interview at Purdue went better. The reason for that was because Purdue was probably the only university or college that had a tenure-track regular faculty position to teach the Bible as literature.

A distinguished professor, Harold Watts, was retiring. He had been teaching such a course since the late 1940s. In 1949, he'd published *The Modern Reader's Guide to the Bible*. I read it thoroughly before flying out for an on-campus interviews. It was erudite and crafty. Professor Watts acknowledged many good reasons for reading the Bible. For one thing, a reader gathered the background for understanding much of Western art and music and literature. Professor Watts even said, tongue in cheek, it would help doing crossword puzzles. The reader could follow the progress of thinking about God over millennia. He suggested there might even be an underlying theme from Genesis to Revelation. Thereby he gave a brief noncommittal nod to the Christian tradition of reading the Hebrew Bible as a run-up to the New Testament, a la St. Paul. But he didn't dwell on the idea. Rather, he used the word *intuition* to identify the kind of religious thinking that produces biblical literature like any other and claims the reader must read the Bible intuitively as well. I thought that was a clever term. It carries the idea lightly that there might be underlying truths in the intuitive flourishes. But the term more directly says its writers *imagine*. They do not speculate or assert.

During my campus visit, I met Professor Watts privately at his house in West Lafayette. His gracious wife served cookies and tea.

"Okay, let's cut to the chase. How would you teach the Bible? I don't have to say you need to pick your way through minefields. And you've told me you read my book. You certainly don't have to do it the way I did."

"I like your book. I mean that. Like you say, Bible stories can be lyric, tragic, comic, farcical, meditative—like stories found everywhere. And in your book, you read them like that. And I will too. The Joseph story is a ritualistic dressing and stripping of Joseph until, after starting out as a callow, vain kid in a flashy cloak, he's dressed like a noble in disguise so he can arrange for his brothers to express their sorrow for their treatment of him, and thus redeem themselves. The David story is like Faulkner's *Absalom! Absalom!,* a classical tragedy of a character who fails because he does one thing too well—forgiving everyone, even his rebellious, patricidal son, Absalom."

"But my basic strategy is to get students to read the Bible book by book as if each was a hunk of polished Fordite."

"Fordite? Never heard of that. Have you, dear?" he asked, turning toward his wife.

"Sounds like men-talk to me."

"Okay, first let me show you a piece." I pulled from my pocket a cookie-sized lump I put in the professor's hand. It had a smooth, shiny gray matrix in which appeared swirls and dots and lines of various colors, all polished and gleaming. In miniature, it looked like a painting by Paul Klee.

"It's beautiful," he said, turning it over, rubbing its sides. "But what is it? Some kind of gemstone?"

"It's a chunk of paint. Actually, many layers of paint sprayed on cars being manufactured. Over time on the assembly line, layers of different colors pile up on top of each other and harden, and lumps start sprouting on walls and machinery like mushrooms. Periodically the lumps get chiseled off. If shaped and polished, different colors intrude on each other like pieces of jasper or agate. The idea caught on. Now there's even jewelry made from it."

"Okay, fine. How is Fordite like a Bible story? Surely you're not saying something like it's Jesus turning water into wine."

"No, no. It's just an analogy or metaphor. Bible stories are all layered, made of different episodes, added together, combined, edited, redacted. Palimpsests, like monks writing something new over an old writing on parchment or vellum. Some of the original writing shows through. But you can never be sure of the motives of later editors who might have added stuff consistent with their own sense of the meaning of the Gospel. The end result is the thing. The stories are manufactured—literally—handmade over time, layer upon correction, upon redaction, elaboration. What I like about the comparison is that the layers of paint or different versions get put down without any painter able to imagine the final product in their mind. The story grows and twists its words, like colors juxtaposed in a kaleidoscope."

"Have another cup of tea. Explain what you're talking about in terms I can understand—so I can understand your point."

"After reading your book, I also looked at the styles of standard biblical scholarship I was already familiar with. Not because I wanted to use any in teaching, but to avoid making stupid mistakes or reinventing the wheel or overlooking sound facts.

"There are three basic types. No one using any one of the three really reads the Bible as a library of literature to be read for insightful pleasure.

"In one, a sectarian scholar pans for the gold of doctrine obscured by what the scholar will sometimes complain about being annoyingly badly written texts, in Greek, Hebrew, or any modern translation. There's tons of that. I can't do anything like that. Like you said, that would be like sowing a mine field in a secular classroom, especially one filled with different kinds of believers.

"On another hand, Biblical anthropology looks for anything in a story or poem that aligns with physical evidence or known history. Lots of hard digging goes into that. Some of it is foolish, like looking for wood from Noah's Ark or the True Cross. Where anthropology follows the protocols of science, the evidence is spare. There's no solid evidence that there ever was a historical King David; nor evidence about exactly where Jesus was executed. Or that the Red Sea parted. Or more disturbingly, even that Jesus existed—except in the stories told about him by people with a vested interest in trying to prove he did. However valid scientific findings like this might be, they never substitute for anything written down—except to suggest that what's written probably didn't happen that way. Joshua did not lead an army of ten thousand men to conquer Canaan. In fact, you can go further to say, whatever the underlying facts, they do not matter. A writer implies that Israelites knew how to fight. Or that Jesus did rise from the dead. That's as far back in time or place as a reader of literature can go. What does *that* mean?

"I have to be more careful with the third kind of traditional biblical scholarship: academic textual analysis. Learned linguists of Hebrew and Greek—or any other languages spoken in the milieu of the ancient Jews or early Christians—can trace timelines of compositions and editing and redacting of the texts whose final assembly cannot be exactly dated.

"But for me to bring any of this kind of scholarship up is dicey. If I relied on it overmuch in class, it would be inferring that to read the Bible properly, you'd have to be learned in ancient languages. Which is fine. Except it reserves 'reading' to the experts. You can't call literature anything only scholars can pretend to understand.

"Sound textual scholarship is useful to keep me from making any mistakes. Not for guiding me how to read a story well. I once read slowly a finely combing commentary on the David story in a translation of the Hebrew Bible by a learned literary scholar, Robert Alter. Having done that, I then read the whole story as a literary work to see if my understanding of it had been deepened. It hadn't. It was in the end, just a story, albeit a fine one.

"Okay, here's what I'll do. Simply read the Bible as it comes to hand in the binding of an accurate, readable book. It *is* fragmented. Parts of almost any story were composed, recomposed, redacted, edited, etc., many times. Of course, a gimlet-eyed scholar can detect cracks, crevices, palimpsests, overlays lurking in the canonical texts.

"But even this scholar at leisure can appreciate, even enjoy, the way the fragments were ultimately brought together—like the story of Jesus at the lake appearing in the narrative after the story of Herod in the palace. Or take the three different words used for God in the Genesis Creation Account. *El, Yahweh, Elohim.* That does suggest that three different groups of writers wrote different parts of the story. But the literary question is—what do you make of the jumble that the final editor allowed to stand? Isn't it beautiful and provocative?"

I reached into my pocket again, and this time, brought out a polished agate stone. I handed it to Professor Watts.

"Look, the swirls of colors you can see in this gem come from different minerals like quartz or limestone. And in turn, the elements of the mineral brew are the chemicals lithium, calcium, manganese, aluminum, sodium, and others. Imagine the Bible composed from a periodic table of many different writers from many different places at many different times. Then see it blended and molded and polished by the editors who saw it into print. What marvels can you see as the work and art of their hands?

"The Bible is like that. It's beautifully polished. Reading the Bible as literature comes down to seeing it shine.

"The reason why I think Fordite is a better example is that it's made by hands using tools. Like I said earlier, no worker intended to produce the final, layered chip of material; although someone like a jeweler did intentionally cut and polish the chip that shimmers in the hand.

"There. I've said it. What the Bible means to me. I don't know if I'd pass around an agate or a piece of Fordite for the class to look at, at least not until we felt comfortable with each other and the way we were reading the Bible as literature. But that's the model for what I'll be doing that I'll leave hidden to finger in my pocket. But for now, I've got some other gems back home. You can keep these two as house gifts from me for your hospitality."

"What do you think, dear, pretty?" he said, holding out the stone to his wife.

"Gorgeous," she agreed. "I think he's going to do just fine filling your shoes. He's entertaining at least."

Harold laughed as he turned back to me. "Bravo. I give you my blessing. My method as you saw in my book is to read the Bible as a collection of ancient stories, comparable to others. Yours looks closely at the texts as written—even edited. In either way, it's looking at the text as it appears on the page *now*. But the important thing is to get students to read Bible stories for pleasure and provocative thinking—without closing off the stories with sectarian pronouncements. Many Purdue students who take the course come from conservative evangelical backgrounds. You can't let that get in the way of getting them to see how, after all, the Bible tells its stories as stories. Not elaborated dogma."

Harold must have given his approval. I got the job. When I left his house, I looked to the west and was delighted to see the tops of blue mountains.

I didn't think the Rockies were that close to Indiana, I thought with wonder.

They aren't. In my East Coast parochialism, I had mistaken blue clouds for blue mountains.

When we moved to Indiana, Helen and I packed our belongings around the Triumph TR-3 sports car we had driven into the bed of a rental truck. It caused a sensation among the faculty and families from the English department who showed up to help us unload. After we cleared enough for Helen to climb in, she drove the car out of the truck onto a ramp, waving her arms as if she were a Shriner in a parade.

"There was a car in there!" the people cried. They laughed about it for years afterward.

We did well during our first several years in Indiana. Purdue's English department was huge—over two hundred regular faculty and another hundred graduate students. The department hired six other young faculty members the same year it hired me, with smart, enthusiastic young families, many with small children right from the get-go. We had dinner parties and trips to the park and helped each other with house renovations. Ours needed more than most. The only house on the market that met our criteria for having a fireplace in it and being affordable on my small salary had once been a fishing shack on the Wabash River seven miles from campus. There were holes in the wall. Some of the electric fittings hung from wires coming out of the ceilings. When the toilet flushed, water erupted on the narrow lawn between the house and the river. There apparently was no septic system. But it was dirt cheap—only five thousand dollars in 1972. We got a mortgage from a local bank for thirteen thousand, which was enough to buy the materials to make it livable.

We moved in and went right to work. We put on a new roof, dug a septic system, and redid the plumbing and wiring with the generous volunteer help of our new faculty colleagues. We got a good deal on a household-sized lot of cedar board and batten siding we nailed to the side. The place did look good. Nothing like the splendors of Shadowbrook, Weston, or Virgil Barber House of course—our starter house actually did reflect the spirit of a vow of poverty.

We were young and in love and on the way. It was an easy seven-mile commute to Purdue from the nearby village of Battleground. It was named after the Battle of Tippecanoe, where William Henry Harrison defeated a confederacy of Native Americans defending their homes against their confiscation. That led to the people's forced exile, following Thomas Jefferson's policy of Indian removal to open spaces for White yeoman farmers. We lived on a small ridge directly on the river that had been the site of the original Indian settlement.

Max, our first son, was born in March of that first year, which added to our bona fides as fully sanctioned new marrieds. I stood by for the climactic moment as Max slid out into a bright room to a boom of spring thunder. I passed around cigars to everyone, male and female alike, saying, "If it had been a girl, it would have been donuts."

A climactic *social* moment for us was the surprise party friends arranged for my thirtieth birthday. I had been complaining of my apprehension at entering a forbidden age already marked by the 1960s maxim "Never trust anyone over thirty." Several dozen friends gathered outside our bedroom at 5am on February 2, 1974, singing "Happy Birthday": two of them in Finnish. At first it seemed a dream. When we woke up enough to look through the window to see all the smiling faces, Helen and I jumped out of bed and ran to the closet for bathrobes. Several said later it was gratifying to see we both slept naked. By the time we got into the living room, our friends were pouring through the front door with strawberries and champagne. Everyone was tipsy by 7:00 am. As William Wordsworth put it, "What bliss it was in that dawn to be alive, but to be young was very heaven."

A short time later, however, a friend who was part of the birthday party with her husband, appeared in the window of the same front door while Helen and I were sitting before the woodstove on a frigid night. She was crying. She told us her husband, who had been hired at the same time as I had, had asked for a divorce in order to marry a graduate student. We talked and listened and cried with her. Later that night, alone in our bed, which I had made out of the oak frame of an old corn crib, Helen and I hugged each other. We pledged our hope that something similar would never happen to us.

A Woman With an Afro

1972

*I am black but beautiful . . . as the tents of Cedar,
as the curtains of Solomon.*
—The Song of Songs 1:51

I assigned eight short papers. Students would be asked to juxtapose two parts of a story or a poem in the Bible, like say Herod at the party and Jesus at the Lake, or two creation stories, or the episode of Absalom, son of David, hanging by his hair in a tree as he died to the scenes in the Gospels of Jesus hanging from a cross. Could the Gospel writers have channeled the former?

How close could students get to imagining what kinds of thoughts emerged from the juxtapositions that appeared to be arranged just so such sorts of thoughts would emerge. "Like yours!" I would say. I would grade all the papers overnight to return them the next class period with red-marked comments written in the margins. The idea was the students needed immediate feedback to whatever they had written for the procedure to have any hope of doing any good to develop both writing and speaking skills.

One trick I used was before handing back the papers at the end of class, was reading salient, graceful sections from various papers to the class—especially papers that the student who wrote them would soon discover were almost drowning in red ink—as a way of showing everyone, especially that student, that the task of writing clearly and well was within the capacity of anyone with any major. You didn't have to be specializing in English, as few students at Purdue would do. This one time I took the paper on the top of the pile and said, "Ruth Brown . . . ?" Early in the term I had not memorized student names yet—which I would do to make sure to call on everyone to say something in every class session by the semester's end.

The paper made a case for the dove Noah released from the Ark that did not return—indicating it had found land on which to roost—was imagined by a Gospel writer to be the dove that descended upon Jesus at his baptism by John the Baptist at the Jordan river. Jesus was set free to roam the land until his soul flew away.

A Black young woman with an afro sitting in the first row raised her hand. Two detonations went off in my brain. First—an image of the woman with an afro standing up to her knees in the water at the edge of the beach in Puerto Rico more than a decade ago. Second—the shock—a Black woman who writes like an angel sits in this classroom at Purdue where there are few Black people except those from impoverished, industrial Gary, Indiana in the far north, adjacent to Chicago. I couldn't help having the first image spring to mind out of the waters of memory. It would turn out I was right about the second. Ruth did hail from Gary, Indiana, she would eventually tell me.

My face registered neither memories nor astonishment. Instead, with professional aplomb I announced to the class "Let me read a paragraph from a very fine paper indeed . . ." which I did. Ruth glowed. I handed out all the papers and dismissed the class at the end of the period. But I let Ruth know right away that we needed to talk.

"You have an astonishing flair for language. You write clearly, with wit and insight. I want you to know I'm very impressed with your first paper."

She smiled with a little embarrassment and said quietly, "Thank you."

I didn't tell her that her writing radiated with talent like only a handful of student papers I had yet read in my career, and as it would turn out, yet *to* read. I would call on Ruth in class about the same number of times I'd call on any of the other students—not to show any favoritism. But I listened closely to what she said, and almost always, chatted with her a few minutes after class when the others had walked out about what she had said or written or thought.

"You're the first White man I've ever talked to," she said shyly.

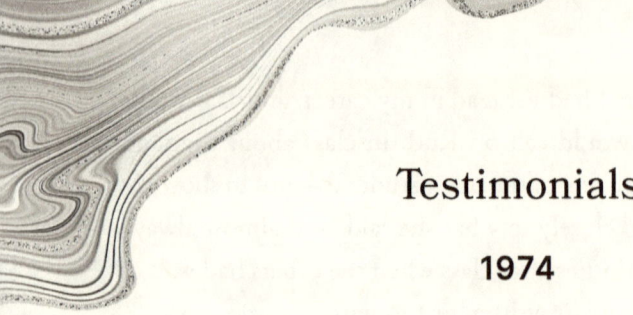

Testimonials

1974

God said to Noah, "Come out of the ark..."
—Genesis 8:16

At the time I met Ruth, I was planning to imitate what AJ had done at Boston College, to stage outdoors, on campus, some medieval mystery plays from the back of a pickup truck. For staging the Mystery Plays a la Antoon, I had gotten the promise of the lend of a battered pickup truck from a neighbor farmer friend to stand in for the cart. I pressured several faculty friends and some graduate students to appear in costumes from the theater department to act out the plays on a good fall day at the end of the semester—during Reading Week, between the end of classes and the beginning of exams. The play was about the story of Noah's Ark.

I asked Ruth to play God. She would stand on a ladder behind a large screen setup on the truck bed. It would be painted blue with white clouds with the word *Heaven* written on it. At various appropriate moments, God would suddenly appear above the heavens to render some judgment on events going on down below on the truck bed. It had a sign on the bottom that said *Sea*.

It would be wonderful theater to present God as a Black woman to any audience at Purdue or in Indiana.

At first Ruth said, "No, I'm not good at memorizing lines."

"No problem. God doesn't have much to say."

She agreed to do it. We kept her role a secret, making sure she didn't look to be part of the cast before the show. She didn't wear the robe or halo until just before her head popped behind the screen to shout "Yar!" That was the word in the text with which God began every pronouncement. The audience gasped. She was a smash hit. The actors at the curtain call stepped back from where she was standing for her to receive for a moment the full roar of audience approval.

There was a cast party for the actors later at my house on the Wabash River. All toked up lightly, as was the social custom of the time in the 1970s. At one point I was leaning on the railing of the deck of our house overlooking the Wabash River, next to Ruth, both of us deliciously lightheaded.

"Where are the animals?" asked Ruth with a giggle. Then, pointing to the sky she shouted, "Yar!"

I asked her whether she had told her family about her triumph.

"Oh, no, I couldn't do that. My family is so religious they would be angry to hear that a woman had played God—even if it was me, their own daughter."

I gasped. "You just testified to the best possible reason for you or anyone else to take a course like the Bible as literature. Thank you for that. For whatever you got out of the course, you've just given me back a great gift."

Another moving testimonial came from three Jewish women who took the undergraduate course as special students. One of them had survived the Holocaust as a young girl. The others were her younger sister and her daughter. The three of them told me that they thought the readings of the Old Testament books got them right—their humor, wisdom, and their encouragement for readers to think on their own. I was moved.

Another time, a young father holding his son's hand recognized my voice in a hardware store. He reminded me he had been a student in my class. "It changed my life. I joined a church, went to seminary, and became a Christian missionary in Turkey—where my son was born," he said, pulling the giggling kid up by the hand. "We loved it there. Thanks for showing me the way."

An informal caucus on campus of Jewish professors in various disciplines organized a Jewish Studies group. It published an inhouse periodical called *Sofar*. I was invited to join, went to collegial meetings, and published some essays in the journal. I got word of a Jewish Studies Conference to be held in Boston. I submitted a proposal for a talk on the Book of Ruth and was accepted.

"It's the only book in the Old Testament in which nobody gets killed," I told students.

With the help of a tutor, I read the Old Testament Book of Ruth in the original Hebrew. My paper claimed the errancy of a thousand years of its clerical readings. Traditional scholars, I argued, rabbis in particular, kept trying to understand the very loose use in the story of the traditional Talmudic rules about the Levirate marriage. These were the rules that prescribed that a man was obligated to marry his brother's widow. Boaz in the story did not fit the bill in marrying Ruth. And what was worse, he gets approval from the religious elders of the day sitting in council at the village gates. They should have known better. I argued all of the characters simply improvised the holy rules in order to bring about a happy solution to the couple's perfectly legitimate love affair. They were riffing or improvising on a traditional theme.

When I presented the paper before the Jewish Studies Society of Boston, several young rabbis in the audience were beside themselves, leaping up in frustration at their need to wait for me to finish. They waved open books. They yelled citations at me from the Talmud that did indeed, they insisted, prove the Book of Ruth was orthodox. No improvisations at all.

My cryptic response was, "As Henry David Thoreau said, 'You can't get anything without giving something up.'" Some people in the audience laughed and clapped. One of them, whose name was Ruth, became a lifelong friend. She bought me a drink afterward. Her testimonial was, "You convinced me," which she said with a smile.

I published the essay in a good literary journal. Which, along with the testimonials of students and audience, validated teaching the Bible as literature. It did some people some good.

Yet, years later I was miffed to discover no subsequent studies of the Book of Ruth by biblical scholars mentioned the essay. My reading didn't rate notice. Just as I had been at the end of the presentation on the Gospels at the Divinity School, or of the Book of Ruth before the Jewish studies conference, I was alone with my ideas.

However, there was a period in the 1970s when I developed an academic following. Faculty from small, Midwestern sectarian colleges came under government pressure to no longer give academic credit for sectarian Bible courses. I got invitations to demonstrate strategies for reading, all of which in some way or another replicated the style of reading the Bible from within—as I had in prayer as a Jesuit—juxtaposing scenes from already faceted stories and poems for the second thoughts they inspired. One accessible example: the scenes at Herod's court followed by the scene at the lake. Then I opened the discussion by offering to demonstrate how to read any part of the Bible the audience would suggest. By this point, I knew the Bible almost by heart.

These experiences led to another, intriguing validation of my teaching of the Bible as literature. I spoke to the faculty at an evangelical college in Iowa. Then with no forewarning, I was invited to attend what was apparently the daily religious congregation of the students and faculty in a huge amphitheater-like room; then, after I listened to some announcements and prayers, the man in charge turned and asked me to speak. On the spur of the moment, I put together a brief Bible as literature homily about Jesus appearing suddenly in the closed room with his followers, right after the doubting Thomas declared he did not believe the rumors Jesus had risen from the dead. I pointed out Jesus's and the narrator's pointed turn to the reader, indicating they should also "see" what Thomas "saw" in the closed room of the story, as a literary flourish to persuade the reader to emulate Thomas's declaration,

"I see and believe it for real." I drew no conclusions.

I could sense that the chaplain at the college was uneasy afterward. But remarkably I heard on the academic grapevine afterward that a female student, after hearing the talk, left the school, apparently because what I said about narrative chicanery undermined for her everything the college stood for. I was gratified. What a validation of the revolutionary chops of reading the Gospels as literature!

But despite successes in the classroom, and on a sectarian college circuit, I plied an orphan trade. The Bible was emphatically not considered to be literature by its professional interpreters working under the rubric of biblical scholarship. There was also little interest among secular literature types. For one thing, there was trepidation for entering the minefield of sectarian tensions. For another, there was little interest in the Bible, given its reputation for being rough-hewn stories and poems too politically prickly to invite close readings.

Eyes would roll on the faces of either biblical or literary scholars after I'd respond to "So, what's your specialty?" The Bible as *literature*? I stood alone in the field.

There's considerable snobbery among academics. You're judged by the prestige of the university where you teach. The Ivy League universities trump all, of course. But most academics carry around in their head a ranking system that puts those elites on a level with Berkeley, the University of Chicago, Johns Hopkins, Stanford. Just below them are the better large public universities like Michigan and Virginia. And so on down the line. Purdue falls in the middle of the list. It's a land-grant university after all, with emphasis on engineering, agriculture, and science. So, not the place where humanists go to live in academic heaven.

"I got a graphic example of snobbery," I told Professor Watts at coffee one morning. Smiling, I told him, "Before we met, I went to the annual Modern Language Association meeting two years in a row. The first time, looking for a job, I had a name tag listing my university affiliation as "Yale." Pretty, young graduate student women smiled and parted ways for me encouragingly. The badge was sort of an academic babe magnet, like a puppy on a leash. The next year, after you helped me get my job here, the name tag said *Purdue*. None of the pretty women looked twice. If anything, they shouldered me out of their way. I joked to myself that I should stop them and say, 'Look, last year I was just a graduate student, and now I'm an assistant *professor*.' No one would understand what I was talking about. Maybe it was all in my mind."

"Maybe the young women had been angels leading you to Purdue as the promised land."

One reason for my smiling while I told the story was being reminded of the class prejudice which had vexed me as a child. What had happened to me since then hardened me—or softened me—it's hard to say which; so now anything like that seems useless, risible, and just plain stupid. Of course, even now, teaching at a plebian university like Purdue, I would have likely been one of the five thousand listening to Jesus at the lake. Then as now, I lacked the legacy that earns a ticket to the palace.

The snobbery had an element of truth to it. While a graduate student, I wondered if I might have the talent to take another step up the academic ladder to gain a professorship at a place like Yale or its exalted equivalent. Who initially ever has a sense of defining limits to ambition? I looked closely at the persons just more advanced than me on site—the junior faculty at Yale—who had been given the next handhold to pull up. I read their stuff. It was remarkable. I recognized it was more than I was capable of emulating. Those young scholars had more precise judgments and more felicitous prose. I'd probably—if not certainly—never make their grade.

I was right. I would publish in prestigious journals, occasionally. I published books, but not with elite academic presses. I didn't have elite chops.

There was a blessing in disguise here that, once again, Gospel guidance provided. Having an academic teaching position, but without any recognized academic identity, I was free to experiment.

Lee Perron, a gifted poet, one of the seven young faculty hired at the same time, asked me to take over teaching a course of his own devising: the Literature of Ecology. Lee had resigned his position at Purdue to pursue a life of poetry.

The books he had assembled for the course included Aldo Leopold's *Sand County Almanac*, Henry David Thoreau's *Walden*, Annie Dillard's *Pilgrim at Tinker's Creek*, Ernst Callenbach's *Ecotopia*, Rachel Carson's *Silent Spring*, John Muir's *The Yosemite*, David Rain Wallace's *Idle Weeds*, Edward Abbey's *Desert Solitaire*, and a student favorite, *The Monkey Wrench Gang*. I told the students reading Richard Bautigan's *Trout Fishing in America* was like being stoned in the 1960s. "Too bad you missed it."

This was a religious literature of sorts, drained of anything formally sectarian: how humans should live morally, ethically, poetically, seeing themselves a part of the natural world. At first, I didn't think I was interested in taking on the course in addition to teaching the Bible as literature.

Lee insisted I read Leopold before saying no. Within ten pages, I was hooked. Leopold described his students doing a statistical analysis of Canada goose groups and discovering they were mostly in even numbers. That flocks were aggregations of pairs. Thus, he concludes, "We are free to mourn with and for the lone honkers as bereft."

Wow, I thought. *Science done in order to validate emotions. What a marvelous poetical point of science as traditionally practiced as strictly objective analysis. A good thing to teach in a practical-oriented university like Purdue!*

Fascinating students enrolled from all over the university's departments. I taught it for a decade in tandem with the Bible as literature. The signal of its success was that the Horticulture Department in the School of Agriculture came to require the course of all its undergraduate students. After fifty years, I still correspond with some graduates. It was particularly gratifying for me to teach a required course outside the humanities curriculum—being as, within it, I practiced an orphan trade.

But the book in the course that influenced the next turn, or station in the pilgrimage of my professional teaching career the most was Wendell Berry's *The Unsettling of America*, a diatribe against the industrialization of farming. Berry wrote with the passion and verve of an Old Testament prophet. He was a self-declared subsistence farmer in Kentucky who farmed with horses. Although one blemish on his bona fides as a prophet of healthy living was his cultivation of tobacco. He called it an almost perfect crop since its own internal poisons precluded the need for chemical pesticides. He was also a sharp-witted pastoral poet of the Midwestern landscape and culture with, it turned out, a large readership in Indiana. Most intriguing, his foil throughout the book was Earl Butz, who had been the dean of Purdue's School of Agriculture before being tapped to be Nixon's secretary of agriculture. (May opprobrium be heaped on his shoulders!) Many Purdue students grew up on chemically fueled farms praised by Butz and condemned by Berry. The book spoke to these students because their youthful reactions were strong. And convoluted. They loved the family farm that they could understand was being undermined by the policies of industrial productivity pushed by ag schools like Purdue. The viable size of a profitable, productive modern grain farm was becoming much larger than any family could manage or afford.

The head of the English department, Jacob Adler, and former colleague and friend of Berry's at the University of Kentucky, agreed to invite Berry to campus as a guest to give a poetry reading and perhaps to talk about his farm book. But I impishly thought how much more spectacular and intriguing would be having his visit cosponsored by the School of Agriculture itself—home to Butz, Berry's nemesis. I crossed the state highway that cut through the campus, isolating the School of Agriculture from the rest of the university. That day, I noticed the squirrels that ate walnuts that grew on both the humanities and the agricultural sections of the campus crossed the state highway that separated its two great lawns. Before crossing, the squirrels dashed left and right to see if the road was clear before attempting a crossing.

Proof on the local ground of the evolution of species. They learned at the university too.

I got an audience with its friendly but skeptical dean. He had a huge office and was very short behind a large desk. His office was much bigger than Jacob Adler's. Butz was no longer dean, although he could still be seen on campus. Butz always wore a black suit and a black fedora and looked like a gangster. My argument to the ag dean was whatever Berry would say *would* be provocative. But that his ag students were going to be encountering his ideas and his way of thinking anyway in their careers. What better prep than to have those ideas exposed and critiqued by their own teachers. The dean said he'd think about it but gave no timeline.

I began showing up at every public event or program the School of Agriculture sponsored. I was curious how these people thought. The programs were highly technical: how to kill weeds and bug pests efficiently. How new machinery worked. I always chatted with the dean.

After one program, to my surprise, the dean came over and said, "Come back and see me about your Berry idea." I did. The dean agreed. I got the English department to agree to cosponsor the visit, to include a public poetry reading. I wondered whether I had been unconsciously politically savvy in settling this up.

At any rate, I had the temerity to write to Wendell Berry himself. Berry wrote back to say he no longer accepted public speaking opportunities, but he would make an exception to speak at Purdue. He knew what the political underplay in agriculture was. He packed the house.

The title for his talk was "Solving for Pattern," which was puzzling to me at first and probably other members of the audience as well. It meant a farmer juggling the natural givens of farming—the weather, the pests, the need for fertilizer, the market prices, the necessary loans into the sustainable pattern, within all their variations, of producing healthy food in healthy soil. The opposite of current farm policy that imposed economies of scale and corporate power over the farms and that smothered any efforts to balance the health of the farm, the farmer, and profitability nonetheless.

"Mr. Berry. Who's going to decide who's going to starve if we go back to farming your way."

Wendell Berry had heard that question before. He didn't smile. His small head on his lanky frame bobbed like a squirrel hanging in a tree branch.

"Who's going to decide who starves is always a political question. My concern is for feeding the most people healthy food sustainably."

The pattern was intricate, shifting. Like reading the Bible as literature, I thought, drawing scenes and characters together. Where industrial farming like the Purdue School of Agriculture promoted resembled sectarian, specialized assumptions—what to do to make agriculture more and more productive. I thought ag academics were like the students of the Bible at Divinity School, always with an eye toward making the stories useful in advancing fundamental notions that there was an underlying truth packed inside to preach and teach about. Both systems were linear, driven by goals. Not melded layers in a piece of Fordite.

I couldn't help thinking Berry's farmer kept having second thoughts in order to adjust the possible pattern, weighing contradictory industrial demands against what the farm in hand could sustain. No resolution could ever be final. The variables kept changing. Second thoughts offered the key again.

During Barry's talk, I hunched down in a tweed sports coat and a bow tie in the back of the auditorium of mostly men in plaid jackets and some bolo ties. I worked to make sense of the mood and interchange of people and issues new to me. I used my standard way of thinking. The big guys in the high towers of Purdue's ag school work the fields for profit. The people at the picnic gather at the lake to listen to Jesus for good words and good food. Berry says, "All the improvements from agricultural research have been to the pump, not the well."

Simple notions jelled for me: "Keep showing up," like I did and "Be true," as Berry said to be to the land.

I met the ag dean in the hallway outside the auditorium afterward. He smiled at me and asked, "Wasn't that fun?" I was relieved. He didn't see any threat in the way Wendell Berry thought agriculture should go. His boys would remain in charge.

After the success of Berry's talk, and with the ag dean's approval, I arranged to bring to campus three other writers critical of American agricultural policy. I dubbed the series with the unlikely but notable name: The Annual Purdue English Department and School of Agriculture Lecture Series. Jim Hightower, Mark Kramer, and Wes Jackson all had different ways of presenting Berry's ideas. After all, wasn't a university supposed to be "universal"? Contributing to my motives was, again, having no real, or recognized academic discipline of my own. While still taking to heart Rene Wellek's admonition to think of comparative literature as cross-dressing with other sorts of human culture, I saw farming, for all its dust and drudgery, manure and money matters as a work of art. Like Fordite, worked by many hands, polished by humane stewards of the land.

Saving the Bible as Literature

1978

... in the heart of the fire ...
—The Song of the Three 1:1

After classes started in the fall of 1978, the head of the English Department, Jacob Adler, called me into the departmental office.

"You're due to come up for tenure review next year. We like the job you're doing 'teaching.' That's the first of the triad for tenure. Your work with the ag school is remarkable. That covers 'service.' The problem is the third, publishing, a.k.a. 'Publish or perish.' You've published some articles. But not yet a book. That's usually required for tenure here. I think you need to have one either published or well along if you're going to make it. We do want you to. We like what you do for us. Think about it."

I did think fast, right there during an awkward pause, in a swirl. I had published eclectically. Essays on Tolkien, Rilke, Emerson, Erasmus. I got an essay on the Gnosticism in Luke's Gospel into a collection of Bible as literature essays published by Indiana University Press. The Purdue Jewish studies caucus invited me to join. I edited some articles for them and published an essay on the David story in their small journal called *Sofar*, or "ram's horn," that only circulated among Jewish studies departments. I was gratified that they welcomed me as a member and contributor because of my devotion to the Hebrew Bible, (albeit in translation) despite not being Jewish. I published two translations from German for the Divinity School course I took in hermeneutics. No possibilities I could think of to expand any of that into a book. I wrote a monthly column on fishing in Indiana rivers for the *Hoosier Angler*. That wouldn't count much.

I sighed, looking into the sympathetic eyes of the department head, Jacob Adler.

"I feel boxed in. There's no interest, I don't think, in any kind of Bible as literature book. And I haven't even started thinking about what to do instead."

"Start thinking," he said simply and leaned forward from his desk to pat me on the shoulder. I went back to my office and sat down, cradling my head in my hands.

I was at a crossroads. I loved the Bible as literature for its crackling variety, big pictures, shining polish. It was as good as anything Homeric. The Bible had become a "Lady" for me, her limpid eyes looking back into mine. She'd led me through my youth, the Jesuit years, into a job teaching wonderful kids. Now, like a damsel in distress, would she help me get tenure to keep her vital in my life, and those of my students? Or so I thought in another quick, panicked, mental run.

I took a breath and took a chance. I went back to Professor Adler's office.

"What about that medical ethics project that's been floating around? It requires a medical ethics course to be cotaught by a biologist, physician, and faculty person. I've heard no one in the Philosophy Department wants to do it. Nor anyone else. Could I try that? I think there's maybe a book in that?"

The head of the department had a look on his face like Rene Wellek had as chair of comparative literature when I'd asked about writing a dissertation on biblical interpretation.

He had the same smile. And said almost the same thing.

"See what kind of a proposal you come up with. I can't predict how it'll fly with the university tenure committee."

Right after I left that office, I got an appointment with the Office of the Dean of the School of Arts and Sciences who had sent out inquiries about the medical ethics grant. His office was big, but not as big as the ag school dean's office, although it had more books on the shelves. He had a big picture on the wall of himself hugging the great funny man George Burns, who I had heard was a distant cousin.

"Could I apply for it?" I asked.

The dean said the same thing. "See what kind of proposal you come up with. I can't say whether the grant people want an English professor to do it. But give it a try. No one else wants to. They're busy frying their own fish."

I applied. I offered to team teach a course on medical ethics. For a qualification I mentioned my degree in philosophy from Boston College. It included a course in medical ethics that mostly grappled with the difficulties the Catholic Church had with human reproduction. But its scope had been wider than that.

I proposed to write a textbook to be used in the course. Students would debate the key issues after reading my original real-life stories of people caught up in medical dilemmas. Each chapter on a topic would follow the stories with a comprehensive review of the best ethical thinking current on the topic I could find among scholars, journalists, moralists, and ethicists.

I proposed it would be the kind of book a nonspecialist could do, assuming the guise of a fully informed citizen of today's world, synthesizing the best that had been said or thought for the benefit of citizens without medical or philosophical expertise. I did not propose an original ethic, or any new ideas about medical ethics per se. I could assume that for now, everything that could be said about it had already been said. Now was a time to choose.

On the Feast of the Epiphany, January 6, 1978, I got a letter saying I'd gotten the grant. The grantors apparently really wanted the course taught at Purdue. Nobody else wanted to try it. The grant allowed me to buy out of teaching one course in the second semester—Jacob Adler agreed to this. And to pay me as much for the summer as I would earn teaching summer school. Bonanza!

To start, I immersed myself in the university library, reading into the controversies about abortion, death and dying practices, birth control, the distribution of scarce medical resources, and the like: the government-mandated vaccines posed for certain religious groups. I thought, *A lot of this stuff runs around in the shadow of religious thinking, much of which derives from bad readings of the Bible.*

Dualities ran through everything—the technology of new medicine developed fast and far in advance of the culture's traditional assumptions about what was health and the good life. A key example, just in the news at the time, was what to do about a young woman apparently brain dead who continued to breathe normally and appear as if she was only sleeping. Was it murder to pull the plug? *Do not kill.* Doctors fearing lawsuits complied, although the case went against their physician's oath *Do no harm*—in this case—perpetuating a life worse than death.

I found patterns in the arguments, such as people favoring letting natural life take its course, life over artificial intervention; keeping a fetus or having it surgically removed; keeping a comatose person from dying; giving a scarce liver for transplant to a young dock worker or an elderly state senator. Arguments would run the gambit from emotionally regarding a nonviable fetus as bearing a God-infused soul, to coldheartedly regarding it as inconvenient tissue.

After reading the real-life-like stories used as examples, I made up new ones, describing the ethical crisis of a woman confronting the dilemmas of finding herself pregnant with an unwanted fetus. Was the possibility of an abortion given the same moral, emotional weight for a woman pregnant from a rape; for a mother of four who didn't feel her family could support any more children; for a young, unmarried career woman on her way up the ladder of success? Following laying out three different kinds of moral dilemmas, I summarized the best arguments pro and con for each instance. Then the reader could draw on the survey to argue about whether what the people in the story did was ethical in their view or not.

Teaching the Bible as Fordite provided structure. I would bring together incompatible-appearing arguments like the layers of hardened paint, one against the other, and have readers or students make sense of them, having "second thoughts," whereby one idea didn't cancel the other but, instead, extended thinking to the point of an educated decision.

I thought the key idea of being nonsectarian—as in teaching the Bible as literature—would be to stress that whatever your heartfelt thoughts on any matter were, say on abortion, you still had to respect, even gratefully, opposing ideas. Only then would you discover the true cost and depth of your own. So, although I'd be technically working like Ruth "amidst alien corn" out of my field, the Lady of the Bible of Literature would show me the way.

After a semester's reading, I got the gist of the field of medical ethics—so that as with knowing about traditional biblical scholarship, I could avoid making mistakes. Now I needed time to write the stories and clearly condense the best thinking going on about the issues. I gave myself three summer months in order to have something to put on the table in the fall of 1978 for the tenure review.

On the Feast of the Ascension, May 4, 1978, Helen and I decided to spend the summer writing the stories for the medical ethics book where the air was clear and cool. The Indiana air in spring and summer aggravated my asthma. Tractors cultivating the vast fields of northern Indiana spewed dust into the air. The intensely hot summers good for growing corn labored my breathing.

Maine had been wonderful during our honeymoon. We looked at several places to rent on the coast through a booklet provided by the Maine tourist office. We found a place to rent called Under Cliff on Cape Rosier, near Blue Hill, Maine. Caroline Robinson rented out cabins on a cove of Penobscot Bay. She and her husband made their fortune publishing *The Have More Plan after the War*, to encourage Connecticut suburbanites like themselves to become subsistence farmers intensely cultivating the open space around the house with vegetables, not just growing a lawn. Helen and Scott Nearing lived just down the road. They were famous for the book *Living the Good Life*, urging a comprehensive withdrawal from the capitalist economy.

We rented a cottage called "The Casino" built on pilings off the end of a rocky jetty. There was a pleasant sound of tidal wash coming up through the floors. Caroline Robinson said that in the 1930s, during Prohibition, it had been a small booze and gambling house for tour boats that used to tie up to the jetty.

There was a small nook that had been used as the bar where I set up a study. It rained everyday for the first month we lived there. The kids were restless. I was often frazzled trying to play with them when I really wanted to get back to writing.

The sun came out for July and August and things got better. The family sailed, clammed, fished, and played wiffle ball. I stayed up late most nights writing in the nook. The writing was going well. I began to feel at home, albeit in a "rental field of study."

One morning Max was not in his bed. We heard him cry from the other side of the floor. I rushed outside. He was standing up to his knees in sea water next to a piling holding up the floor of the building—in his pajamas with the tide rising. I grabbed him up into my arms, soaking wet.

I cried, "Oh, Max," in fear and relief.

Clouds thickened on the day Helen and I drove past a small house nearby with a for sale sign nailed on the front door.

"Let's look," Helen said.

"What for?"

"We'll see."

We stopped and looked around and met the owner, Ivory Peasley, who told us he had built the place himself as a young man. Six acres came with it, including a path that led through the woods to a small but fiercely flowing tidal river called Horseshoe Cove. The selling price was twenty-five thousand dollars, which seemed remarkably cheap. The outside steps looked rotted and needed replacing. There were stains on the ceilings, indicating the roof had leaked.

When she saw me looking doubtful, Helen said, "You're good at fixing things like that. Look what you've done in the Wabash house."

As we drove away, I said, "It's tempting of course to think of getting our own place in Maine for the summers. But we really can't afford it on my salary. It's enough time and expense to keep working on our house in Indiana. And I'm not tenured yet. If I don't make it next year, I'll have to start looking for another job. And with my weak resume, especially after being practiced at teaching the Bible in a way no one else wants, what'll we do then?"

Helen scoffed. "Oh stop it. You'll get tenure. We really should look into this before we say no. It might be cheaper to own a place like this than to keep trying to rent places for the summer here."

We found the reason for the cheap price was that there were more than thirty small liens on the place. Ivory had mortgaged it in bits and pieces to friends and relatives to get the funds to build it. I thought that was reason enough to forget about trying to buy it. Helen insisted we talk to a local lawyer. The lawyer estimated it would take him six months and cost about one thousand dollars for him to clear the title.

Back in Indiana for the fall term, we argued while lying in bed one evening.

"No, I'm too nervous. We're not rich enough for this."

"We really shouldn't pass this up. Nothing like this will happen again. Maybe my father could help us."

When she said this, I pushed her shoulder in frustration. It was the only time during more than fifty years of being married that I ever did anything physically aggressive to a wife. Helen didn't appear to notice. She kept pressing.

I finally relented. "Okay. But let's see if the tenure thing happens before we look into hiring any lawyers. One worry at a time."

I had finished the book at the end of the summer. Purdue Press published a softcover quickly to be ready to use by the spring of 1979 titled *Muted Consent*. It would sell well beyond Purdue. Apparently, it got picked up for courses in medical ethics at various medical schools. It would eventually go through ten printings.

The Monday after Thanksgiving, the English Department head, Jacob Adler, pulled me into an empty office.

"You made it," he said with a sigh and a smile. "You got tenure."

Immediately a text came to mind: "When the day of Pentecost came, they were all together in one place. Suddenly a sound like the blowing of a violent wind came from heaven and filled the whole house where they were sitting. They saw what seemed to be tongues of fire that separated and came to rest on each of them" (Acts 2:1-4).

Apparently despite my iffy research record by the usual English Department standards, the department wanted the Bible as literature to be taught. *Muted Consent* saved teaching the Bible as literature for the rest of my working life. Just in the nick of time, the elegant Lady was safe in my hands. Later, she'd give me one final gift after a series of unexpected turns in the pilgrimage with her whereby I almost lost her again.

The glorious spring semester of 1979 I got to teach the book. A biology professor and a local physician and a local lawyer came to some classes. Students from all over the university signed up for it. A few already thought about going to med school after graduation. Most of them had experienced some medical crisis in their families or for themselves. The discussions were lively. What was particularly fun was assigning a student to take part in a class debate in defense of the actions in one of the stories that the student *didn't* agree with. I told the students "When it comes to ethical dilemmas like these, your best resource is listening to someone who's very good at arguing against what you think. That's the person who lets you know the real price you have to pay for doing what you think is right."

What surprised me right from the start was how the participants in the class kept jumping the net. The stories were complicated enough so as not to allow simply plugging in an idea in the summary sections to resolve the dilemma it posed. But after a quasiformal debate at the start of each session, where students debated from assigned positions, almost everyone wanted to bring up a personal experience of some medical moral crisis often more convoluted than the one I had concocted. The discussions became lively, my role a referee to keep them decorous. One student came in a wheelchair. She told us she had contracted polio the same week of the announcement of the Salk vaccine that immunized against it. She argued for using medical and technical advances in medicine vigorously regardless of any religious scruples. Another student was a devout Christian. She argued from the premise of what she called "natural law"—what God had made, humans dare not alter. She was vehemently opposed to abortion.

The biology professor and geneticist who worked with fruit flies responded.

He started with a joke. "Flies are as promiscuous as humans." He wasn't joking when he startlingly compared medicine to sex, which he saw as the efforts of an individual to alter his or her own genes via the recombination with another set that might produce more hardy offspring.

"Just as parents of a child have rights to decide how to educate a child, so a woman has the right to decide not to have one to educate."

The physician (who had helped deliver my sons Max and Vlad) said everything he did in his practice required ethical thinking. How to explain risks to a patient, what calculus to use in prescribing medications, whether to mollify a patient's suffering or seek to end it. Rarely did he ever see any cases as dramatic as those fictionalized and surveyed in the book.

"I sympathize with all my patients, even ones who choose to make a decision about whether to have an abortion or not that I would not personally believe in."

A local attorney who attended class sessions said the Supreme Court decision Roe vs. Wade was ethical because it allowed individual women to make their own ethical decisions, regardless of what someone else might think. Law at its best allowed ethics to flourish.

"The law has yet to catch up to what modern medicine could do unfettered on its own." But the lawyer did say the stories in *Muted Consent* represented the kind of work lawyers did in preparing to try cases reaching judgments in support of or in dismissal of the results desired in his or her case.

I had my own ethical crisis as a teacher over the chapter on abortion. The woman who often evoked the "natural law" told us she vehemently opposed abortion, to the point where she insisted proponents were damned to hell. She actually said this during a class debate. Her judgment met with absolute silence. Not even the other antiabortionists wanted to go that far—at least in public. She declared the same conviction in her paper on that section of the course.

Before returning the paper to her in class, I invited her to my office. I urged her to rewrite it.

"I sympathize with your views on the matter. Many people believe like you do. And you've thought long and hard about them. That's admirable. But in a course like this, in a secular university, you can't get an A if you cannot bring yourself to at least admit your opponents have goodwill. Otherwise, you allow your religious beliefs to prevent you from having a valid academic experience of objectivity. Certainly, while doing that you can still hold your own beliefs."

"I'll take the B and save my soul."

I eventually gave her a failing grade on the paper, although she did pass the course. I still wonder whether that was the right thing. To grade on the basis of *how* a student thinks, no matter *what* the student thinks. But regardless of that, I hope she saved her soul.

My experience with the student was as close as I got even after a decade of teaching the Bible as literature in insisting religious beliefs could not withstand the ethics of openminded university teaching on any subject. You can believe anything you want. But you can't restrict what another thinks without violating the universal doctrine that requires everyone to entertain—at least in my own personal terms— "second thoughts."

The semester I taught *Muted Consent* I also taught the New Testament as Literature as usual the second semester. The Old Testament the first. (I didn't use the term *Hebrew Bible* since by definition and canonical fiat, it did not include the lively stories about clever triumphs over oppression that Jews wrote in Greek in various periods of exile or political oppression. Thus, absent the stories of Judith, Esther, Daniel, Tobias, The Song of the Three and others.)

By dividing class time between the ethics and a literature course, I found myself reiterating having second thoughts, in the sense of having two objects (class subjects) suspended adjacently in my own thinking. *Muted Consent* gave rise to a startling, new understanding of the Bible. Both were *scriptures*, a word reserved for those literary works (which transcend propaganda) that appear composed to instigate decisions. Both had stories and plenty of discussions of morality and what it meant to be human and what humans thought about God and what human life should be like for humans who thought about God.

Both books (forgive the impertinency of comparing a very little book to very large book, even if only rhetorically) were composed in fragments, as in the analogy to Fordite, stories and ethical standards that intentionally did not precisely mesh—bits and pieces of old writings often incongruent brought together to inspire the thinking that arose out of the provocative discrepancies. I had suggested to the publisher the cover design of *Muted Consent*: two adjacent puzzle pieces that did not exactly fit together.

With this insight I taught the Gospels that semester with a new reverence and restraint. I loved the Lady more tenderly. She allowed me personally the benefit of the very odd academic pairing.

I was also teaching Literature of Ecology, which qualified my teaching load as "three preps," with all the reading and attendant piles of papers to grade. Most academics in regular positions, not adjuncts, consider this a penal sentence of hard labor. But I found myself wondrously awash in different discourses, words, stories, and provocative musing, fingering a brilliantly colored hunk of educational Fordite.

Scenes of Jesus curing the blind, lepers, the lame, and doctors learning to understand the feelings of their patients. Muir's praise of the water ousel's exuberant freedom; Jesus pointing to the birds of the air flying free of worry; Leopold's geese; Thoreau's owls and loons—Muir and Thoreau and Jesus and Leopold and Berry and the poverty of human spirits before land and heaven. Characters like the woman at the well chiding Jesus for his religious bigotry and me discussing abortion with a zealot. Poetry, stories, close thinking, the natural world, animals, birds, doctors and lawyers, a poet, farm kids, a literature professor seeking common ground and language. A heady mix, requiring pedological discipline to keep courses clean of each other, while reveling in their indiscriminate stimulation of my thinking.

At times I wondered briefly if common themes or notions underlay all three courses and their objects of study. Something like a yearning for humane science or satisfaction with an earthly moral life beguiled by the beauty of the earth and the goodness in its people. But I resisted. The three inquiries had their own languages and points of view. It would only trample nuance to blend them. It would be like confecting a biography of Jesus by cobbling together stories that did not intermesh in either composition or as literature. It would be like crushing all the wondrous bulk of the Bible into one thin idea: the sin in the Garden led to the redemption on the cross.

A second thought came to mind. When they were ten and seven, Max and Vlad and I walked into a campsite in the Adirondack Park on a truck trail—one wide and smooth enough for Rangers to use in jeeps to get into the interior of the wilderness. It was easy for young kids. We set up at the first campsite on the trail, about five miles in. A scarlet tanager perched sideways on the door of the outhouse I had left open for the view. I'd never seen one that close. The first evening, we set up our tents on a level spot next to a small pond like the bottom of a bowl rimmed by vertical cliffs of granite.

We played with echoes we could get bouncing off the walls. Then came the magic. Two owls in nearby trees began hooting, their hoots doubling and trebling against the walls and harmonizing with our echoes of laughter. As if that wasn't enough, two loons on the pond began their eerie calls that picked up echoes and played like natural jazz improvised with the owls. My sons and I listened mesmerized to the medley of ever-changing hoots and calls and echoes.

It was fun to think maybe the owls started hooting on purpose—to sing themselves into our echoes. Then the loons picked up the melody. Maybe the birds did it for our benefit—because they liked us, or perhaps had gotten a good report from the scarlet tanager on the outhouse door.

But that was not a serious thought. We could not assume we understood the language or intentions of the birds for the moments of their concert together with the rock cliffs. Their motives were opaque, however wonderful their mingled cries.

I always think of that scene whenever I am tempted to find meaning in some comparison between unlike things, squeezing a definitive out of what is naturally a jumble—like the strata of Fordite—like reading the Bible as literature or assembling a story of a life like mine following unexpected lures to turn *this* way, and then *that*.

At any rate, the ferment in that semester would not occur again. In the middle of the next fall's semester, while I was looking forward to teaching the same three courses together again, the dean of the School of Arts and Sciences called me into his office. He still had the picture of him hugging George Burns on the wall. But the mood in the room was not comical.

The dean introduced a young philosophy professor who insisted an English professor had no right to teach a philosophy course on medical ethics.

Now somebody from philosophy speaks up, I thought.

"But I wrote the book. Surely, I can teach from it."

The dean said no. The young philosophy professor looked down at his shoes.

"Well, I can at least recommend what textbook you use." The young philosophy professor continued to look silently at his shoes. There was shit on them.

After the dean said his no, I got up, walked out, and slammed the dean's door. I felt fierce as I drove home too fast.

After I told Helen what happened, I almost shouted, "I'm disgusted with this place. Let's hire that Maine lawyer."

As he'd predicted, it had taken the lawyer months to clear the title to Ivory Peasley's house for a fee of one thousand dollars. With the provisional contract I had with Purdue University Press for *Muted Consent*, I received no royalties. But at least it had earned me tenure and gotten me pushed into a series of happenings that led to buying another cheap, run-down house.

We managed a small down payment with what little savings we had. With tenure came a five-hundred-dollar raise—the same amount I'd received upon leaving the Jesuits. A local Maine bank was willing to give us a mortgage. The lady we talked to at the bank said she had grown up with Ivory.

"The price is cheap because he built it cheap. Two-by-four studs on twenty-four-inch centers with no insulation. But it'll be fine if you don't live there in the winters."

Muted Consent continued to sell well after it was knocked from my hands. "Somebody else was willing to teach from it," I muttered to myself. It received one backhanded positive review when another publisher, without receiving permission, reprinted its introductory chapter in a collection of essays on medical ethics.

I got one more chance to talk about the book. The dean at the medical school of the University of Alabama in Mobile invited me (to my amazement) to lecture on medical ethics before the entire medical faculty. During the visit, I got to attend Mobile's Mardi Gras parade and caught an armful of plastic beads.

We bought the place just before leaving Indiana that spring to move to Maine for the summer. We met the neighbors on the road that ran in front of our house. Our favorite was Dot Gray, who kept a few cows and raised a small flock of sheep on the other side of the fence between our two properties. We bought her unpasteurized milk the kids liked to drink and home-grown garden vegetables. Dot introduced us to some other neighbors, one of whom was her sister. Her husband worked at a boatyard. He helped us find a small used sailboat to rent that was larger and in much better shape than *Flotsam* had been. We moored it a mile away at the mouth of Horseshoe Cove.

For several years, we lived in Indiana for the winters and Maine for the summers. Life was good. Helen and I gardened using the manure from Dot's sheep. Unfortunately, we'd always have to drive to Indiana in August before the tomatoes and corn ripened. The kids loved sailing and swimming, exploring the tidal pools on local islands, digging for clams. Helen joined a course in weaving a local woman offered with two other women who became friends of ours. On many days I felt like I was back again in my childhood, relishing the sea, wind in the sails and hitting my face, fishing off the back of the sailboat in Yeats's "mackerel crowded seas."

But right from the start, I found it exhausting—to renovate the Indiana house during the fall and winter, and then, after a long three-day drive to Maine, to start doing the same thing on another old house during the spring and summer. I'd get snappish with Helen and the kids too often.

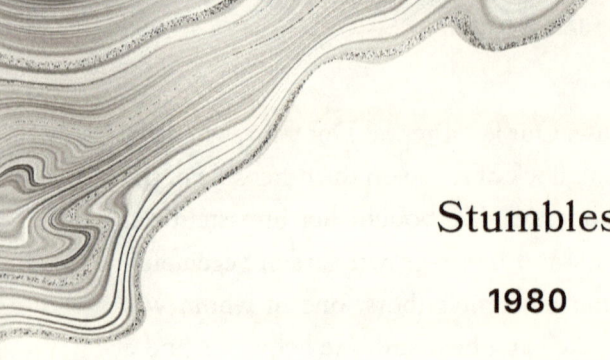

Stumbles

1980

Never let yourself think that you are wiser than you are.
—Proverbs 3:5

By 1980, small things were gathering in a cloud around us. Ever since I had known her, Helen smoked in the house. She'd open a window even during the winter to vent her exhales out.

"Could you stop smoking, Or, try to? And while you try, can you go outside to smoke? Perhaps it's the mold from two old houses, or the ash from the woodstove that's causing it, but I'm using my asthma inhaler too much. It feels like it did when my parents smoked inside the house when I was a kid."

"You knew I smoked back in Munich. You haven't said anything about it before. I'm not sure I want to quit at all. I've tried before and it's excruciating for me. And this isn't the right time."

She started putting on a coat and going outside to smoke. But she didn't like it. But both of us at the time admitted tersely to each other it was necessary. And this was one of those bumps that happen in any marriage that lasts.

Eventually, Helen stopped smoking. She put on weight. I told her that bothered me, which was a mistake. She went on a draconian diet that slimmed her body down to what I told her I found very sexy. To my surprise, she got mad. She started to gain weight again. This was a trivial crisis, I now admit. It led to further disagreements. I'll remain silent about them to protect both my own and her integrity. But suffice it to say, I take all the blame for all the bad that followed.

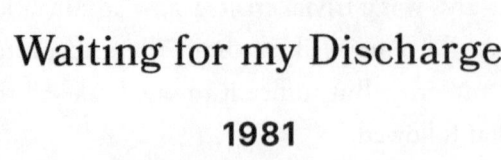

Waiting for my Discharge

1981

Take up your bed and walk.
—John 5:9

After eleven years of marriage, after breakfast on Good Friday, while the kids slept in and the Wabash River flowed past the Indiana house high and brown with spring run-off, Helen said in an even voice, "I want a divorce."

I was devastated. I told her again I was sorry for my failings. I loved her.

"You don't love me. You only love being married."

Her reasons still puzzle me. Although, as my friend Don, who'd been through several divorces himself, put it bluntly, "Stop fretting. In these matters, the woman is always right. It's the husband's fault. I know. I've been through a few divorces myself."

After Helen had moved out, and the two kids were asleep in the Wabash house while the river flowed darkly past the house with a moon on its back, Don came over with a bottle of bourbon we emptied while sitting alone on the floor of the silent Indiana house. I told Don about the premonition that something bad was in the air.

"During the school vacation the week before Easter, just before her announcement, I had been inhaling a lot of dust while I finished a long project of trimming the house with baseboards and around the window and doors. It had taken me years. A large apartment house was about to be demolished in town, and free access was given to anyone who wanted to salvage the crown molding and elaborate beautiful woodwork, which I began to do with crowbars and hammers. The wood was free. But the cost to me was the worsening asthma attacks caused by the dust and mold of the demolition.

"I think the attacks were also the result of my subliminal feeling Helen had grown dissatisfied with me. I continued to complain about the difficulties of constantly working at renovating two old houses five hundred miles apart, with the only respite the three-day car trip to get from one to the other.

"Our feelings erupted after she dropped the D-bomb. During an hour of my pleading with her, a severe asthma attack brought me to my knees, and a grim Helen drove me to the hospital.

"I was hospitalized on Good Friday in what appeared to be an otherwise empty, tomb-like wing of the local hospital where both our sons had been born. A call went out to my allergist. While I waited, I agonized trying to breathe. No nurse responded to my push of the call button. I rolled out of bed to crawl out of my room and then down the stairs, desperate for relief. Nurses discovered me on the stairs. They angrily pulled me back to my bed. The allergist finally arrived. I remember looking up into his face as he delivered into my arm a strong dose of adrenaline that was utterly wonderful to feel clearing my lungs immediately. It was as miraculous, it seemed, as when I'd recovered from some awful hornet stings in the infirmary bed at Shadowbrook.

"Later while I was resting, recovering, and waiting for my discharge, Helen came to visit. She told me she'd wait in the car until I came out. What seemed strange to me at the time, was that shortly after she left the room, Neil and Lorna came in—two close friends at Purdue. They were genuinely sympathetic and comforting and deeply concerned. Helen had not been. After they left, still waiting for my official discharge, I thought ruefully that Helen had waited for me to finish trimming the house before announcing her decision. She planned on taking possession of the Indiana house in the divorce settlement.

"I walked out of the hospital on wobbly legs on a bright Easter Sunday morning. And now, on the feast of the Epiphany, I'm sitting on the floor drinking whiskey with you."

"*Na zdrowie*," said Don, who knew that much Polish.

Without Helen now, I no longer had a strong woman in my life, like my mother or Donna or her mother had been. A female presence but also the wisdom and bodily assurance that I had been born lacking and never acquired on my own—probably because I'd never had to.

It was very lonely during the week when the kids were with Helen. I sat every evening for an hour reading the Gospels in *The New Testament Student's Workbook*, published by the Liturgical Press. Every page of the Greek and Latin and English texts appeared side by side. I could switch between them to savor the different inflections. I had a leather-bound copy of Luther's translation in German to add into the mix. It made reading the Fordite easy, since the differences in language made the layering of the stories easy to feel at the fingertips.

Once, I thought to try the old Gospel Guidance trick called *tolle et lege*—"pick up and read." Saint Augustine had used it when he was trying to figure out what to do with his wrecked life. The idea was to open up the Bible at random. Pose a question in the air. Then drop a finger on a passage to be read as an answer from the inspiring spirit within. Of course, when Augustine tried it, he hit on a passage from Saint Paul thundering at him to mend his dissolute sex life. I knew I deserved to receive the same message for having done the same stupid thing. But that's not what came up. By chance, my finger fell on the end of John's Gospel at one of my favorite stories. Jesus has risen from the dead. He's cooking fish on the beach while his disciples fish off shore. They don't recognize him. He tells them to throw their net to the right. They haul in a huge catch. They come ashore, by this time certain it must be the magical Jesus who told them how to fish. He feeds them fish for breakfast as they chat. Jesus engages Peter in particular. In their conversation, Peter asks what's to be the fate of John, the disciple who leaned against Jesus at the last supper. I had never before paid much attention before to what follows.

Jesus retorts: "If it should be my will that he wait until I come, what's it to you?" That saying of Jesus became current in the brotherhood and was taken to mean that the disciple would not die. But in fact, Jesus did not say that he would not die; he only said, "If it should be my will that he wait until I come, what's it to you?" (John 21:23).

Reading the Bible as literature, I often came across gems like this that had been overlooked before. This risen Jesus was loose enough to use what sounded like slang: "What's it to you?" And to compound the matter, the narrator stops the story to explain a part of it, as if the reader was one of those dim-witted disciples. He repeats Jesus's off the cuff remark, "What's it to you?" It sounded brash in Greek *ti pros se*—τί πρόσ σέ—and Latin *quid ad te*, and even more challenging in German *was gebt es dich an*, which carries the flavor of "Mind your own business."

If by performing this trick, I was allowed to think the message was also directed at me reading it; there was some consolation in being told indirectly by the passage that—like Peter—I was an idiot. Jesus didn't seem to be worried about it. I felt some release. That was better than moping around thinking of myself as a tragic figure.

It was consoling to apply to myself Thoreau's great line, "I never dreamed of any enormity greater than I have committed; I never met a man worse than myself." It's a liberation to admit that. No excuses needed.

After waiting a year, as friends said to, I dated a few women. It was too soon. I was lying in bed with a woman one time who had recently been divorced herself. We were crying in each other's arms. I was determined to go back to living as a celibate again until the brain fog cleared.

It did, although the pain endured. At one point I said to Helen while we were negotiating further details of postdivorce arrangements, with desperate tears in my eyes, "You're going to take my sons away from me."

I recalled hearing the despairing cry of "No sons!" while walking in the moonlight at Shadowbrook.

"No, I'm not!" she insisted. "We're going to raise them like parents. Lots of people do this who have kids when they break up."

"Let's promise each other that no matter what we each might be feeling, we will never say anything negative about the other to the kids."

"Done!" she said. "I know you love them, and they love you."

That is a promise I keep. It's not certain Helen has. And that's okay. She deserves to handle matters as she sees fit. But trying to stay a parent to Max and Vlad proved hard. It took several years to build back a fatherhood with Vlad. With Max, it remained a failure for decades.

Mrs. Ellen ran the daycare center in West Lafayette where the kids spent parts of the days for several years before the divorce, and afterward, when Helen was taking classes and I was teaching, and we were living apart.

Miss Ellen said to me once, "Max is the happiest child I've ever had. He's full of fun and is kind to the other kids. He always finds new things to do with the toys and shows them around."

One time, after picking him up at Miss Ellen's just before Easter, Max was standing alongside while I adjusted the car seat in the back of the car. I heard a frightening screech of car brakes. I ran around the back of the car and found Max with his stomach against the grill of a car he had run out in front of. Max had a smile on his face that seemed to say, "I can get away with anything." The driver's face was pale with horror. But he had braked in time. I ran out and picked Max up and immediately ran to the driver's side window and blubbered an apology and gratitude the driver echoed. As terror drained, my knees buckled. This time I held one hand on Max firmly while buckling him into the seat with the other.

On the way home, we drove under a bridge. Max looked up from his child seat and began to intone as if chanting:

> Now is the Time,
> Now is the Time
> To take all the Easter Boys
> And all the Easter Girls
> To the Bridges. To lock them up
> In the Bridges.

After his near-death experience, for several months Max spontaneously recited other poems he improvised:

> I have special eyes,
> So I can say anything
> Like—'invisible trees.'

and

> What does yes mean?
> I know what trees mean.
> Trees mean trees grow.
> But I don't know what yes means

and

> The waves hit the rocks.
> The rocks cry.

The poems rose from deep within his awareness of himself alone, on his own, in a world of his making.

A profoundly painful consequence of the divorce from Helen was that Max could never seem to forgive me. For years Max would refuse to speak to me. Christine, my second wife, and I read books about how to address the difficulties children have with their parents' divorce and their reactions to any remarriages. One book said that mathematically there were more than seven hundred permutations possible: one parent remarries. Both do. One parent has more children with a second spouse. Both do. The new spouse brings to the second marriage his or her own children and the original parent and second spouse have further children of their own. Ad infinitum. Each permutation brings with it its own complex dynamic, making it difficult if not impossible to negotiate well. Only the children of divorce can decide how to make it work was the disconcerting conclusion, since with Christine and me, at least initially, neither Vlad nor Max were willing.

Eventually I rebuilt a loving relationship with Vlad and his family. But not ultimately with Max. I once asked a friend who was a divorce lawyer to speculate from his experience when I might expect a reconciliation with Max. He said, "When he turns fifty, or you're on your deathbed."

Max has already turned fifty. So now I know how long I still have to wait.

Right Down the Alley

1983

A stranger in a strange land.
—Exodus 2:22

I stood alone at the window looking at a parking lot. At first, living alone after the divorce, homeless, in one sabbatical house-sit after another, riding herd on two edgy kids on weekends, feeling alienated from friends who had either taken Helen's side, or with whom I was too ashamed to socialize, I hadn't the slightest idea how to begin anything that would be any better.

The next stop on the pilgrimage road would lead out of Purdue and into farming ventures of my own—something that *would* be a lot better.

My friend Bob pointed the way. Bob was an entomology technician who had dropped out of the PhD program in agricultural entomology at Purdue after he realized he was preparing to learn how to professionally kill the bugs he had come to admire for their resourcefulness. He also ballroom danced with Miss Ellen, the kids' daycare center teacher.

Now his professional task was to gather specimens in the field to bring back to the labs. This way he got to see how they were doing on their own before anyone figured out how to eradicate them.

"What are they doing now, Bob?" I always asked him when we ran into each other on campus. "They" meant bugs.

Bob's eyes glistened. "The lab people found a chemical molecule that killed corn borers dead right after they take a bite. Within a year, I began collecting strains that have developed a chemical secreted from their pointed proboscises into a chain saw of sorts that cuts the molecule in two. The cut separates the deadly molecule into two components they love to eat. One more round for the bugs. Speaking of which, here's one to put in your ear."

Bob told me about a project he had heard about. The Kellogg Company that made the corn flakes also distributed charity through the Kellogg Foundation. It now advertised the availability of competitive grants to agricultural departments and schools to fund programs to explore and teach about the social, political, and economic ramifications of modern agriculture.

"From what I've heard, no one in the ag school is interested in applying. Too softheaded for them. But it sounds right down the alley of your medical ethics thing."

Once again, I asked around. No one in the other appropriate departments like history or sociology or economics or philosophy was interested in applying for the grant either.

Once again, I asked my department head and the dean of arts and sciences if I could apply for the grant. They said yes.

"Something else for you to do, now that you can't teach medical ethics," said the dean sardonically.

I proposed writing a book on the model of *Muted Consent*. Chapters would start with stories about farmers and farms in crisis. Often facing the question whether to "Get big or get out." The stories would be followed by a review of the most persuasive arguments I could find about the need to use chemicals to grow large crops to feed billions of people versus the moral obligations to cultivate the land with organics to feed the local people.

I talked to people at Purdue Press. Conveniently, funds were available from the continuing sales of *Muted Consent* for the Press to agree to publish what I provisionally titled *The Arguments of Agriculture*. I found a professor in the ag school who was willing to coteach a course with me using the book.

I won the grant—one hundred thousand dollars. Big money in those days. One of its conditions was attending an all-expense paid trip to the Epcot Center in Orlando for officials from Kellogg to tell applicants in greater detail what they wanted. As Bob had predicted, it was right down my alley. It was fun being the only humanities professor at the open bar in a tweed coat and bow tie among the aggies in polyester plaids and string ties.

This time when I submitted the amended application, I made sure to write in generous support for myself to spend another summer writing in Maine and to pay down the mortgage. Helen had been right after all. The money showed up *after* we decided to spend it.

The course was to be offered jointly by the English Department and the School of Agriculture at Purdue—a first. Just like the speakers' program cosponsored by the ag school and the English Department.

I started reading everything I could get my hands on discussing the problems and promises in modern industrial agriculture. Everything from Wendell Berry's diatribe: "All advances in agricultural research for the last century have been for improvements to the pump, not the aquifer," to advertisements for aerial spraying of poisonous pesticides: "We Cover the Territory."

Again, perhaps because of my penchant for thinking in terms of contrasts, I juxta-opposed arguments that when placed adjacently gave rise to "second thoughts." And because of my experience writing the medical ethics book, I discovered a fundamental duality running through the arguments. One line of thought promoted "sunny farming," using sun-powered practices like crop rotations, animal fertilizers, and integrated pest management to produce sustainably modest amounts of healthy food at often high prices. The other, "oily farming," relied on herbicides, pesticides, fertilization of the ground, and the clearing of fields using petroleum-based chemicals that produce prodigious amounts of grains and hefty animal bodies at the price of ravaging the countryside and poisoning public health.

Each chapter started with three made-up stories of farmers in crisis, "Should I get better, or bigger?" basically. This was followed by a survey of the best writing to be found in favor of sunny or oily farming. The book sold well for several years as ag schools, particularly Cornell's, bought up classroom-size lots to use in their own survey courses.

This time the students who signed up for my course were mostly from the ag school at Purdue, who had mostly grown up on Indiana family farms. Bright, smiley kids with freckles.

"Be warned," I told them. "You'll hear a lot of things said in this course you don't agree with. It's intended to help you understand your kind of farming and understand what its most articulate critics say about it. As you've probably already experienced living on farms yourselves, you always need to know more about what you're already doing."

I liked the students. They were bright and honest and proud, touted far and wide in Indiana as the hopes for its future. The course went well. It piqued my curiosity about what their Indiana farmer parents were doing on those vast green fields that spread like an endless sea to the horizon. One woman student wrote a powerful paper. She described standing at the fence of her family's farm while a large tractor pulled a cultivator through the soil. Its blades dug out and then chopped up a mother rabbit and her litter. The woman wrote that she began to cry for the rabbits. She stopped when she said she realized her feelings were powerless. The drivers of big farm machines would never realize what they had done.

"How could I tell them?" she wrote.

She became for me the model student, like Ruth had been in the Bible as Literature class I'd taught years before. Someone who lived on the edge between doctrine and personal feelings, entertaining second thoughts between what they had been taught was right and what they felt was wrong.

As with *Muted Consent, The Arguments of Agriculture* received another informal review when the dean of the agricultural school at the University of Warsaw invited me to lecture to its faculty during the very week in which the Solidarity Party won the election that drove the Communist government out of power. I retraced Gramp's pilgrimage.

While teaching the course, I decided, like my friend Bob, to get out in the fields. It was time to meet real farmers for the first time. Up to now my sense of the environmental and social crisis in American agriculture had come from reading lofty writers with grand perspectives, like Wendell Berry and Wes Jackson.

I drew on widened contacts within the Purdue School of Agriculture. People I knew there who knew local farmers recommended me to those farmers who might be willing to talk with me. This time I applied for a grant to the Indiana Committee for the Humanities. I proposed a public slide show featuring the words and pictures of current Indiana farmers and their families. It would show the public what farmers did for their living, but more significantly, what they thought about what they were doing—still living on family farms, most of them inherited, yet farming vast fields with heavy machinery and great infusions of chemical fertilizers and pesticides.

The project this time would have three parts. One, to interview modern farmers for their thoughts. Two, to canvas the current literature about what was good or ominous about the kind of industrial farming the farmers were doing. But this time, in contrast to *Muted Consent* or *The Arguments of Agriculture,* there was a third part: an archival component. To visit museums and archives throughout the state that held diaries and letters of early Indiana farmers dating from the middle of the nineteenth century—to find out what they thought they were doing. There was a trove of old paintings and photographs to illustrate what they did, along with original manuscripts recording what they thought about it. The show would compare former and present Indiana farm practices, while showcasing the attitudes the farmers had—to see what had changed and what had remained the same. Remarkably, consistently, even the earlier farmers had used the biggest machines they could afford, worked the land as hard as they could, and beyond wanting to make a living, hoped to pass the farm and their gumption to their children. Reproduction inside and out.

Maury Wills, the president of the Purdue Agricultural Alumni Association, was genial when I crossed the highway again (along with the squirrels) to seek a recommendation but initially skeptical.

Maury would later say, "I was suspicious: what could a bow-tied, tweed-jacketed English professor say he understood about agriculture?"

He invited me back to his office to meet with some of his advisers in the ag school. They listened to my spiel silently. They agreed to provide a critical recommendation but warned they would have to see the show ahead of time before they would agree to any further sponsorship—like presenting the show to any farm groups. That was fine. The great gift Maury provided ahead of time was introductions to a number of local Indiana farmers he knew who might be willing to talk honestly and freely.

With Maury's backing, I got the grant. Partly because it was rare, perhaps even unique, that a humanities project would treat Indiana agriculture benevolently. Like literature, not politics.

I recruited Natalie Leimkuhler, a gifted local photographer, to take pictures of the families being interviewed at work with their animals and crops. She, with her husband Ferd(inand), belonged to the circle of close friends Helen and I had made. He was dean of Purdue's School of Industrial Engineering. He'd made his academic fortune designing automated shelving systems for libraries. She took great pictures. Her techniques were flawless. Her warmth cast an aura of trust in which her subjects basked.

The title became *The Gumption of Indiana Farmers in Pictures and Words. 1840–1980*. Maury booked me into meetings of alumni associations and ag extensions throughout the state. Several times Maury even arranged to fly me on the university's plane to remote areas of the state that otherwise would have taken a day to drive to. He often introduced me at meetings of the ag alumni chapters we both attended, describing his initial suspicion of "a bow-tied, tweed-jacketed English professor who had, nonetheless, something to say about agriculture."

Gumption did the farmers justice, for the nobility of their motives in their hard, skilled work. Over and over, they echoed what their elders had written about their deepest-held hopes to farm in such a way as to be able to pass the farm on to the next generation. But there was a melancholy subliminal theme. The modern families knew they were ruining the land with their necessary harsh treatments of soil and crops—the land that they hoped to pass on to their children. Often people in the audience would come up afterward with tears in their eyes. They were moved by the integrity of the voices of people like themselves they heard. They rued their own grinding doom.

They were prescient. When I followed up with a revised version of *Gumption* almost forty years later, available on YouTube, I discovered not a single family I interviewed in 1980 still owned their original family farm. The average size of an Indiana farm had grown to one thousand acres, the net profit from which in an average year was thirty thousand dollars. That was below the poverty level for a family of four. Only corporations could afford to farm on that thin a margin.

Spending time on the road with these honest, hardworking people softened my own sadness—exiled from marriage.

And one night that road led me to Christine's door.

We first met when she was sitting attentively in the first row of a *Gumption* performance on the Purdue campus in early January 1982. I found out later she had been invited to a reception afterward at the home of a mutual friend who had surreptitiously set up an introduction between us. Christine was a newly hired professor of accounting in the Purdue School of Business. She had grown up on a family farm in Nebraska. We began seeing one another, mostly for lunch on campus.

Remarkably, prophetically, one of the things farmers who had seen the show said to me afterward was, "Why don't you try farming yourself?" I would honestly respond, "I wouldn't have the slightest idea how to begin," which at the time was true. Christine changed that.

Early one cold morning on my birthday, February 2, 1982, several weeks after we met and after I had driven back from French Lick, a town in Southern Indiana where I had presented *Gumption*, instead of going to the sabbatical house-sit, I rang the door-bell at Christine's house. It was 2 a.m. She opened the door wearing a bathrobe with the belt untied. She smiled and let me in. She led me to her bedroom. Two weeks later I moved in with her and cooked a Valentine's dinner of beef heart for two.

Several months later, in late April, we were driving toward a cross-country skiing vacation where her brother was teaching mathematics at a university in the upper peninsula of Michigan. Max and Vlad, spending a week with us in shared custody, were asleep in the back seat.

Christine asked, "How long do you think we should be living like this before we make a decision?"

"A decision? You mean, to get married?"

"Yes."

"Are you proposing to me?"

"Yes."

I paused only for a moment to think of the right thing to say.

"Yes. But you have to accept my children and our spending summers in Maine."

"I do," she said. Then she added with a giggle, "Although for this to be official, I need to say this to you while we're getting married."

Max and Vlad had moved away to begin living with Helen, who had moved to Virginia. At the end of the academic year for Christine, the two kids flew out to spend the July with us in Maine. Christine and I drove east to meet them. When we pulled up in front of the Maine house, Christine looked out the window.

"I like the looks of it. Not too grand. Comfortable. But even from here I can see it needs a lot of work."

A Sacramental Relic

1983

Why did you stay among the sheep pens?
To hear the whistling for the flocks?
—Judges 5

The next day, Christine and I stood outside Dot Gray's door, at the next house down the road from mine. We had walked along about an acre of fenced-in sheep pasture between our two houses. There were a dozen sheep in it watching in still, simple silence.

"I've always liked sheep," Christine said. "One of my jobs on the farm was helping the ewes give birth in the spring."

"You and Dot will have something to talk about."

I knocked on the door. We heard a great hullabaloo of dog barking, then Dot shouting, "Shut up!"

Dot opened the door. "Good!" she said with a big grin, looking at Christine. "It's nice to meet you. Your man's written me about you. It's clear he needs your guidance. He'd been kind of a sad sack, moping around here for the last few summers."

Walking inside, Christine and I had to walk around a ribbon of flypaper hanging from the ceiling.

"I like this place," Christine said simply. "And the looks of your sheep. He's already told me you're his best next-door neighbor."

Just as Christine finished speaking, to our amazement, a small sheep walked into the kitchen through the door of the next room. It bleated with an edge of annoyance. Both Christine and I gasped. The sheep began to butt me in the knees.

"Baby! Stop that," cried Dot. She pulled the sheep by a collar around its neck just as it began to urinate, then defecate on the floor. She pushed the sheep back into the room it came out of—where I could see several dogs laying on the floor and a couch who didn't even look up.

She shut the door and turned to us. "You'll have to excuse her. You can't house-train sheep. And Baby gets jealous if I start talking to somebody. That's why she was trying to butt you out the door."

Dot grabbed paper towels and a spray bottle and started to kneel down to wipe the floor.

She was slow. "My damn knees," she complained.

"Wait," I said quickly, "I'll do it," and took the bottle and the roll and squatted down and started wiping up.

Dot was surprised. "Well, ain't you nice."

Christine said, "I want to start off on the right foot with a nice local like you. But first tell us," she asked laughing, already at ease enough with Dot to ask a personal question, "do the local people who live on the road keep sheep in the house like you do?"

"No," Dot smiled, embarrassed, "and usually not even me. Baby was a bottle lamb I started feeding in the house when she was born during a bad cold snap late in the winter. Her mom wouldn't feed her, and I found her shivering and half dead on the floor. I brought her into the house to get warm. I started feeding her lamb milk replacement from a bottle. I should have put her back with the others after she got on her feet; but one thing led to another, and we both got used to each other in the house, and she's comfortable with the dogs. I like having her around. She sits next to me on the couch when I watch the Red Sox on TV.

"Her time is about to come, however. My daughter Sami, who you'll meet, has told me either Baby goes or she goes. Well, she's about to go anyway. Sami just graduated high school and is about to get married. But to make her happy while she's still here, I will shove Baby out the door one of these days."

After the wonderful introductions to each other, Christine and Dot became fast friends. "Your farm is like the one I grew up on," she told her. We both asked her to be a witness for our marriage, which we were planning to take place in our flower garden at the end of July.

We bought groceries from her huge freezer full of lamb and beef, and the vegetables from her huge garden. We drank unpasteurized milk she milked herself. She eventually relented and pushed Baby back into the flock.

Sami later told us what happened after that.

"Mom and Baby cried on either side of the door from the kitchen into the barn for a week. The problem was, while she lived in the house, Baby came to identify with the dogs rather than other sheep. That's made things really hard for her. Now, you'll see Baby running with the dogs outside and they're much faster. She'll bleat plaintively trying to keep up, sometimes falling over when the dogs change direction. The dogs never look back."

Dot told us she felt bad about Baby, but then told us, "She'll be slaughtered for lamb before she's six months old this fall, so my agony won't last long." Dot's lack of sentiment brought Christine and me up short.

Dot noticed our wince. "I admit, it was a big mistake for me to give her a name. Makes it harder on me, but not in the end on her. The whole point of farming is to produce something to eat. I'll give you some chops later, and maybe that'll help you feel better."

"We'll give it a try," I said hesitantly.

"That'll be nice," Christine said forthrightly, undoubtedly drawing on her lifelong tolerance for the bloody business of the farming she'd grown up with in Nebraska.

We did get some chops, as succulent I had to admit, as the local lobsters we dropped alive in boiling water to cook.

Dot had a mantra she'd repeat whenever asked how things were going: "If no more breaks than is already split—I'll do just fine."

The first time I heard her say that, I had to ask her to repeat it, just to get the sense. She did. Then she pointed to the leg of the kitchen chair whose split was held tight by hose clamps. "Sort of like that!"

"I like the sound of it," I said finally. "It reminds me of my mother's threat to break off my arm and beat me over the head with the bloody stump when I did something bad. But what does it mean?"

"I'd like to meet your mother," Dot replied after a pause. "But to answer your question: we all live"—she pointed her thumb to her chest and her index finger to mine—"on the fine edge between split and break. You've got to keep your balance."

"Thanks for the good advice."

Sami invited us to her upcoming wedding. Christine asked if she could help Dot with a dress since Sami wanted her mother dressed up for the wedding.

Christine took Dot to a fabric store in Ellsworth, the biggest town near Blue Hill, where, unlike my mother, they were docile customers. Eventually, Dot did get to meet my mother.

Christine decided they should ask my mother to make the dress.

"You told me she was an award winner as a seamstress."

My mother and sister, Jill, drove up from Connecticut with a sewing machine.

Standing on the chair with the split leg, Dot told my mother, who was pinning up the hem, "You raised a nice son. I like how you threatened to beat him over the head with his own arm if he didn't shape up. Looks like it worked. I should have said something like that to my own daughters."

My mother growled, "Hold still."

Dot smoked two packs of cigarettes a day. Several years after we met her, she collapsed in Sami's arms while heading back to the house from weeding in her garden. Her last words were "Shit, I'm not ready to go yet." I recited Frost's "Reluctance" at her funeral. Dot was an "old salt," that would not have been out of place as a deckhand on the disciples' fishing boat Jesus finally called ashore.

Several months after Christine came to Maine for the first time, and several weeks after Sami's wedding, we were married standing in the flower garden outside the house in Maine. We had custody of the kids for the summer. A friend from down the road who was a lawyer married us officially. Maine had a tradition of allowing lawyers to perform marriage ceremonies from the days when long winters prevented other officials from getting around easily. We had invited friends to bring a dish to add to our menu of lobster rolls, beer, and a homemade wedding cake. Dot was my best man. Ed, the friendly mailman, was Christine's maid of honor.

Max and Vlad were present, but not happy about it. My mother had driven up from Connecticut to babysit while Christine and I took a short honeymoon to Boston. We attended a Red Sox game. On the first pitch, Paul Molitor of the Brewers hit a home run that was the only scoring in the game.

The next day we drove to Walden Pond in Concord. We swam together. Only when we got far enough offshore did the beach noise fade to a rustle in the leaves. We heard a loon voice a melancholy cry from the end of the pond where Thoreau had built his cabin.

"It's a descendant of the loon Thoreau once chased around in his rowboat. Both he and the loon laughed when the loon kept popping up unexpectedly." We both listened to the loon. Only one, and no owls this time.

We swam back to shore and ate sandwiches and talked while sitting on a blanket on the artificially created sandy beach.

When I looked at Christine, she was smiling. She ballooned into a colossal figure of serene assurance and patience.

"Take a walk with me to Thoreau's cabin site, a sacred place for me. I went to it a lot when I used to bike here from Weston College. There's a path from here to the other side of the pond. But first, put a handful of sand into an empty sandwich bag. You'll see why."

We walked hand in hand on the path around the pond from the beach to the cabin site. There is no building there now. In its place sits a square space marked with cement bollards at the corners linked by chain.

The scene evokes the rubbled ruins of the Sybil's lair at Delphi: a large pile of stones nearby.

"People bring stones from all over the world to put on the pile as homage. The pile stays the same size over the years, since some people take away a stone as a memento."

I took the plastic bag from her and poured some sand into her hand and my own.

"Our ritual of homage will be pouring sand into the pile. No one will ever carry our grains of sand away. This will seal our deal."

For a memento, rather than take someone else's stone, I led Christine to a cleared area near the cabin where there were stumps in the ground arranged in a large diamond pattern.

"When Thoreau left the cabin, Emerson, the owner of the land, asked him to plant pines in what had been Thoreau's bean field. Thoreau did—in a diamond pattern. The trees were all knocked down by a hurricane in the 1930s. But the stumps still hold the pattern. To hold a piece of the stump wood in your hand is like touching a sacramental relic. Almost like a piece of the True Cross. So, pick a stump."

She pointed. "How about that one? It also has two saplings growing right next to it. They'll stand for you and me." She added with a snap of thumb and finger, "How's that for an improvised ritual?"

When we got close and knelt down beside the stump, we saw pollinating moths flitting between tiny flowers on the saplings. I asked Christine coyly, "What do you suppose the moths stand for in your ritual?"

The fragment of wood I broke off the stump was roughly the shape and size of a good trout. Later, I mounted the piece in a wooden frame and gave it to Christine. It now hangs above the desk where I write this reminiscence.

At the end of the summer, we took the kids to Ellsworth—the biggest town in the area—to shop for their back-to-school clothes. We also took them to the dentist, then to the airport for their trip back to Helen in Virginia. We loaded up the car and the trailer and traveled through Pennsylvania endlessly again and back to Christine's house in West Lafayette, Indiana. The school year began.

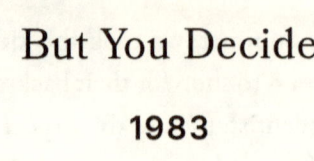

But You Decide

1983

You will see deliverance.
—Exodus 14

Trouble for Christine started on her first day back in her office in the fall after we were married. An older colleague walked in unannounced, called her his girlfriend, and said he wanted to give her a hug. Christine asked him not to call her that. He laughed her off. He said similar things to her during following visits and she tried to be firm in telling him politely not to talk to her that way.

"It makes me very uncomfortable."

"It's okay. I'm just having fun."

She wasn't sure what the legal status of his unwanted behavior was. So, she met with the campus police for clarification. She was told her colleague's behavior met the criterion for sexual harassment. She then went to her department head in the business school to ask him to intervene. He told her just to ignore the problem. "That's just him."

Sometime later, she was told her contract with the business school would not be renewed.

When news of this got out, many women on the Purdue faculty begged Christine to file a suit against the university.

"Yours is the best case we've had so far to address this kind of thing, which is rampant all over the place here."

I told Christine she should fight it too. But she said no.

She really didn't like teaching in the business school anyway.

And now, no matter how anything went after this, she would find it impossible. She began applying for other teaching jobs.

I told her to see what kind of offers she got. But if it meant both of us leaving Purdue, I'd give up tenure and go with her and try to get what work I could.

"I learned my lesson again to let the woman take the lead."

"I'm not going to ask you to do that," she said.

For the rest of the school year, she applied for jobs all over the country. I continued to go on the road presenting *Gumption* to farm groups. Invitations for interviews at universities around the country poured into her mailbox. The phone rang a lot. Professors of accounting are a rare commodity since getting a doctorate in accounting easily led to lucrative positions in industry. She received five invitations from universities in Boston alone. Together the five arranged to pay her expenses for a week's visit to all of them.

That was extraordinary. Especially in comparison to my experience. I applied to every university she did. Most never acknowledged the letter. At this point in time, no universities needed another literature teacher, especially one who taught the Bible as literature, medical ethics, and the arguments of farming.

I called up the chair of the English department at Boston University while Christine was being interviewed there. The chair, in some exasperation said, "Half the faculty here are adjuncts. We have no openings. We get dozens of unsolicited requests like yours. The dean of the business school wants to hire your wife and hopes we can take you on, too, as a sweetener. I'm sorry." She burst into tears and hung up the phone.

The only offer we got that included me was from Clarkson University in Upstate New York. Neither of us had ever heard of the place. Clarkson was building an accounting program and was eager to hire Christine. It turned out the humanities program followed a great-books-model curriculum. One of the great books was the Bible. Currently no one on the faculty had any background in the Bible. I was offered a half-time, one-year adjunct position on probation for the sabbatical leave year from Purdue I had coming up.

Christine took the accounting job, and I took the Bible as literature job from perhaps the only university in the country besides Purdue that had anything like a regular position for that. Saved by the Good Lady again—one last time. Gospel guidance at another twist in the pilgrimage road. We would decide what to do at the end of teaching a year at Clarkson. I would either return to Purdue alone or resign and take my chances at Clarkson. The dark speck at the end of this tunnel looked adamant.

Christine put her house in Indiana on the market. We moved into a rental apartment in an old schoolhouse in a small village outside of Potsdam. Potsdam itself had two small universities: Clarkson, like Purdue an engineering school, and SUNY Potsdam, one of several dozen small regional colleges in the state system. This one fortuitously had the only music school in the state system. There was lots of free music playing there all the time.

We liked the jobs. She had an esteemed regular position; I, a humble part-time adjunct position. But a wife. And the colleagues in my area were smart and welcoming. The students were just like the students at Purdue in that the best of them were there to study engineering, so they already had to be motivated to do hard work.

Christine called a "table talk" meeting at the end of the first semester. You had to say what was on your mind, listen to the other person, and make a decision.

"I want to give it a try here. Do you want to go back to Purdue? I'm not sure I want you to. But you decide."

"Let's look around for a place to live here. It'll be our home. I'll resign from Purdue. I was going to tell you, yesterday my department chair here upped my position to full-time adjunct for next year. I'll make enough to pay the taxes. If I don't get a permanent job here, I'll look for something else to do. I'm not sure what. But I'll look."

We looked at an old farmhouse for sale in no better shape than Dot's.

"It reminds me of the place where I grew up in Nebraska."

"It reminds me of the Wabash house when Helen and I bought what had been a fishing shack."

"Let's not forget the Maine house with its leaky roof. We should both feel right at home."

The elderly couple who owned it had allowed trees to grow up around all the outside windows. Their shadows darkened every room even when the sun was shining. The floorboards squeaked. The plumbing leaked. The electrical outlets weren't grounded. The basement was dry, however. And we were impressed to see rafters in the basement and that under the roof still had bark on the rough unplanned sides. The core of the house dated from 1826 and was still standing.

While we were making up our minds—whether I wanted to live in and restore yet another decrepit house, we spent weekends walking the roads that spread out from the driveway to see what kind of neighborhood we would be getting into. One thing we already liked while walking right down the middle of the mostly empty road that ran in front of the house was that, probably because the property was seven miles outside the village, it was very quiet, with little traffic. No sirens or students shouting.

Another benefit of buying the house was the 160 acres of woods that went with it. Along with that, a short distance down the road from the house, between the road and the surrounding woods, and part of the land that went with the house, was a well-established beaver pond. We could see an active lodge at one end piled with sticks and mud twelve feet high; no coyote was going to be able to dig through that. The dam was very high at the woodsy edge of the pond but very solid since bushes and trees had taken root on top. But the pond looked shallow and was choked with lily pads from end to end.

"It's the same size as that part of the lake I could see from the windows of Shadowbrook."

"It doesn't look like we could swim in it," Christine said with some disappointment in her voice.

"I wonder if the plants die down and the water freezes for skating in the winter," I said hopefully. "We'll have to ask someone about that."

After scouting around the pond on one visit, we got back on the road and kept walking until reaching another farmhouse. This one had an active barn surrounded by fenced fields filled with dairy cows. An elderly couple sat rocking on two chairs on their porch. They waved us over as we were walking by.

"Lemonade?"

They were Argie and Madelaine.

Christine told them, "We're trying to make up our minds about buying the farmhouse down the road to the north of yours. How long have you lived here?"

"As long as the twentieth century is old," Madelaine said proudly.

"You've had a head start on us," Christine quipped.

"What about the big pond between your house and ours? Can you skate on it in the wintertime?" I asked them hopefully.

Argie said, "Well, yes, if you're lucky. After the first frost, the plants all sink down, and the water freezes smooth when it gets cold. But you've got to be lucky to get on the pond before the snow comes and ruins it. We've skated on it with our kids our whole lives. Our son runs the farm now. His kids sometimes get to skate on the pond. And sometimes, when the ice gets really thick, we'll plow the snow off with a tractor. We know the pond comes with the place you're thinking of buying, but we've always considered it belonging to anyone who wants to use it. I used to trap beaver there, but I don't anymore. They got the right to live here just like we do."

Christine quickly assured him, "If we buy the house and get the pond too, please skate on it just like you're used to."

"Well, thank you, that's kind of you to say, but we don't do that kind of thing anymore. Nowadays we just drive by and look at the geese and ducks in the fall and spring. But we'll be sure to tell our grandkids it's okay to skate."

Waving a hand toward his wife, Argie continued, "When we were kids, your pond was once a large potato field with a stream running through it. Before the beavers moved in. You'll find a foundation next to it that marks the house of an old lady we knew as kids who used to sit on the porch smoking a pipe."

"That was early in the century, when we were five," his wife Madeleine added, handing us each a piece of pie. "That's when Argie and I first met. And it was right here! Our house now was the schoolhouse we attended then. I remember the first day. Looking over in the corner where he was sitting then—and he's sitting right outside now in the same corner as was then—I said to myself, 'That Argie is some cute.' We've been together ever since."

"That's because I'm still cute at ninety," Argie chuckled, striking a pose with a crooked smile.

Madelaine added, "And he's still mouthy about it. Our house is related to yours, did you know? I mean if you buy it. Our teacher in this school was Mrs. Doud, who lived in the farmhouse you're thinking about. She raised sheep there. We used to sled down her hill in the winter."

Christine sounded intrigued. "It's interesting that your house used to be a school. We're renting an apartment in another building that used to be a school too. Are there a lot of them?"

"Yes," Madeline said. "There used to be more than thirty one-room schoolhouses between here and Potsdam. That's because the school had to be close enough to where kids lived for them to be able to get to it every day by walking or riding a horse. No school buses then. Still, lots of learning. But as you can see, we never learned enough to move away."

"It doesn't look like you had any need to," Christine said.

After the visit, we walked back down the road to the house we were considering; this time, instead of asking for another look around inside, we took a path behind the house that curved down to the right bank of the West Branch of the Saint Regis River that actually ran through the property. We found a tumble of great gray boulders and sat on one. We listened to the sound of the river.

Christine broke the silence. "I like the neighbors—both the people and the beavers," she said. "This is a good place."

"We like it better each time we see it, which I've heard is a good sign."

"Let's make an offer," said Christine decisively. And we kissed on that.

"Now are you sure you're willing to give up tenure at Purdue to start a new career teaching here? Are we going to live here together?"

"Yes," I said at once. "This is the next twist in the pilgrimage for me of teaching the Bible as literature, which is what I've been doing for years now. It's just the same when I close the classroom door and start to talk. But when I open it again and drive home, I want to find you there."

I meant it. But it hurt. I cherished the only life I had made on my own. Leaving Purdue would be like leaving the Jesuits, not knowing who I was if I walked away again.

It would turn out to be another turn or twist in the road of the same pilgrimage I was already on. And at this point, I was almost used to this, almost felt that taking this next blind step was another in the natural errancy of my life.

It's a hunk of Fordite too, I thought. *All these places and ways of life and things I do that layer on each other, without seeing any one of them coming beforehand.*

Our next experience of the culture of the area was a profound act of generosity that followed from our decision. It validated sticking to the program we had chosen for ourselves—almost a sign from on high.

The owners insisted on a selling price that was two thousand dollars more than we could afford. Christine was still paying the mortgage on her Indiana house, as I was on the Maine house. Mr. Plumley, the local realtor, was a longtime friend of the sellers. He argued with them to accept our offer.

"It's the first you've received in ten years. No one before even came back to look at the place a second time. I know you're ready to move to Florida."

They would not budge. In exasperation, Mr. Plumley decided to forgo his commission fee in order to shrink to zero the gap between the asking price and the offer. The deal went through.

The house certainly was a mess to start with. Every time we took a step inside, something broke. A pipe began leaking. A split floorboard popped loose. Some large sheets of fake wood paneling were propped against the open studs for a renovation project that stalled.

Christine said ruefully, "I think the problem is we walk around differently than the old folks did here for fifty years. The house gets nervous about the new vibrations, and to paraphrase Dot Gray, 'what's already split, breaks.'"

"It reminds me of flushing the toilet for the first time in my Wabash River house and seeing a geyser of water erupt in the lawn."

We renovated with middle-class aspirations in our hearts. We tore out walls and brought the plumbing, wiring, and interior design up to date. We made most of the downstairs one large open space with areas for cooking, eating, and sitting before the woodstove in the winter.

On weekends and holidays, I began systematically clearing the old sheep pastures around the house of the sumac bushes and early invasive birch trees that had grown up where sheep no longer grazed.

One evening, while the kids were asleep, Christine convened another table talk.

"Our original agreement, 'prenup,' included my promise to spend summers with you in Maine. I'll stick to that if you insist. But what if we instead decided to settle into one place and stay in New York year-round. Less travel. And we've gotten ourselves into another house that needs work. Isn't it time, do you think, to 'simplify, simplify, simplify,' as your buddy Thoreau urges? Like I said, I'll stick to my promise if you insist."

We put the Maine house on the market. It sold in one day—with the shortage of working-class housing in an area dominated by the homes of rich summer people. I made four times the amount of money from the sale that Helen and I had paid for the place. Once again,

Helen had been right about the decision to buy the place to begin with. It was my only and best venture as a businessman. We sold two acres of pasture to Sami Gray that lay adjacent between us.

The New York place had already begun taking hold of how we lived—almost as if we were being guided by Dot Gray's invisible hand. It began by leveling a patch of ground terraced on a south-facing slope that would be a good place for a garden. I had never cultivated one before, although I had watched closely how Dot did. Christine, of course, was a seasoned veteran.

We bought seeds and books for me to read. The garden doubled in size two years running. It became addictive. Salad greens, tomatoes, and cucumbers to start; then corn, potatoes, squash, beans, peas, pumpkins, eggplant, carrots, and so on, row after row. For six months of the year we could get by eating only our own fresh vegetables. We canned enough to get through the winters. She taught accounting. I taught the Bible as literature.

Weeds popped up. Bugs ate plant leaves. A ravaging woodchuck family raided to wipe out what the nibbling rabbits missed. The weather could conspire against the garden with too little or too much rain. The frost could come late in the spring, or early in the fall.

In our second year, crows descended into the garden just as the first green sprouts of the corn poked their way clear of the soil. The sprouts were little green flags showing the crows where the still mostly ungerminated kernels were hiding. I replanted the corn. Then the crows did it again.

I got up before dawn one day and hid behind the woodshed waiting for the crows. As soon as one alighted on the ground, I stood up, shouted, and took a shot with a .22 in the general direction of the crows, missing of course. But then I cut out a cardboard shape of what I thought looked like a dead crow with its limp wings extended. I glued on feathers from an old cushion, and spray painted it black. I hung the effigy from a pole in the middle of the garden. And by gum, it worked! No crows ever came back to raid the corn again—and for years afterward. The original crows taught their young to stay away.

"You don't want to mess with that nasty man," they told them in Crow.

I spray-painted pebbles red, the shade of strawberries, and sowed them among our plants while new berries were still green. The chipmunks that gnawed and the birds that pecked the painted pebbles gave up on the garden before the real berries came ripe.

Both tactics were satisfying, of course, and fun. Applying an "organic pesticide," you could say. But the skirmish was only the opening salvo. Christine and I and my son Vlad, when he came in the summer, crawled through plants, pulling up unending invading weeds and pinching off crop-sucking bugs. Some stank, like the stink bugs on the squash we tweezered off into a can and then stomped to death on a rock.

I built a fence around the garden to keep out the woodchucks and the rabbits. They tunneled in anyway. So, I strung electric wire on the fence. One day, while I was walking outside the garden, I noticed some Colorado potato bugs on the luxuriant potato greens above ground. I leaned over the low split rail fence on which was affixed the electric shock wires. As I reached out to pluck and pinch a bug—to prop myself—I inadvertently pressed my knees against the electric fence wire. At first nothing happened, since I was wearing rubber boots that insulated me from the shock. But as soon as I touched the potato bug, my finger grounded through the bug, and I got hit with an electric shock powerful enough to knock me back flat to the ground. In my whirling mind I thought in dismay, *The bugs have superpowers!*

There's an old Chinese proverb: "The best fertilizer is the footstep of the gardener." In other words, "If you want to live out of your garden, you have to live in it and wear hobnailed boots!" What's missing in the naturalist myth about gardening with images of baskets of vegetables and a happy person whistling at the birds while cultivating is that gardening exposes a person to the rough edges of the natural world. Things eating other things. Weeds seeding themselves and sucking up the fertility and moisture of the soil the good plants need. Unsympathetic rain and drought and winds and frost. The gardener walks the border in his mind between green, quiet rows of organic produce and ravenous nature, red in tooth and claw, trying to rip it apart.

Brer Rabbit Punching the Tar Baby

1990

I know my sheep and my sheep know me.
—John 10:14

I stood by a chair in the kitchen after breakfast. I listened with some trepidation as Christine, again, announced it was time for another table talk. This was our standard ritual, whereby each spoke truthfully, without irony, about what we were doing and what we should be doing. We each had to listen.

She said with a solemn tone, "Dearly beloved, you've received your tenure here again. It's clear to both of us you're not likely to get another job anywhere else, or another shot at tenure. You've found your place—your only place, the place to die for, and eventually, to die in."

"Ouch. That's pretty heavy. Let me think about that for a minute. Pour me another cup of coffee."

"Take your time. I need to brew another pot."

She got up from the table to grab a bag of coffee beans to grind.

Ominously, her tone hinted, I was about to be impelled toward another station in the pilgrimage.

She was right about my prospects for the few academic humanities jobs that occasionally did come open. In my academic career, I had by now published seven books, one a translation of Horace's Latin *Odes*, another on Luke's Gospel as literature—with a special chapter on my version of the juxtaposition of Jesus teaching at the lake with Herod cutting off John's head. A bona fide Bible as literature book after all; my Gospel guidance never stopped pushing me this way and that.

I had won five teaching awards. But all this was too eclectic, unfocused—improvised one could say—to fit me into any tight professorial slot, as they were always elsewhere. I was fortunate to get as far as I did. I taught the Bible as literature in the only two places where it was taught. Which was a kind of minor coup that earned me no clout anywhere else.

A student who was a drummer in a jazz band once asked if I listened to jazz. "Your class sessions work like a jazz piece. You establish a theme each class, then start free associating impressions of the book under discussion, calling on students by name for reactions, and then extrapolating from what was said, as if after you set the theme and tone, you call for solos of improv yourself."

"Yes, I think you're right. Actually, even before I learned to love jazz, I had found my own mind worked through a process of improvising on themes brought forth by bringing images of different things together."

I continued to wonder about the authenticity of this way of thinking—either as it got transformed into a way of praying or as it morphed into a style of teaching. I looked into precedents outside my own experience. One approach was to see these mental movements as internalizing the rhetorical trick called *parataxis*. That is the juxtaposition of words or images without describing any relationship between them, except by their very proximity. The classic example is Julius Caesar's boast: "I came. I saw. I conquered." Caesar leaves the audience to assume that he was a man of decisive, thoughtful action and just the man to lead the nation. The logical gaps in the rhetoric allow the audience to imagine whatever connecting tissue of meaning they wish—and even to imagine they themselves are the authors of what they imagine. A more recent delightful example is Winston Churchill's speech late in the winter of 1942 before the Canadian Parliament in the midst of WWII. He said that in order to justify their own shameful capitulation to the Nazi's attack in 1940, the French Vichy puppet government predicted, "In three weeks England will have her neck wrung like a chicken."

Churchill brought down the house with his paratactic flourish—"Some chicken! Some neck!" He was the chicken. His ample neck allowed him to hold his head high as—he implies without making an overt boast—"I am the man who so far as saved England from such a fate."

Rhetorical parataxis is a technique of public speaking, of course. But it works because it plays off the way all thinking takes place. In Albert Einstein's phrase from a letter to Jacques A. Hadamard, "Combinatory play seems to be the essential feature in productive thought." This falls close to what Saint Ignatius called *the composition*, or what I call *second thoughts*. Close enough to consider it a valid rule of thumb.

I needed to be cautious. To plumb one's way of thinking back to something essential about thinking itself runs the real danger of pretentiously justifying something personal, trivial, (how your own brain works) by tracing it back to some core of underlying wisdom. "I think—therefore I am as smart as anybody."

So, I proffered to myself an extended experiment to test the idea. The experiment grew from a dilemma facing anyone teaching college freshmen composition, as I did for forty years. At the beginning of my teaching career, I was frustrated about the amount of plagiarism and cheating in student papers, which grew worse as increasingly greater masses of writing and information became available at the snap of a finger on a computer screen. Some students became adept at finessing others' words into their papers.

So, I assigned what might appear to be absurdist topics. "Begin with a scene from Homer's *Odyssey* and another from a Donald Duck comic book. Cite the scenes. Select evidence. Speculate what's to be gained from reading them against each other. Prove it."

The students would groan when they heard such an assignment. I'd say to them, "Look, this is a teaching exercise. No big corporation is ever going to hire you to figure out a connection like this. But it is going to hire you to figure out how to resolve a persistent problem in management or engineering or science that the existing data doesn't yet explain on its own. Consider topics like this mental calisthenics to tone you up before getting called up to play in the big leagues."

Initially, I'd find that one-third of the students could figure out how to do the assignment right off. Another third never could. The third in the middle could do it if they got lots of assignments graded and returned to them quickly for a tight feedback loop, and then got a chance to talk to me in private. That middle group provided the most exciting field for a teacher to work in.

It required a student to excise genuine, original ingenuity to point out—for just one example of where you could go with the assignment—that the original mythic hero Odysseus could carry on conversations with different people speaking different languages, as well as with monsters and gods and animals, without a translator. And then that Donald, a duck, could speak English to other ducks as well as other kinds of animals, and like Odysseus, talk his way out of any mess he found himself in.

Underlying both their stories could be found the entertaining comfort that any intelligent being, at root, spoke the same language as any other. Translations could always be found. That extended to between languages, as say using math or science to translate raw data into a working hypothesis.

Sometimes for a puzzle to solve, I'd ask a desperate student initially trapped in the second group to select two items on my office desk—say a broken pencil and my car keys.

"Okay, right now, tell me something both of them say about who you think I am."

Possible answer: "Works hard, but not so hard that he isn't eager to go home." Another example would be to ask, "From the way a cat walks and the way its body is shaped, what is a cat?" Possible answer: "A stealthy predator."

To call this teaching strategy "experimental," it should produce verifiable or validating results by studying student successes over time. But it was impossible to trace all my students from college to career. There were many of them. They flowed in and out of my classrooms as salmon swimming in currents in a river. In addition, successful college students are taught by the whole faculty, the whole experience of living away from home and thinking about unexpected things. So, I could provide no longitudinal studies that would isolate the variable of those few who took courses from me.

Nevertheless, there was anecdotal evidence. After their initial suspicion, the students didn't seem to mind the assignments and became deft at them. As I mentioned earlier, another useful technique I used, before handing back edited papers at the end of class, was reading out loud a good line or phrase in a paper—with praise and even appreciative analysis—especially from a paper with a lot of red ink scribbled over its errors. Thar's gold in them thar hills. The student whose paper was chosen would glow while you read. Like Ruth had at Purdue. Then the student's face would wrinkle with consternation to behold the red ink bleeding across the essay I handed back. There was another example of the juxtaposition of opposites—praise and criticism—that the teacher would hope might, in Paul Ricoeur's term, "give rise to thought" in the student.

For a sample size of one, as evidence the teaching trick could work, one former student I had in class at Purdue as an undergraduate grew up to eventually become my dean at Clarkson. When we met in the hallway once, the dean confided, "Your writing teaching stuff was good. Look where it's gotten me." We both laughed.

It occurred to me, during this tightly packed digression about my praying and teaching career that Christine's table talk announcement triggered, that one advantage to working in underrated universities like Purdue and Clarkson was that none of the academics in any of the major universities took any interest in what I was doing, which was a kind of freedom. It was the noble Lady of the Bible as literature that had shown me an errant path to a comfortable success as a teacher, writer, husband and father, gardener, and as a clearer of pastures. Could all of that taken together validate the very method of reading the Bible as literature—the engine that pulled the other cars? At least living like the Bible was composed made *one* life possible.

Christine returned with a steaming pot and two mugs. She continued. "So. Let's decide to settle here regardless, and as Voltaire said to Candide, 'cultivate your own garden.'"

"I am happy to agree, since that means we don't have to worry about finding another place to live—for good. And we are already doing fine gardening."

After Christine secured a mutual agreement to "Let's stay here," she took another deep breath and the next logical step: "Let's raise sheep."

I gulped, "Where did that idea come from?" as I knocked over a cup of coffee.

"Listen to me," she said emphatically. "Their grazing will keep down the brush we've cleared. We both learned to eat lamb from Dot. We've got the right place for it. We know from deed records and what the neighbors say that previous owners raised sheep here. We lived next door to Dot while she raised Baby. We can always call her for advice. We can read books like you did when we started gardening. We can take a course. We can ask other local people who raise sheep how to do it.

"You'll like it. We'll be 'pastoral' in ways different from those ancient barefoot Greek shepherds you read about wooing nymphs in the undergrowth. For real. And there were certainly lots of sheep running around in the Bible. Right up your alley."

Following my general philosophy of always letting the woman take the lead, I took an extension course in sheep raising. I found a shepherd named Shortie who sold us six starter black-headed Suffolk sheep and promised he'd be available day or night to give us any advice we needed.

One night at 3 a.m. on a cold spring March with the temperatures at fifteen below zero, I walked to the barn in the moonlight. I heard loosening sheets of ice grinding in the high water of the spring runoff on the West Branch of the St. Regis River that ran through our land. When I got inside the barn, a ewe was still lying on the floor two hours after I had gone back to the house for a break. She was exhausted from trying to birth a lamb that seemed stuck inside. Our Great Pyrenees sheep guard dog Sirius was lying next to the ewe giving helpless comfort.

With a phone crooked between my shoulder and ear, at the end of a long, coiled cord attached to the wall of the barn, I asked my sheep mentor Shorty the shepherd for advice on how to pull out a lamb with a head too big for the ewe to expel naturally.

"She's been rolling around on the floor for two hours, grunting." I sighed wearily. By now, I was leaning against the large warm body of Sirius (named after the Dog Star) who lived in the barn with the sheep and kept predators at bay by just smelling like something the coyotes didn't want to mess with or woofing at lesser vermin like raccoons and foxes intent upon our chickens.

"Feet against her thighs," Shortie ordered. "It won't hurt her. Tie a cord around the lamb's hooves; it won't hurt the lamb either. Curl into a ball, stretch out, and pull!"

With a groan from both the ewe and me, I cried, "It's out! Bless you, Shortie!"

Shortie chuckled and said, "I'm going back to bed."

The lamb lay flopping and gasping on the barn floor packed with manure-laden straw, about the size of a salmon finning in the shallows after I'd landed one. I cleared its nostrils of the slimy, bloody birth sack, held the lamb with one hand, and dragged it over to the ewe's teat with the other. The ewe wasn't ready for that and kicked both me and the lamb. I pinned the ewe against the side of the pen with my shoulder and, with one hand pulling the teat tight, tried to pull the lamb over with the other. At this point the ewe began shitting black pellets in my face, which initially I didn't mind since that appeared to calm the ewe down enough—after all, she was getting a chance to make her point clear about the business going on.

Nonetheless, squinting my eyes mostly shut (like at the Boy Scout Jamboree) against the splatter of pellets, I finally pulled the lamb over, squeezed its cheeks, and attached the little warm, wet mouth around the leathery teat. Once the lamb held on, I fingered the lamb's anus—what the sheep-raising books said was the stimulus for a lamb starting to suck. And the lamb began to suck.

While I kept the ewe pinned until the lamb got enough colostrum in its stomach to weather the late winter cold—the ewe continued to pepper my face with pellets. I laughed in spite of myself, just like the father in the poem "The Night Before Christmas."

Here I am with a doctorate, letting a sheep shit in my face. Why am I doing this? It's winter; it's 3 a.m.; I'm tired; my colleagues are asleep in their own clean, warm beds and Christine in ours. I grew up next to the sea. I lived like a monk. Where does this scene fit?

This time I tossed in Plato's theory of reminiscence.

Plato believed in reincarnation. A person could get back to what had been important in a previous life by reminiscing about what was important in *this* life and thus get closer to understanding not only who he or she really was but what endured over time and so was eternally true. One followed second thoughts back to the truth. The truth was I had loved the stink of low tide and the dirty septic beds of Shadowbrook. Pretty much like manure on a barn floor. I had always followed my nose.

The steaming, slimy, wiggling truth on the floor of the barn and the effort it took pulling it free and giving it a chance expressed my sense of the meaning of living on the edge of where food became excrement and life went dead but shook itself free again. The oysters and the rats and the cats, the linked horseshoe crabs, crayfish clinging to the corpse of a dead salmon, "Everything that is holy now," in Blake's phrase. Or maybe, "Truth is Beauty; Beauty Truth; that's all you know on earth, and all you need to know" in Keats's. Or Frost's holy "scraping and cheeping" of life.

As an old hymn put it: "How do I know? The Bible tells me so."

Gun Bona Fides

1998

. . . never walk alone in the darkness.
—John 8:12

I stood in the driveway in slippers on a cold and windy winter's night. A few minutes earlier, I had taken a shot with a .22 over the head of a fierce-looking, barking dog that was leaping outside the fence of the west sheep pasture.

"Don't shoot, goddammit," and some other curses rang in the air. A few minutes later three pickup trucks came roaring into the driveway, with angry men pouring out.

"We're coon hunters," they yelled. "Coon hunters have legal rights to follow a coon dog following a coon—even over private property." This was startling news.

The dog was actually, I was soon to find out, leaping at the fence to get at a raccoon that had been treed in the lower branches of an apple tree in the pasture.

I yelled back, "I raise sheep, and what was I supposed to do when in the middle of the night I find a rabid dog jumping up against my sheep fence?"

"He's not rabid," they shouted.

I could see Christine looking out the second-floor window of our bedroom. She looked calm, as if watching a play unfold—say the last scene of *Hamlet* before the bodies fall.

Vlad, who was visiting, had followed me outside. He was chatting and chuckling with one of his friends whose father was one of the shouting men. Vlad knew him from playing box lacrosse locally whenever he visited. The sons looked like they were enjoying themselves. I began to feel a little foolish yelling.

I held up a hand.

"I didn't hit the dog. You didn't get the coon. And I don't care if you have a legal right to run a dog on my land in the middle of the night. I raise sheep! What do you expect me to do in the middle of the night when I hear a dog barking in my sheep pasture? Do you expect me to say to myself, 'Oh don't worry, it's probably just my neighbors having some fun'?"

Everyone more or less calmed down. The men went out and retrieved the dog. By this time the coon had run off. I never heard from the dog or the men again. Or the coon.

If gardening brought us to live on the edge between benevolent rows of vegetables and the hostile natural world, so raising livestock brought us to live on the edge of the world of feral dogs and men with guns.

Several months later, a month before Easter, when Christine and I got home in the evening from school, we heard a funny noise coming from the barn. I took the .22 again to investigate. This time I found a feral dog was ripping out the entrails of a dozen pregnant ewes. I tried to corral the dog, with the idea to test it for rabies. It kept running back, and then lunging at me. After it lunged back at a bleeding sheep, I shot the dog and called the sheriff's office.

A deputy came out to the crime scene. He looked at the wounded sheep and the dead dog.

"You know, I could arrest you for shooting a dog without knowing who it belongs to."

Before I got over the shock to protest, the deputy smiled and said, "But no jury would ever convict you." The town tax assessor showed up with the deputy. The assessor told me some of the money from dog licenses went into a fund for compensating farmers from dog attacks on livestock.

Looking at the pile of bloodied sheep up against the back wall of the barn he said, "I figure roughly, you'll get forty-five dollars."

"It's good to hear that," I said sarcastically. "But it won't cover a vet's fee."

After both men left, I spent most of the night pushing sheep guts back into their bodies and sewing their leathery hides closed with a large needle and black thread Christine provided. All the patients survived and went on to give birth to healthy lambs at Eastertide. Resurrection all over again.

Several months earlier, Vlad saved me from an even more frightening encounter with the barrels of a gun.

Vlad had come down for a visit. Christine had encouraged us to go down to the pond and skate. "It's a beautiful New Year's Eve night, quiet and cold and washed in full moonlight. You can come back later, and we can watch the ball drop and have a drink."

We had just pulled on our skates when a man emerged out of the shadows pointing a double-barreled shotgun at my head and shouting, "You get the hell out of here."

I was flabbergasted. And looking right down the two holes of oblivion, I quavered, "We're just here to skate," pointing at my feet.

"You heard me—git," he said with a bit of an alcoholic slur.

Foolishly trying to sound reasonable, I trembled, "But I own the pond."

The man growled "No you ain't." I could hear him cocking the weapon, the tick of hammers being pulled back—another one of those little sounds that opens up holes into another universe.

Vlad broke in and said tensely, "Pop, get back in the truck. We'll do what he says." I drove the pickup truck back to the house with my skates on.

When we got back to the house and told Christine what happened, she was alarmed, of course, and demanded we call the sheriff right away. I hesitated.

I was afraid. "If we get whoever this guy was mad, he'll come after us later."

"Right now," she repeated. By this time, it was two in the morning on New Year's Day.

The two deputies were alert and genial as they stood in the living room taking down our stories. One was blond, the other dark-haired, and with their hats off inside you could see they both had butch cuts. They already knew who the guy with the gun was by his MO, and where he lived.

"Are you going to press charges?"

I hesitated again.

"Pop . . ." said Vlad, exasperated again with my timidity.

Christine barked, "Of course you will."

The deputies took the man with the gun to be arraigned at the local justice of the peace, Wayne Williams, who was a friend of ours. He told us later that when he typed in the man's name, thirty-six pages of the man's rap sheet slithered through the justice system's fax machine. It turned out this time he had poached a deer out of season and hidden it in the brush near the pond. In his alcohol-muddled mind, he was afraid we had come to steal it.

The sheep farm location profoundly affected our lives beyond the lure of the garden and the barn and the pond and our good neighbors. We lived on the edge of the divide between village gentility and rural vitality. The road in front of the house delineated the outside limit of the Potsdam Village School district, seven miles north of the village center. Potsdam was home to both Clarkson University and a campus of the SUNY, which housed the Crane School of Music. We didn't know at the beginning of moving in that wonderful music by students, faculty, and visiting artists was available just down the road, much of it free. "Oh Fortuna!"

We didn't live in the village—just within its cultural embrace.

Many of our neighbors who lived even a little farther out from the village than we did—on the far side of our front road—needed to send their kids to a rural school system. Those families rode four wheelers and owned pickup trucks, often with gun racks in the back window. Many worked in nearby Massena (almost equidistant from our house as Potsdam) at one of four large manufacturing plants run by Alcoa, Reynolds, and General Motors. The plants took advantage of the cheap electrical power generated by the mass hydroelectric dams on the Saint Lawrence River that provided the water depths for the locks that brought ocean shipping into the Great Lakes.

There had been deep blue-collar prosperity for forty years. And the workers, many of our neighbors, were resourceful. A number of families on our road lived in houses they themselves had built on land inherited that used to be small farmsteads. They were the equivalent of the people on the road in Maine who built boats.

"All this skill in the hands," I would say with admiration.

Some of these handy neighbors would help us build our own barn and do renovations on our place. But they also held guns. We often heard firing, counterpoint to the snarl of chainsaws detonating in the background, and sometimes too close for comfort.

On yet *another* occasion, I complained to a neighbor who lived nearby about his continual, unnerving target practice.

"We can hear you shooting when we're trying to relax on the deck after work. So, at least, please don't shoot in the evening." The shooting continued. Later I found a dead squirrel in the mailbox. Then a pile of dog shit.

I called the sheriff again, just to ask this time if we had any recourse beyond a friendly conversation with our neighbor.

"Unfortunately, no. As long as there is a certain distance between properties—and there is—and a safe background behind the targets, all is perfectly legal. Of course, it is a federal crime to tamper with your mailbox. But you'd need some solid evidence to prove that guy put the squirrel in it."

But a week or so later, a sheriff's car did stop at the farmhouse. The officer asked if there was still gunfire, and we said yes. The deputy said nothing more than we had already been told but expressed sympathy. He drove away. Whatever he did after that, the shooting stopped.

"Liberals like us," Christine noted, "usually automatically want more gun control. Most of our neighbors hate that, and if there's any single voting issue around here, it's anti-gun-control. But it's curious, nobody ever shoots anybody around here. They hunt deer, often shooting more than the law allows, for meat for the family. Otherwise, there'd be even more collisions with deer on our roads. They poach fish for food too, have gardens, and often with friends and family build their own houses on land inherited from the family."

"There's improvised justice in this land," I agreed, following up on her thinking.

Christine responded thoughtfully, "Maybe we're just far enough away from the settlements so even the rules get blurred in the trees."

"The deputies improvise just like jazz musicians."

"We inhabit edge habitat. Right on the edge between often different things or people, we weigh both sides in the scales. It's the having 'second thoughts' thing, which we're bound to do if we keep living our kind of life right next to, right along the same road as these people living another life. Or like you, the man conveniently living on the edge right alongside me, the woman," Christine said impishly, and placed my hand upon her breast, which I squeezed gently.

"About you," I whispered huskily, "I never have second thoughts."

As our form of play along these lines of rule, Christine and I made clear to neighbors our gun bona fides. We allowed an extended family to hunt deer and waterfowl on the large wood lot and adjacent pond. We allowed another young man to trap—"always sustainably," he promised. "Just enough to stimulate a gradual increase in the species population." But he agreed, "No beaver."

We cultivated a beaver population explosion. Beavers were left on their own to build dams to contain small ponds to back up the overflow rivulet from the big pond—all the way down a corridor through the woods between two stony ridges. It was another flow of water through the woods like the stream that froze that winter on the far end of Lake Mahkeenac.

Under the guidance of a local forester, we permitted the wood lot to be logged three times in forty years of ownership. One of those times, when many trees had stopped growing after a bad ice storm broke off the crowns, we kept three men employed for three months harvesting timber.

One veneer-grade black cherry tree fetched five thousand dollars. We milled some of the hemlock they cut into the timbers used for the framing of the sheep barn. Hemlock under shelter gets harder with time. Now I can't drive a nail into a stud without bending it.

The sheriff deputies who presided over the Pax Ruritana on both sides of the road were usually young and always genial, and we called upon them occasionally for other problems. The road in front of the house had been one of the roads to the town dump when we first moved. Garbage would fly off the back of pickup trucks, which rarely had the required tarp. I carried a large plastic bag whenever I walked the road with the dog and policed the shoulders. I separated out the returnable cans, which I gave to a neighbor woman who was a serious scavenger. She earned enough to provide her daughter spending money at college.

Eventually, the town closed the dump about the same time towns all over the country did, shifting to transfer stations for environmental reasons. Almost immediately, certain citizens started skipping transfer fees by dumping garbage along roadsides, and even along the dirt roads in our woods.

I found a pile of garbage bags on the road going into our woods. I called the sheriff's office again.

Over the phone, a deputy said, "You need proof of a name before any charges can be filed. Look through the bags for a mailing envelope with a name and address. If you find one, call us back."

I descended upon the pile of garbage with glee, toting a fifty-five gallon black plastic garbage bag. Wearing surgical gloves, I picked through the pile while filling the bag, looking for a tell-tale envelope.

Eureka! A doctor's appointment card with a name on it the dumper hadn't filtered out. A deputy came to the farm.

When he saw the name on the card, he barked sharply, "Oh, *that* guy! I know where he lives. He'll get a ticket. But do you want to have him come and pick up the garbage?"

"No," I replied. "I've already taken bags of it to the transfer station myself."

"How much did that cost you?"

"Twenty-two dollars," I said.

The deputy said, "Wait here. I'll be back."

Later that day the deputy did come back and poured twenty-two dollars' worth of quarters into my hands.

"It's from his change jar," the deputy said with a grin. "Just enough." He had fined the dumper independently of the judicial system.

While we were chatting, Ralph, the turkey tom, made his move. He was smaller than normal turkeys. We were raising about fifty of them a year for the local Thanksgiving market. Local Amish families would process the live birds into nice meat bundles in plastic bags for only two dollars apiece—a cost we passed on to customers happy with local, organically grown, free-range turkeys for the table. We put them out to pasture late in the summer, after a deadly parasite in the soil fatal to turkeys would finish its life cycle. Then the turkeys free-ranged to fatten up some on bugs and grass and seeds.

Ralph was a loner. And sneaky. He kept an eye on me. If I wasn't looking, Ralph would sometimes come up silently behind me. This time, the turkey came up behind the deputy without either of us being aware. Then, as was Ralph's habit, he thrust his head between the deputy's legs, and gobbling sharply, expressed sperm on the ground between the deputy's feet. He gobbled in triumph.

"Hey," both the deputy and I shouted in surprise. For one wild moment I was afraid the deputy was going to be really angry at both Ralph and me.

The deputy laughed out loud instead. "Now, that's some cute. How did you train him to do that?"

"Ralph learned that on his own. That's his name, the turkey."

"That's what I would name him too," the deputy said with a laugh. "He's a ralpher, all right."

Then I was inspired. I could make the deputy happy, thank him, and get rid of an annoyance all at once. "Say, would you like this turkey?"

"Yes, I would," he said quickly, enthusiastically, and expertly picked Ralph up by grabbing him in the elbow of his wings and holding him up to shake him and laugh some more. There was a cardboard box in the garage, and the deputy loaded Ralph into the box, closed the lid, and deposited him in the trunk of the squad car. Again, a square deal made independently of the judicial system.

We got used to the background noises. Gun pops, chain saw snarls, the high-pitched roars of four wheelers and snowmobiles racing down the road over the snow in the winter after I groomed trails in our woods with a borrowed snowmobile. ("We have nine of them; you can borrow one for the winter," said a neighbor.)

We invited friends to use the trails for cross-country skiing (mostly people from the colleges and village). On certain days of the week, to make sure the skiers and snowmobile drivers didn't cross paths, neighborhood snowmobilers were welcome to roam and further groom the trails. We invited the snowmobilers who groomed the trails to ski them—although they never did, living as they did on the other side of the road.

Christine and I lived on the farm longer than either of us had ever lived anyplace else. Bred as liberals, we almost never voted for any winning local political candidate in the rural neighborhood. The main issue in every election was always gun control, which the local men always feared occurred on a slippery slope toward prohibition.

We gained local respectability and drew electricity from solar panels. Recycled. Heated with wood from our woods I cut and split and stacked. We sponsored and boarded students from Africa, India, and Colombia through their college years, and later still, a homeless nephew from Boston who needed a quiet place to write a book.

"You have stars in the skies at night," he noted, pointing up through the trees one night, admiringly. "Nothing like that over Boston."

We also, for a decade, shared living with, and eventually nursing Christine's mother until her death.

Closing the Book on the Bible as Literature

1998

Be assured, I am with you always, even to the end of time.
—Matthew 28:20

I stood up next to the chair in front of another dean's desk. The dean had just told me the department would no longer have me offer courses in the Bible as literature. Which was a shock.

I sat down.

The dean said dispassionately, as if he was assigning a driver a new morning milk route, "You've done well with it here. But time's run out. There were forty students who signed for it this year, but only four for next fall. I think the popular interest in religious topics that flourished in the 1960s has petered out (no pun intended). You've got to find some other course you want to teach. Think about it. Course descriptions for next fall are due in a month at the registrar's office."

As was the case in the principal's office, and in the offices of a succession of advisers, department chairs, and deans, the acceptable response to these momentous career-pivoting announcements was to smile, get up, leave the room, and go someplace quiet to nurse the hurts and have second thoughts.

Like Purdue, Clarkson primarily attracted majors in engineering and the sciences, who didn't usually incline to taking literature courses.

Or at least those of the traditional sort that would focus on a great writer like Shakespeare or Wordsworth or the imaginative writings of a particular time period, like say the nineteenth-century novel or medieval poetry. But situated as the university was in a rural, woodsy area of northern New York, it drew on a student body mostly from New England and the mid-Atlantic states, many of whom enjoyed the outdoors and traditional recreations like hunting and fishing and camping.

To try to keep vital the spirit of the forcibly retired Bible as literature course, I outlined a course titled "The Literature of Fishing." The course would begin reading the sublime *The River Runs Through It* as the first book in the course to set the hook. By way of introducing the book, I planned to read my favorite passages from the Gospels about fishing. The stories to shadow the radiant opening line in the novel: "In our family, there was no clear line between religion and fly fishing."

That book would be a good start to the course. It was utterly ravishing writing, and although about the author's growing up with his mother, father, and brother, and so a *bildungsroman*, it's told from the point of view of the author as an old man, standing alone by the river he and his sons used to fish together, mentioning the concern of his friends he was too old to fish anymore. Instead, he reminisces about the fishing and religion all mixed together in their lives.

My take on "the no clear line between religion and fishing" would be that Presbyterians believe in predestination, a harsh doctrine softened by the notion that the preselected elect would radiate God's good intentions by bathing the individual sinner with lots of success in his or her life. Thus, the crisis for the author's Presbyterian father-pastor when the younger son, magically gifted as a fisherman, dies young in a bar brawl.

The first assignment in the fishing lit course would be comparing one scene in the book to its rendering in the movie starring Tom Skerritt, Brad Pitt, Craig Sheffer, and Emily Lloyd (which the students loved, and which gave birth to the rave in the early 1990s for the merchandizing, teaching, and widespread fascination with fly fishing).

Other works included Hemingway's *The Old Man and the Sea* and his short story "Big Two Hearted River." Before being pulled relentlessly out to sea by the massive swordfish the old man, Santiago, hooks from his small rowing boat, he muses, "I would like to fish with the Great Dimaggio. They say his father was a fisherman."

Richard Brautigan's comical and druggy *Trout Fishing in America.* Herman Melville's classic *Moby Dick,* which raised the troubling question long before the births of Hitler or Trump, "What if you discover the captain of your ship is mad, and you can't get off."

Linda Greenlaw's *Hungry Ocean*, the adventures and success of the only woman captain in the North Atlantic sword-fishing fleet. I used this occasion to say in class, "Remember this, you young female students—and you too, you young male students—when you get piped aboard your first working boat. Recall the strong smiling figure on the cover of the book of Linda Greenlaw, with the sea wind tousling her hair as she captains a working boat of rough men better than any other male captain at the time in her fleet. In her book, she continually mentions the tendency of male captains in the fleet to attend too slavishly to fishing in traditional ways. She improvises."

John Casey's *Spartina* was about a fishing village in Rhode Island losing its shore fronts and dockage to the swarm of wealthy summer people building elaborate summer vacation homes. It turned out many of the students who attended Clarkson themselves came from towns and villages rife with similar conflicts between traditional working-class natives and flatlanders from "away." The novel raised to the level of high, entertaining, and even sexy art the students' musings about their own home towns. And reminded me silently of my own growing up in East Norwalk.

In a tongue-in-cheek imitation of the lab-component that many technical and scientific courses at Clarkson required, I offered optional evening instruction in fly tying. One project: to tie at least one original fly out of litter picked up on campus—cigarette butts and pigeon feathers and silver gum wrappers. I requisitioned the basketball court when it was empty for the loft and range provided for teaching fly casting. The final exam was catching a trout with a fly the student had made at a spot on a local river that in the spring I knew had just been stocked with trout. Everybody passed.

But the heart of the educational experience of the course would be again the exacting work of writing short papers comparing short sections in various books together—which—if not as far-fetched as comparing Odysseus with Donald Duck, or bloody Herod with nurturing Jesus, did require exercising thought and measured prose.

The course might work well for the rest of my career teaching perhaps, I thought, because it recovered the spirit of a jazz standard. In music a standard is a well-known piece like "Summertime" or "Take the A-Train" or Brubeck's classic "Take Five." The listener who recognizes the theme grasps a template for appreciating the improvisational genius of what the musicians come up with this time. The very act of fishing— for whales or trout or lobsters or swordfish or bass, or even clams—is always an act of humans intervening mechanically in the natural world of wet, in order to exploit the natural habits and instincts of ancient animals trying to live on their own terms. The only way any fishing can continue is if it's restrained by laws and codes of restraint. The trade ends if vast nettings sweep the ocean clear of fish in a fortnight—as indeed had become the case. In this way, the literature of fishing is about living an ethical life in a natural world.

Whenever I might meet up at a conference with a colleague I knew from a more traditional and usually more prestigious college or university and was asked what kind of courses I was teaching, if I described "the Literature of Fishing," I'd watch as the light in their eyes dulled out in contempt of the need to pander to a common taste and theme to keep students in their seats. There was no point in trying any justification. I would just smile and nod in feigned helpless agreement.

When I thought about what the point of all this was—why would someone smitten by Gospel Greek be teaching literature written mostly by and always about anglers?—what helped was a second thought arising in my mind. The unexpected juxtaposition of an image of me with the image of an elder Norman Maclean: thoughts about the fitfulness of mourning the dead alone on a river—itself a symbol, a metaphor for the pouring of life and death up and down the river. The loveliness of remembering wonderful literature is the dissolve of time and space fishing for reminiscing about both.

Here emerging from the tomb of the Lady of the Bible as literature, was another offspring, living waters still flowing, to walk riverside still. I taught the course during the spring semester for the rest of my academic career. The final book in the course was James David Duncan's funny love story between two young anglers on different pilgrimages who meet spontaneously at a fishing hole and find in each other what only makes their lives whole. Students loved it. Several romances appeared to begin between members of the course. A good book to read in the spring.

In one memorable paper, an electrical engineering student lamented that the crew of the *Pequot* whaling ship in *Moby Dick* got to work with rough rope they could hold in their hands. All he could look forward to in his career was typing with fingers on a computer keyboard.

I Need to Live with You

1999

For now, as for what is inside you, be generous with the stranger . . .
—Luke 11:41

I stood outside the bus door; I queried softly, "Blaise Tine?" Imposing at six feet, two inches, fit and handsome, Blaise Foncou Tine from Cameroon in West Africa stepped off a Trailways bus in the village of Potsdam, hesitating before looking up at me and whispering, "Yes."

Later Blaise said that shaking my hand was the first time he had ever touched a White man.

"When your hand felt like any other, I began to think I might survive as a stranger in this strange land."

Blaise arrived as a beneficiary of a new program in the Clarkson International Student Program called "Host Family." Faculty and staff were invited to welcome new foreign students into their homes for several days before their official orientations. The idea was to have them meet people who knew their way around what was undoubtedly a disorienting new corner of the universe. All we knew about Blaise was that he spoke French, a tribal language, and some English. Soon we learned that at age thirteen he had programmed his pocket calculator to play the Cameroonian national anthem in beeps. He was already a gifted artist in drawing the human figure—in pencil because he couldn't afford paints. Now he wanted to fulfill his childhood dreams and build robots.

Christine, her mother Virginia, and I spent several pleasant days with him. Blaise tried fly fishing and helped weed the garden. He knew a lot about Christine's roses, which they delightedly talked about with a mixture of French, English, and hand gestures. She was amazed to discover some of them also grew in Cameroon.

The evening before Blaise was scheduled to move onto campus, he asked me to take a walk. He looked up through the trees and was surprised to see Scorpio, the same constellation he could see over his village in Cameroon.

"I wonder what other constellations you could see from Potsdam and Cameroon?" Blaise asked.

"Let's make sure we get around to figuring that out."

Blaise hesitated. He spoke quietly. "I wanted to get into the dark before asking you this. I'm sure it would work. I've been studying you and Christine for two days. I need to live with you for the next four years. My father can only pay my tuition for one semester. The whole village had to put all its savings into his bank account for one day in order for him to be able to show US Immigration there was enough family money to support me for four years. The families took the money back from the bank account after one day. I will work for you for room and board and figure out how to pay for the second semester. Maybe I can tutor French."

I was taken aback. The two of us went back to the house. Christine and Virginia sat down with us. I repeated what Blaise had asked. All four of us looked at each other appraisingly. Christine already had a smile on her face. Her smile was the only conversation needed. We both took a deep breath and said yes.

It worked. Blaise tested out of courses to shorten his double degree program in electrical and computer engineering to three years. We cosigned for a student tuition loan. He earned straight A's. He was accepted into the honor's program and received its scholarship. He won a scholarship from the National Society of Black Engineers. I accompanied Blaise to their national convention one year and spent the night sleeping with twelve other Black student engineers on every flat surface in one hotel room. Not one of them appeared surprised or asked why the older White guy was there.

The summer between his junior and senior year, Blaise worked as an intern at Microsoft in Seattle, Washington. Afterward, Microsoft offered him a permanent job as a software engineer following his graduation in December 2001. He paid off his loans and financed the emigration out of Cameroon of his parents and three sisters to Canada, more open to the outside world than the US—unfortunately for the US.

Blaise went back to school after working in industry. He received a PhD in computer architecture (AI) from Georgia Tech and was hired as a professor at UCLA.

"They're giving me five million to set up a lab and assigned me five graduate students. The beach is right outside my window!" he told us excitedly.

One afternoon, while he still lived with us, I had been asked to help a neighbor lift up the framed side of a home he was building. The neighbor had taught me and Christine how to build our own barn stud by stud. Blaise came along. A dozen other locals already stood in line waiting for the signal to lift the lattice of two-by-four studs that would form one side of the house. They hadn't noticed when Blaise and I took up positions at one end of the wall. When the signal came, Blaise and I started lifting, but the wall didn't move. We looked up to see why the others hadn't begun the hoist. All the other men were standing stock still, looking gap-mouthed at Blaise—perhaps the only Black man they'd ever seen in their remote, very White, rural world.

We looked up what stars shone over both the North Country and his village near the equator. A computer program simulated the Cameroonian night skies.

There turned out to be quite a few stars in common. Amazingly, just overhead in northern New York State was much of the same familiar sky as over Cameroon.

My curiosity piqued, while Blaise continued his engineering studies at Clarkson, the English professor in a tweed coat and bow tie crossed over another road. I signed up for an introductory night course in astronomy at a nearby community college. Rob Dixon, its accomplished professor, became a firm friend and fellow stargazer whose technical expertise helped me get over a big hump.

I had discovered Clarkson had a small observatory off campus that had been abandoned by the physics department. I got the key. I could not figure out how to bring the telescope into focus. Everything looked like a white blob. When I told Rob of my frustration, he set up a date on the spot to show me. An exemplary hands-on teacher, Rob Dixon was.

After that, there was still a lot of headache work learning to navigate the heavens. What you see by eye might be a single bright star surrounded by smaller white dots. When you look through a magnifying telescope, the field opens into a vast array of blurs and dots scattered around it like fireflies lost in the woods. A basic technique for finding your way around is called *star hopping*. You decide what you want to see. Perhaps a cluster of stars too faint to see with the naked eye. You locate the cluster on a sky chart, then select a bright star nearby to center in the eyepiece. Then you look back at the chart to see the pattern of stars that lies between the bright star and your target. You "hop" from star to star in your telescope field, which will now match your chart field, until you can center the cluster in the eye piece. Now you can consult a star guide to study the magnified intricate pattern the cluster forms, plus facts about how it was formed, how old it is, how far away it is, etc.

It helped to get the hang of this by thinking the process was a lot like having what I've called second thoughts, juxtaposing one image of an object with another, until getting to the *next* starting point for another hop. Like arranging the order of stories in the Gospels.

Still, it took a lot of practice to learn how to star hop. It's like playing scales while learning a musical instrument. It's one thing to try it while you're alone with yourself before the telescope, in a timeless zone of the heavens magnificently, eternally arrayed. It's another to try to do this when people standing close by start impatiently stepping from foot to foot, waiting to look through the scope themselves. The sky scout gets nervous. The hopping gets stuck in cosmic dust.

For several years, I opened the observatory up to the public every clear Friday night. School groups and Boy and Girl Scout troops came and very often parents with school-age children. I changed the focus and provided stools for small observers and put together programs suitable for showing off the best of the night skies on any given night. I started an astronomy club at Clarkson. Its students built a small research shack to house computers to run simple experiments in observing. They fashioned a simple radio telescope from discarded large TV satellite dishes, the bandwidth data from which passed through a Korean War military broad-beam radio receiver borrowed from the Clarkson Radio Club. Astronomy Club students helped run the show on public nights. Several matriculated into graduate studies in astrophysics.

When Blaise did his senior honor's project, he built a robotic arm for guiding the telescope to find stars in the sky at the push of a button. Now an operator typed a desired object to view onto a computer screen hooked up to a motor on the telescope, pushed a button, and waited patiently while the telescope hummed and buzzed, turned left or right along the horizon, up and down from ground to the zenith. *Bing!* There it would be, what you wanted to see in the center of the field in the eyepiece.

Now, with this device, I could put together a program to look at a series of objects sequentially that would represent the various stages by which a cloud of cosmic dust becomes a star. And how a star eventually blows up into a cloud of cosmic dust and the cycle continues. Or we could look at fuzzy balls of dust from exploded stars, or clusters of the pinpricks of a million stars in a distant galaxy like our own.

When he attended Clarkson, Blaise cooked delicious crepes and introduced us to fried bananas and peanut soup. It was hard at first to get him to wear boots and gloves during the Potsdam winter because he stubbornly insisted boots and gloves held the cold in. One morning he ran out of the house to catch his ride to school barefoot in the snow—still not used to footwear. He found the homegrown raspberries too tart. But three and a half years after he first stepped off the bus, Christine and I experienced the empty-nest syndrome as a beloved child outgrew his primal needs.

On the night before he left our home to fly out to Seattle, Christine and I sat down with Blaise in the same chairs we'd sat in when we mulled, only briefly, his request to move in with us three years earlier. We were teary.

Blaise asked with a quiver of emotion in his voice, "Why did you do this for me? How could you decide almost immediately to say yes when I asked you about living here?"

Christine and I were silent, startled by the question, uncertain how to answer because, one, we weren't sure, and two, as Christine quipped, "We didn't want to sound mawkish."

Blaise waited a beat. "You were a Jesuit once. Do you think the Jesuits taught you to be kind to strangers—from that old saying 'you should always be kind to strangers since the one at your door might be Jesus in disguise?'"

Christine and I barked with laughter.

"What about me?" Christine said in mock dismay. "I said yes too. I was never no Jesuit. And, no offense, but Blaise, you didn't remind me of Jesus when you showed up here out of nowhere. Your hair wasn't right."

I tried a serious answer. "In a few words, Blaise, your courage just coming to a new world and living with us in our little version of it for a few days made us think it would work. We liked you already. Beyond that, I'm not sure why. However, let me take up the Jesuit thing. The Jesuits never taught me or any of the rest of us about how to be kind or generous or open to people—not in any formal way. We influenced each other sideways, being around each other. These were the most extraordinary people I had ever met, aside from Christine here. The day I first showed up at Shadowbrook, I was a stranger, like you were coming here to this strange land. Yet, right off the bat, they called me 'brother'—"

"Uh oh," Christine broke in. "Now you're going to get mawkish."

"Let me finish," I scolded her sharply. Pointing at her. I said, "When you decided to invite me in that night I knocked on your door, it wasn't because you knew who I was. You were hooking up with a stranger too, just like Blaise stepping off the bus.

"So, it seems to me, we took chances on what we intuited about each other there. We have shaped each other, and by that logic, the Jesuits shaped us too. I'm not sure I left any mark on the Jesuits; their ship sails on. But they certainly made a mark on me—us.

"But when I think about it for a moment, there was once a boy named Juan who knocked on our door. He arrived on a bus like you did, as a Fresh-Air Fund kid from Queens, New York. That was a long-standing program that linked up city kids with rural families throughout the state, for the kids to spend two weeks in the summer out of the city staying with a family. If the relationship worked out, the kid could stay for a month the second summer. Christine and I liked Juan a lot and put in for him to spend a second summer. But he called in the spring saying he had flunked math and English at his inner-city school and had to stay for summer school. We arranged to have him take summer school while living with us. We tutored him in English and math. He aced out. Then his mother agreed to have him attend high school during the year with us. We fell in love with him as a child we never had together. So, maybe, you just seemed to us like another Juan showing up by surprise. We'd been lucky once. Now twice."

I paused for a moment, "Okay, that's enough from me. I think I am starting to sound mawkish. Although I meant every word of it." I turned to Christine, "Okay, your turn."

She smiled at Blaise, pointing to me. "Don't you think he's charming?

But he's also right. Blaise, you seemed to belong here 'at first sight,' probably because of who we were before we first sat down together in these chairs. But let me add to that. We sometimes have 'second thoughts.' Usually the phrase means 'to consider changing your mind.' Like 'I'm having second thoughts about whether I should have another ice cream.' But the way my husband first used it, it meant starting to think about something else—while you're thinking about one thing—just to see how they compare. What they imply about each other."

Blaise interrupted. "Wait a minute. Explain that. The phrase *having second thoughts* in English I think translates into French as *avoir des doutes*. Literally that would come out 'to have doubts.' That's not what you're talking about, is it?"

Christine responded, "You're right. The second thought doesn't question the first thought—it plays with it. An example would be swimming in the ocean, and remembering the last time you went fishing. It would be a 'second thought' that brought you to say, 'Maybe fish have it better than me. They always get to feel this happy.' And then you decide to release a fish you just caught and let it go swimming away."

"I think I got that," Blaise said with a giggle. "You really did think I might be Jesus in disguise when I asked to spend the night—for the next three years."

"Okay," I agreed as we all laughed, "let's go with that. You did bring up second thoughts about Jesus. But let's say a few more about second thoughts like these. Our concept is flexible. It expands if you let it. I often tell my students: 'You think you have one life ahead of you: you get your degree, you get a job, you have a family and live happily ever after. And maybe you will. And maybe that's great. But you might not.'

"What's happened to me is it seems I've had many different lives. One life leads to another, and that to a third, and the third is very little like the first. I was a poor kid, then a Jesuit, then married to Helen. Now I'm married to Christine, and we've just lived for three years with you like you were an adopted son. There was no necessary planning by any of us being pushed along, this way and then that way—"

Christine broke in. "And let me tell you, I know from first-hand information, his life with me is nothing at all like his life with the Jesuits—and I have to say, I'm proud of that."

"Amen to that, sister," I said and then waved at her to continue.

She took a deep breath and said, "We would have been astonished the day we got married if someone told us we'd someday be living on a farm, raising sheep, teaching, raising roses, gazing at stars, and taking in strangers like you. If we had stuck with some original idea along the way about who we were or what kind of life we wanted, we'd never have wound up sitting in these chairs with you today. Each phase led to another—it raised second thoughts about what to do next. We're the better for it. Thanks for asking us to have second thoughts after meeting you—'hey, this guy's not just here for three days. He wants three years.'"

We three started getting misty-eyed again.

What Galileo Saw

2003

Where were you when the morning stars sang together?
—Job 38:3

I stood next to the telescope in a round room filled with people waiting to view the planet Mars on the night of its opposition: when its variable orbit brought it the closest to the Earth after sixty thousand years. More than two hundred others stood outside waiting their turn. Some knowledgeable Clarkson students in the crowd pointed out what could be seen of Mars with the naked eye and named many other stars and constellations. Inside, I gave a Mars bar as a token after an observer had spotted Mars through the main scope.

In preparing for the Opposition program, I had a provocative thrill. One night, I decided to keep looking through the eyepiece at the surface of Mars for an hour. With the planet close, I could see reddish color and the lines of some faint surface features once thought to be canals. I just kept looking. Suddenly, for an instant, I could see craters and hills as detailed as from a NASA Mars probe photograph. I stood up in exultation. In a flash, I was back on my seat gazing at the customary blur.

I could not determine whether I actually saw that detail or whether my mind for a moment imposed a memory of a photograph. And just like that moment when, as a child sailor, I thought I had seen a whale's tail—it made no difference whether it was an illusion or for real. The mind had a nirvana all its own—its revelations rightly earned. Another instance of "the composition of place" I learned to find myself in, remarkably, looking through the empty space between beckoning episodes in the Gospels.

The motorized telescope was Blaise's legacy to Charkson and his host "parents" as he called us.

When I described all this to a friend from Purdue, Don Seybold, Don remarked sarcastically, "You're still looking for God in the heavens."

"No, I wasn't," I said, defensively. "Astronomy starts with evidence. One discovery leads to another, like star hopping. You never get to the end. With God, you don't start with evidence. You start with belief, magical thinking, and go on from there, building on the empty air."

He was having none of it. "You're still looking for God."

We knew each other from the days of my teaching the Bible as literature at Purdue, which we used to talk about then. Don had himself published a fine reading of the Joseph Story in Genesis—that had early on been incorporated into my teaching of the Bible as literature. And we had drunk bourbon together during my divorce.

Don was not prepared to listen to any explanations about the profound ecstasy of celestial second thoughts to be had with a telescope. You start from the ground up. The scope fixed tight to the floor of the observatory, its foundation dug into the ground. And from that humble, immovable spot, the observer sees into a universe vast beyond ordinary imagining. Even with a small telescope, one can gaze back millions of light years at objects that in the intervening time, might have ceased to exist, even as the message line of light continues into your own eyes and up its nerves into the darkness of your brain, where it blinks out. While I did this, I often thought as astronomers do, how intensely inane was human politics and its awful record of brutality for petty points of power. Why shoot anyone for having inconvenient beliefs when we're all fortunate flicks of life on a blue dot in limitless black?

There *was* something religious-like about that sort of ecstasy. I knew I had reached the end of my mind's understanding. There were scientists and mathematicians who went further, until they could only reach a hypothesis on what lay beyond their ken. Scientific knowledge, like literary art, was tentative, evocative, intriguing, beguiling. Just like reading the literary Gospels scene by scene. At the same time, I gained admiration for the scientists and engineers of my colleagues who did have the right chops.

There was doubtless an unbridgeable gap between professional astronomy and amateur astronomy. The latter used statistics to render observations into scientific probabilities progressively. It has no final goal in mind—to know the universe for what it is, say. It accumulates data open-mindedly.

Amateur astronomy like mine is more like bird watching, whereby bird lovers already know what they're interested in. They observe birds and over time learn more and more about what they already admire: colors, mating habits, range, etc.

The final iteration of the Bible as literature in my teaching career was, in silent argument with Don, to design the course on astronomy and literature titled: "What Galileo Saw."

What Galileo saw was that the Church was dead wrong about the universe. He just escaped being burned for his temerity.

The premise of the course was that there have been three models for the universe in western thinking in the past three thousand years. The Ptolemaic, the Copernican, and the Einsteinian. Each model set the stage for the literature told within the shape of the space the model set up.

Aristotle's *On the Cosmos* was a good, accessible summary of the first, the Ptolemaic; and Ovid's *Metamorphosis* related the stories to be imagined within a universe with the gods and the kings at the top, and the nobles and ordinary people making do within the confines of what was allowed. Biblical stories were like ancient classical myths and stories in this way. The stars and the angels and the heavens above set the limits of the earth.

The Ptolemaic first held that the earth was the center of the universe, that planets and moon and sun revolved around the earth. This model saw humans as the highest form of life on the planet and thereby aggrandized human life as the culmination of existence. It was only an extension of this idea to then imagine that there was a natural hierarchy of power and perfection among human beings: thus kings and popes at the top. Then there was a finely delineated descent of value from the top through the various administrators all the way down from princes and cardinals to the serf in the barn.

Galileo's *The Starry Messenger* was a good, accessible summary of the second: Copernican. The sun was the center of a system with the earth and planets revolving around it. At least initially, the stars were to be imagined beyond the sun, but not placed very precisely in their distance away. This pushed human beings away from the center of things and left them on their own to figure out who they were and how the universe worked. Shakespeare's *The Tempest* was a delightful imagining of a fated universe with humans trying every trick in Prospero's books to arrange at least temporarily happy endings. Galileo published his book in 1610, the same year Shakespeare wrote *The Tempest*. No one argued that the book and the play were written under the influence of each other. But they could be read in provocative juxtaposition.

Albert Einstein's *Relativity* as a popularization of his theories for the general public was a good, accessible summary of the third, the Einsteinian. There was no center of the universe, which continually expands randomly. Italo Calvino's *Cosmicomics* is a collection of wildly imaginative and funny stories about the evolution of the universe with characters animating mathematical formulas or primary molecules. "Naturally, we were all there—old Qfwfq said—where else could we have been? Nobody knew then that there could be space. Or time either: what use did we have for time, packed in there like sardines."

The course would pair a scientific or philosophical book with a literary one, if only to illustrate the point of the premise that literature was written within the compass of the reigning universal paradigm. But in the spirit of entertaining second thoughts, in setting up endless and fascinating points of comparison between science and literature, each student would be encouraged to find and celebrate on his or her own.

On the model of the literature of fishing, there would also be a "lab." Observations of the starry skies at the observatory, the equivalent of catching a trout on a self-made fly, and being able to identify a set number of named constellations in the sky.

This would be an appropriate finale to my teaching career. I had made sure ahead of time that each of the three model books were considered legitimate summaries. Aristotle, for example, had only recently been identified as the author of his popularization. Each pairing brought together works created in the same zeitgeist, and so amenable to comparisons of underlying comic theory and stories ranging within the bounds of the universe as it was differently conceived. Even if the course fit no academic curricular paradigm, its contents were validated individually, and the pairings were contemporaneous, like Galileo and Shakespeare's works from the same year. It made possible discovering and savoring provocative juxtapositions and improvising a personal response.

The course required the students to write three vigorously critiqued papers, with encouraged revisions. The writing would supply the academic backbone of what would ultimately be a legitimate university English course. Rene Wellek would approve of the huge range of this course in comparative literature. Don, I hoped, would sanction its secularized search for whatever would be considered an ultimate in the universe. One student became enamored of the clutch of related constellations of Cepheus and Cassiopeia, the parents of the chained Andromeda with Perseus flying to her rescue. He had their images tattooed on his torso. "I love the way they look with steam coming off my body after I take a shower," he told me.

It was a dream course to teach at the end of a career teaching literature at universities that focused on the teaching of engineering, agriculture science, and the hard, quantitative sciences. Elements of them all could comfortably, honestly interact in a course that made no pretense of proving the validity or superiority of any of them but instead presented an opportunity to have their juxtapositions give rise to thought.

I recruited scientists and historians of science to share their thoughts with the students. Notably, Professor Aileen O'Donoghue from the nearby Saint Lawrence University was both an astronomer and a practicing Catholic. She wrote a book called *The Sky is Not A Ceiling*.

While I was teaching "What Galileo Saw" and running the observatory, Clarkson University hired Professor Joshua Thomas to teach large sections of freshman physics. His degree was in astronomy. Professor Thomas contributed to the literature class by providing detailed descriptions of the physics behind the three paradigms of the universe. He also helped run the observatory on public nights. Building on his own PhD thesis in astrophysics, he won grants with which to buy professional-grade telescopes, mounts, tracking equipment, cameras, computers, and filters to perform sophisticated spectroscopy to continue his doctoral research.

This led to his department encouraging him to begin teaching astrophysics to undergraduate physics majors, several of whom went on to gain PhDs in the subject. Professor Thomas's own research earned him a promotion to a regular tenure track professoriate. "By their fruits you shall know them," Jesus said in Matthew 7:15. These fruits were plucked from the high trees the Bible as literature had provided for me—the ladders to climb—starting when I was sitting on a bench as an eleven year old altar boy troubled by an incomprehensible sermon.

Only read as literature could the Bible become a legitimate companion to the teaching of science—or any other human endeavor for the fecundity of the thoughts they together gave rise to.

Via con Dios

2017

Return to your first love.
—Isaiah 63:7

I stood with a dozen former Jesuits in the New England Province graveyard adjacent to the main building at Weston College, where all of us had lived in the late 1960s. It was overwhelming how many men we knew had died. During the 1960s the graveyard had been the size of a tennis court. Now it was the size of a football field. Ola Nelson, who had been a captain of a tank battalion and had been a novice with many of us at Shadowbrook was buried there. He'd succumbed to disease on a mission in Brazil. Some of our former Jesuit colleagues had died of AIDs.

There was the stone of the mag., short for *magister novitiorum*—"the master of novices." Six feet, five inches tall, and gaunt with a pockmarked face, he was rumored to have played collegiate hockey as the team goon. He had terrified his novices. Once during morning meditation, I found myself to my dismay, praying to *him*. Someone said his obituary mentioned him having been a champion marbles player as a child.

At what would end up being six months before his death, Charlie was there with me at the reunion. He had flown in from Colorado. Phil and I had driven from Northern New York. Almost all the other former

Jesuits still lived in the Boston area. For several years me and my old friends booked rooms in an empty wing of Weston College—now the retirement home for elderly Jesuits. Mornings and afternoons, we sat on old couches and leather chairs in what was once the philosopher's rec room. We sang songs and told stories of what we'd done with our lives after leaving, all punctuated with funny stories about our time in the holy trenches together.

AJ Antoon, our most famous among us, died young in 1992 of AIDs. Once for a terrible prank, AJ had dropped a dummy wearing a black habit down an open four-story stairwell while screaming, paralyzing those of us climbing up to our rooms after breakfast. Charlie remembered falling back against the wall, stunned and horrified. "It took almost a minute for me to recover after AJ started laughing viciously at us all."

"You wimps!" AJ had cried. "You all know your end is coming."

Then the stairwell rang with curses and our tentative laughter.

At our reunions we'd have lunch and dinner together in the vast dining room at Weston, half of which was petitioned off for seating the retirees in residence. We'd meet old friends there too. At the last reunion during Halloween weekend 2017, Father Sullivan sat down with us for lunch. He was the priest who had urged us to emulate *pissy Aeneus* at Shadowbrook. One of us mentioned how moving walking around the graveyard had been.

He quipped, "There's been some talk of translating the words on the headstones into English (the latinized name of the deceased; *natus*—'birthdate;' *ingressus*—'date of entry into the Jesuits;' *obit*—'date of death') since otherwise, the only people who could read the Latin would be lying under them."

We all laughed easily. We were used to Jesuits moving away. Even while we were at Shadowbrook or Weston, some close friend would leave to go back to his province elsewhere, go to graduate school, or take a job teaching either in the US or a mission. Then after a few years, you'd run into him in the rec room. So, it always seemed they were just working in another room, or building, or city. We'd get together for lunch and catch up. Given our firm and casual belief in the afterlife, we assumed that death was only a temporary trip away to the other side. We'd meet again for that. For whatever went for lunch in heaven.

This particular lunch, several other Jesuits in residence sat down with us. We had to push several tables together. Some of them were our own age; most were older. We told our stories of what our lives turned out to be after we lost touch, as old friends will. But in this case, we listened intensely and affectionately to each other whether we were former or current Jesuits—it didn't matter which. We'd remained a family after all the twists and turns. The current Jesuits, or at least the ones willing to sit with us, had no animosity toward us or resentments of betrayal.

Brother Connie Murphy had been a coadjutor brother when most of us were at Shadowbrook, that is to say, a man who chose to remain a Jesuit to do mostly mechanical tasks like cooking or grounds keeping, without ordination. He was compact, short, and spoke with a Boston accent out of the side of his mouth. He began every sentence with "Yeah . . ."

He'd worked with all of us while we did our outside *manualia* duties. He was always witty and fun. We held him dearly. He was also now retired at Weston. He joined us for this lunch wearing a particularly well-tailored and very sharp-looking navy-blue sports jacket. We hailed him as a hero when he approached the table. The New England Province had recently published *The Shadowbrook Fire* by Frank Shea. It told the story of the terrible fire that had burned the original Carnegie mansion and killed four Jesuits on March 10, 1956. That happened before any of us reunionists had entered the new building at Shadowbrook several years later. We had all read it. In the book, we learned for the first time about Connie Murphy's heroism that day. He risked his life again and again to rouse and save the many sleeping Jesuits who otherwise would not have survived. We had worked and lived with him for many years and never heard a word about it.

All Connie would say about it now was, "Yeah, what made it tough is how hard you novices slept."

Then Bill, who, together with his wife, had adopted and raised eight children from around the world, our organizer, and perhaps the warmest, most humane of us reunionists told us his best memory of our time at Shadowbrook.

"It was the First Sunday and Pentecost, and so a first-class feast. That meant that after we had all said our Latin graces standing up, we all sat down. The rector sang out, *"Deo Gratias!"* ("Thanks be to God!"). And all two hundred of us—novices, juniors, priests, and lay-brothers roared back, *"Semper Deo gratias et Mariae!"* ("Always give thanks to God and to Mary!"). At which point, all of us would break into applause and happy laughter, since this was a meal in which we could speak to each other in English. Almost immediately there'd be detonations of sharp pops of beer bottles being opened, and a good time would be about to be had by all. There'd be a fish course, steak and vegetables, plus dessert, very often consisting of apple pie and a slice of cheddar cheese—a Boston-based treat the rest of us soon came to cherish. On this occasion, there was an extra level of frivolity. Table by table, one at a time, everyone would burst into a louder laughter. At a distance, I could see something was being passed from table to table, having the same reaction each time. When that object came to our table, it turned out to be an ordinary spring seed catalog but had been addressed to "Mr. and Mrs. Glennon." After every table of scholastics had seen it, Father Rector beckoned that he wanted a look. Every table of priests at the front of the refectory had the same reaction. Everyone looked at Brother Glennon, beet red, with a huge smile on his face. Many of us wagged a shaming finger at him in great zesty gestures. Talk about bringing the house down! And can you imagine any more innocent, gentle, loving humor in a close-packed room of men?

"Everyone started banging spoons on glasses, until finally Brother Glennon, to make that noise stop, stood up and shouted, 'Yeah, now ye know me saychret. Deo Gratias, praise be!' to thunderous applause."

Warm laughter flowed around the table of old friends who cared deeply about each other despite all the many different paths we had taken in the yellow wood.

Angel on a Cell Phone

2018

My heart pounds, my strength fails me...
—Psalm 38:9

I stood outside of Penn Station in Manhattan on 8th Avenue. I fumbled desperately, grasping the empty air where my leather shoulder bag should be.

"I left it on the train! Oh no!" I shouted out loud at that moment. How would I ever manage to get it back? Christine would be peeved. She had bought it for me from an outdoor kiosk in Florence. As if in answer to my sharp cry of despair on 8th Avenue (that no pedestrian passing by paid any attention to), my phone dinged. The train conductor's stentorian voice came immediately to my ear, telling me the bag had been recovered.

"A computer print-out ticket inside had your cell phone number on it. You'll find it at Lost and Found back inside Penn Station."

No angel from the heavens could bear more wonderful news. A man sat at a desk at Lost and Found reading a paperback as I approached.

"Ah, yes," he said in response to my plaintive request. He disappeared through a door, then returned with the bag and a triumphant smile, "This just in," as if he was handing over a lost pet.

I went back out onto 8th Avenue and sat on a bench. I called Christine back in Potsdam to tell her.

She laughed merrily. "It's nice to know that when you get lost in your mind when you should be paying attention to where you are—we've got the technology to call you back before any harm is done."

The Amtrak train from Northern New York ran down the Hudson River Valley directly alongside the river. It toured through many of the spectacular landscapes of the Hudson River School of painting, the works of which Christine and I enjoyed looking at museums and galleries. I had promised to call on my cell phone every day—even before I arrived.

"The train is running down the east side of the Hudson, and right now, I'm looking through the window to where Thomas Chambers stood while painting *View of West Point* we liked so much at the Metropolitan. There are sailboats on the river just like in the painting."

Christine said wistfully, "I really liked that one. It was childlike and almost primitive, with bright colors. But you're wrong. We saw it in an exhibit at the Albany Museum of Art of Hudson River School paintings. Remember? We found Chambers's art much less grand and serious than the Cole and the Durand. Almost like he was winking at the Big Men. I can see it in my mind. Let me just see it again in my imagination. Don't tell me anymore what it looks like to you."

After that, we kept in touch every day of the week I spent in New York City, usually just before her bedtime as I sat in a very primitive hotel room a little bigger than the bed—but one street from Central Park. I walked across daily to spend time in the Metropolitan Museum of Art.

This time I called late in the afternoon; I reported a day well spent, morning and afternoon, in the American Wing. I had met Alison, the young daughter of a colleague at Clarkson, Laura Ettinger, early in front of my hotel.

Alison had precociously graduated a year earlier at twenty-one from Fordham University with a degree in social sciences. She had worked with poor and disadvantaged families in the Bronx. Her first real paying job developed into her becoming the communications director for Riverside Park on the Upper West Side, and she was beside herself, bubbling with joy and good feelings, to have such a job and to be supporting her beloved Eugene, her Potsdam high school sweetheart. He was about to graduate from Baruch College with a degree in political science. They had been living together for several years in the far North Bronx, an hour's subway ride from Midtown.

"But if you know the subway system, we're right next door," she exclaimed. Now they planned to stay together as he had applied to various graduate schools in NYC for studies in economics and political science while she would continue to work at the park.

The three of us spent the morning in the American Wing of the Metropolitan. The couple had never visited. I took them to see favorites by Rockwell Kent, Winslow Homer, Martin Johnson Heade, James McNeill Whistler, and the Hudson River School painters Thomas Eakins and Thomas Cole.

"Eakins and Cole might have taken train rides along the same route along the Hudson that brought me hither to meet with you. You could see the originals of the painted landscapes too if you two chose to take the train back to Potsdam for any visits."

Afterward we went to a vegetarian sushi place Alison had heard about. The food was wonderful, and she, a vegetarian like her mother, was beside herself with joy at the discovery. Eugene smiled quietly through the visit. He knew what gift he had in this almost preternaturally happy young woman.

At one point in the meal, Alison turned to Eugene and said, "Now I hope you do get into the graduate program at Columbia. That's just across town from here. We could come here often."

Several weeks later she would call to say that, indeed, Eugene had been accepted into the graduate program in economics at Columbia. She laughed uncontrollably.

As we walked away from the sushi restaurant that day and were about to head in different directions, I asked Alison, "Do you think you've become a city person?"

She gave me a level look as she took time to consider the question. I had known her since her mother Laura was pregnant with her and watched her grow up on a leafy street in the village. Children like her and her sister Caroline played and rode bikes under large sugar maple trees in the summer. Many walked to their elementary school. Winter was welcomed with skates and skis and snowmobiles, hockey games, indoor basketball, and school plays.

Alison replied carefully. "We're not sure yet," she said, speaking in the first-person plural as Eugene smiled at her side. "It's not possible to tell where we'll wind up when Eugene gets finished. Or maybe I'll get another job. We do love it here now. We don't mind taking the subway an hour to get downtown when we go together most of the way. But we loved living in our small town too. We'll just wait to see where the winds blow us."

They headed off toward the subway that took them an hour north to the North Bronx, and I crossed the park to my tiny room. I wondered if I would have answered the same question her way when I was her age. She was already starting out on a life open to entertaining second thoughts about the life she was living as its possibilities unfolded. In Alison I recognized an avatar of my early life.

I went back to the museum to spend the afternoon in the American Wing. I sat on a bench in any empty gallery to call home. Christine chatted quietly as she sat in her handicapped accessible chair. I told Christine about the lovely visit earlier with Alison and Eugene.

She whispered contentedly, "Through the magic of technology, we are together again New York City and Potsdam condensed into the space between our lips and ears. And this time, Bessie is purring on my lap. Maybe she hears your voice through the speakerphone. 'All is well on the home front,' she's saying, especially since with my free hand I'm scratching her ears."

"I hope you can't hear the sirens outside that I can. That might upset the cat. But right now, I'm sitting on a bench in the museum gazing at the miraculous original of one of our favorite paintings in the

Metropolitan Museum of Art: Martin Johnson Heade's *Before the Storm*."

"Wait a minute," Christine replied. "I'll go wheel myself to sit in front of the print we've got hanging in our back room."

While I waited for her to find her place, I continued gazing on my own. A man with a white hat and red shirt and yellow vest sits on a driftwood log on a sandy shore, looking out at a calm cove at high tide. A white sail lies furled on the beach nearby. The water and clouds are dark gray. A rainstorm looms in the background. The man on the log and a small white dog nearby are watching two small boats coming ashore. Closer in is a man in a white rowboat. Farther out, another man stands next to the mast of a small white sailboat with a cat-rig, about the size of *Flotsam*. Its white sail hangs limp. The tiny figure of the sailor stands up by his mast wearing a red jacket just barely discernible in the background. But there's a weak bow wave that portends the boat will make it to shore before the storm. The painting reminded me of the shoreline in East Norwalk where I sailed as a boy.

After a pause for her taking up her new position, Christine declared, "Okay, now we're eye to eye. It strikes me that from the distance we're each sitting before it, the original and the print look exactly the same. We're sitting next to each other too. The original and the print are second thoughts of each other, in your terms. And each of us in our different seats are transparent to each other. It's got the mood of the calm before a coming storm. The humans in the scene are calm themselves. They're doing the right things to get ready. The man on the beach maybe will help the men in the boats pull them up on shore. But at the same time—and I know we've mentioned this kind of thing before to each other—there are these sharp geometries created by triangles you can draw between the sail on the shore, the sail on the beach, the white hat of the man with the dog. The geometry of serenity."

"I was thinking along those lines myself," I said affectionately, "while waiting for you."

We'd started to visit museums when almost thirty years earlier her osteoarthritis ended our mountain climbing and hiking. Looking at the vast landscapes of New York State in the paintings of the Hudson River School we once again could see mountain views. Fibromyalgia and chronic fatigue crippled her more. She endured another sexual discrimination outrage at Clarkson where she was the only woman in the business school, and its most accomplished researcher. We brought a suit against the university, the adjudication of which lasted five years. She lost the case and her job but received a settlement. We decided to stay put on my salary. She developed a hardy rose nursery of flowers that could survive the northern New York winter. She gave that up as the arthritis tightened its grip. I gradually became more of a caregiver over most of the years of our marriage. As good as I tried to do it, I needed breaks to stay on an even keel.

Christine responded a little sadly, "What's moving me right now is a melancholy, not a nostalgia—which word means the pain of thinking about past times. No, it's my feeling of being suspended between different times and places that blend together while we're talking. There are these distances."

"That sounds sweet to say," I replied softly through the phone so as not to disturb other viewers in the gallery. "But what distances—just between us at far ends of New York State—and only for a week?" I was still a little uneasy that even though we both had agreed upon my need for a break as her caretaker—that my absence might carry with it a taint of abandonment.

"No," she said quickly, as if to assure me our agreement about my trip remained sound. "It's the distance between the now of our talking to each other and the then of when the scene was painted in the nineteenth century. And added to that, yes, the distance between the two of us sitting five hundred miles apart at the same time. It's a little like what people say about your life flashing back before you as you're dying."

"Oh, don't use that word," I said anxiously. "We're just living with the same persons we've always been, just differently now. Weathering a chapter in our story soon to pass."

"Relax," she said, and I could almost see her smile (we were not using FaceTime). "I just mean it's powerful to me to see in my mind these distances blurring together, each transparent to the other, as if for the moment right now they all are suspended together. It's like your idea of composition or having second thoughts. It's just nice. There's something good in the air that you don't need words for."

"I'm also remembering Prospero's line in *The Tempest* where he tells the audience the play's about over, all is about to dissolve:

> We are such stuff
> As dreams are made on,
> And our little life
> Is rounded by a sleep."

Christine paused, aware our conversation veered close to a hard thing for me—more than for her—to talk about. "We both know my 'little sleep' looms. I guess my consolation is to know that, given how your mind works, even at that final distance, I'll always remain alive wherever you find yourself."

With a sigh I said, "Okay, if you put it that way. I'm glad we're having this talk right now. And how nice to have your lips and my ears close together on our cell phones. I see you sitting there, and the man sitting on the log as one image blends into another. Like you say, it's a composition you could only have in your mind—with the help of our trusty cell phones. But you have my word on it. However distant we get to be from each other—even out of cell-service range on the earth—you'll always be with me as long as I have words."

Afterward, I went outside for a stroll around Central Park. The March breeze was cool. I was warm inside with the glow of the intimate chat. On a whim—jiggered by second thoughts about East Norwalk and Manhattan and my mother all transposing on each other—I bought a bouquet of flowers from a lady selling them just over the wall of the park on 8th Avenue. I took the A Train up to Harlem and found the street and the old building my mother had taken me to as a child. It looked the same. I put the bouquet down on the spot where my mother had fallen from the fire escape and lay there for a moment until she resurrected herself to run off down the street. This time, there was no one there like the old man had been on the earlier visit.

For the train ride back home, I made sure to sit on the Hudson River side of the train going north. The conductor started a spiel on the loudspeaker in a deep bass stentorian tone. I recognized the voice as the one I had heard a week earlier, traveling south. Making sure I held my shoulder bag tight under my left arm—figuring the train was empty enough for me to find a good seat on my way back—I walked the length of several cars, looking for the man behind the voice.

I found the conductor filling out paperwork at a table in the café car. I asked him if he had worked the morning southbound train the week earlier. The conductor opened his notebook, and said yes, he had been that conductor. Then I blurted: "Were you the one who found my shoulder bag? I had left it on my seat, a week ago, stupidly, perhaps due to my heightened anxiety that I would do stupid things finding my way around NYC after an absence of twenty-five years."

"Yes," he said dryly, "and when you walked in here with the bag just now, I thought I recognized the bag."

He was a very big Black man, his face obscured behind a pair of dark glasses. He was wearing a large suit, almost black it was so blue, and a stiff, patent-leather shiny-brimmed train conductor hat.

"How did you ever trace the bag to me?"

He said he found the train ticket in the bag, a one-page home computer printout, with one of those little square squiggly QR codes on it.

"I scanned it and found your name, phone number, address, date of birth, the last four digits of your social, and"—he said with a grin—"your favorite baseball team. Actually, that was a ticket stub from a Red Sox game. Don't feel bad. It happens a lot. People get confused when they stand up."

"That's me all right," I added, "You don't look like I imagined my guardian angel would look."

He chuckled and waved his hand deprecatingly. "Just a day's work."

We chatted for a moment. He handed me his card. His name was Sheldon Johnson—a voice actor, the card said.

I asked with admiration, "Do you do voice-overs on radio and TV ads?"

"Yes, and films too."

"I'll listen for your voice from now on. But how will I know it's you?"

And he said, in his deep bass voice, "Oh, you'll know it's me."

"And when I hear you, I'll always remember your wonderful welcome to me back to the city after a long time away."

The train ride back home became even more pleasurable after talking to the conductor who had stood in for my guardian angel. I kept the shoulder bag nestled comfortably next to me on the seat. The trip along the Hudson going north reprieved the flow of the trip a week before going south. Now the Hudson River got progressively thinner as the train hurtled north, and the amount of ice, piled in great sheets like tables, got thicker. It was still a few weeks until it would officially be spring everywhere.

If I scrunched down and used the bottom of the window as a frame, all I could see was the river. It was like sailing in a boat at sea. It was mesmeric. I couldn't take my eyes away from the window at the river going past in the other direction, back toward the great city where it would gradually come to resemble the harbor of the sea.

If I sat upright and, as it were, lowered the frame of reference, there was almost always a sliver of land to see between the train and the water. Here are perched slices of village parks, or sewage disposal plants, or sometimes the back sides of a small village with cars lined up behind a lowered traffic barrier flashing with red lights.

It reminded me of taking the train from Norwalk to Manhattan as a child and young man, along the back side of the fancy facades of southern Connecticut. But it looked nicer here. There was a surprising amount of rough, natural unmeddled-with ground with brush and small trees and branch and leaf litter and sometimes scarves of snow.

I could imagine little animals just starting to stir themselves awake after the long winter's sleep. Sometimes, startlingly, there'd be a house on a spit of land going out into the river, the access to which must have been a driveway that went over the train tracks. You could imagine the owners looking out from the back porch at a serene river while trains rumbled by the front door—living in two worlds at once.

And it was comforting to see very little trash, beyond some busted up masonry from old industrial buildings. Civilization looked good. Lots of hunting blinds visible on the islands offshore. Boats huddled together, tightly wrapped in protective plastic, looked like herds of big toy sheep awaiting their spring reveals and a chance to get back in the water.

Still cuddling with the shoulder bag, I called Christine on the cell phone. Now the magic of our talking would include her sitting in her chair at home, and me sitting in a train seat hurtling through the landscape.

"Tell me what you see out the window," she asked wistfully.

"Right now, we're going by a big blackwater pool. There is a flotilla of little black coots with funny white hats scooting in one direction or another—funny to see, although perhaps it is frantic for them. Ducks in small groups. Even though I have been gone for a week, I suspect our pond back home is still frozen and snowed over. It isn't ready yet for taking on the ten billion geese on the Hudson that I have been counting."

"You're right," she agreed. "I hate to tell you this, but I can still see snow and ice when I look out the window. You'll be traveling back in time coming home."

"Wow!" I broke in, not in shock about what she had said, but at what I could see out the window of the train.

"There are two adult bald eagles standing on a sandbar! They look regal. And there's perhaps a half dozen yearling eagles without their white crowns yet splashing each other in the shallows. The adults look stoical—like two nuns on duty during recess at the school yard."

"Great image!" Donna cried. "I can see it through your eyes."

While she spoke, I stood up to shout out loud about the eagles to the other passengers. But the eagles were already out of sight from the windows, and the passengers looked to be either asleep or on their phones. I did not feel superior to any of them, since my own phone had recently saved a small but memorable sliver of my life when the conductor called me about my bag. Now my phone was keeping me close to Christine while apart. Angels would probably use cell phones if they got sent to earth now with divine instructions.

Alone in the Gray Salmon River

2023

There shall be a great multitude of fish.
—Ezekiel 42:9

I stand in the river at early dawn, up to my knees in the cold, gray, strong current of the Salmon River in Pulaski, New York. I cast flies for chinook, coho, and Atlantic salmon. The fish make their annual autumnal return up their natal river to breed in the shallows. Their fingerlings themselves will one day, some years from now, swim up the same currents to make their contribution to the continuing cycle of rebirth. With luck, I might catch fish on the way up today, and again and again for years to come. Natural resurrection runs through their bodies, and it feels good to touch before releasing them back into the water.

It's the year 2023. It's the eve of All Saints' Day—All Hallows or Halloween—a bookend holiday to Easter. This one commemorates those souls fortunate to enjoy what Jesus's initial resurrection promised his devoted followers—the rapturous reuniting of their bodies with their souls when the Last Day dawns. It's the traditional day for the living to pray to the hallowed dead for their succor toward earning the same penultimate bliss. My late lifelong friends Donna and Charlie among them. I met Donna when we were eight in the third grade in 1952. I met Charlie when we were eighteen when we joined the Jesuit

Order of Catholic priests together right out of high school, more than fifty years ago.

Months shy of eighty, I am careful with my footing on a soft underwater sandbar. The cold hurts my hand when I reach into the water to take out and change a fly. The river is funereal gray, its ripples like rumpled tin. There is little shine on the current from a weak late autumn sun. Few leaves float past now, so there's less of a chance of hooking a leaf, which often feels like the soft take of a fly by a salmon. It's quiet, almost no wind, just a rustle in the few leaves on the trees bending over the stream. Eating an apple sounds loud. A row of ducks flies overhead, quacking, then a V of Canada geese comes, honking.

"They're so earnest," I say to myself. "They know where they're going; no second thoughts for them."

But spawning salmon and migrating waterfowl in vigorous pursuit of their species' natural survival provide some cold comfort to a man grieving the loss of beloved friends. I feel cozy in well-sealed, chest-high waders, wool pants, and long johns, with pads of chemical heat between wool socks and the wader bottoms, a thick wool sweater beneath the fishing vest, and a hat with the ear flaps down. I feel as Ishmael does at the beginning of Herman Melville's great fishing story *Moby Dick*: "The one warm spark in the heart of an arctic crystal."

It's several weeks after the peak of the annual salmon run from Lake Ontario to the headwaters of the Salmon River, on Columbus (a.k.a. Indigenous Peoples') Day, and I had fished with some success then. Christine remained at home. She had insisted once again I take time off from caring for her with food and medicine since her chronic fatigue, fibromyalgia, crippling arthritis, and fatiguing recovery from cancer therapy kept her chairbound. A friend came to watch over her.

For two months in the fall, chinook, coho, and Atlantic salmon that have lived in Lake Ontario for four or five years swim back up their natal rivers to spawn in the headwaters and then die. The salmon do not feed, as their bodies are already beginning to darken and disintegrate with large white splotches as they enter the river. But the salmon aggressively sip up what they think are eggs drifting downstream. They mouth the eggs protectively while swimming upstream, spitting them out where they will most likely hatch into baby salmon fry in the spring. Anglers like me try to trick them with an egg-like pattern. Some use real eggs. I use an imitation fashioned out of a pea-sized ball of deer hair dyed red, with a tiny hook embedded inside.

I can see only two other anglers gesturing and apparently talking to one another a quarter mile downstream. I hear not a word they say. Like seeing men far off in a boat at sea. It didn't look as if they were catching anything either.

I shouldn't be fishing alone, just as you aren't supposed to use a chainsaw in the woods alone; without a helping hand, one false step could be fatal. In the final page of *A River Runs Through It*, Norman Maclean, as an old man, standing in or next to the Big Blackfoot River in Montana, reflects: "Of course, now I am too old to be much of a fisherman, and now of course I usually fish the big waters alone, although some friends think I shouldn't." Like Maclean, I find myself "haunted by waters," the stirring final words of the wonderful novel, as I think back on all in my family I've fished with who've died.

I've been warned against fishing alone. Last night I stopped in at Malinda's Fly Shop in Altmar, New York, several miles upstream from the village of Pulaski and several more miles from where I am standing in the Salmon River close to its outlet into Lake Ontario. I often bought gear at Malinda's, enjoyed a cup of free coffee, and joshed with the other anglers sitting around not catching any fish.

Malinda's face relaxes naturally into a smile. She served in the Army, and wears crisp blue-collar shirts, and runs a tight shop with everything under glass arranged in rows. Waders and vests and rods hang cleanly and accessibly against the walls. It's tempting to take something down and feel the flex or finger the texture comfortably in the hands.

"You'll like it," she'll say with the smile of a saleswoman.

But if I looked half-seriously interested, she'd come out from behind the counter and show me a cheaper and a more expensive model of the same thing and parse out the advantages. I never shop for fishing gear anywhere else.

One time Christine came with me to the shop and sat chatting with the anglers, mostly old men. I was at the counter while Malinda rang up my order. "That's seven hundred thirty-four dollars and fifty cents," she said. She handed me back the credit card.

"Seven hundred thirty-four dollars and fifty cents!" Christine cried out in sharp dismay. All the men laughed. It is an unspoken rule. Never let a spouse know how much we anglers spend on fishing gear.

Malinda looked stricken. She grabbed the credit card back and announced, looking directly at the two of us, "I'm taking fifty off in reparation for my offishness."

One of the men chuckled, "Maybe I should bring my wife the next time for the discount."

Yesterday I stood in the shop by myself, and only after free advice.

"Hello," she said brightly, waving her hand in greeting. She smiled. "You have the frown of someone who needs directions."

"I usually do. Where should I try this late in the season?"

"Well, that depends on your mood. You can fish where it's quiet and beautiful, down at the mouth of the river near the lake and have the place all to yourself. You'll probably catch nothing. Or you can fish where there are fish just upstream from here. But that's where anglers stand shoulder to shoulder, muttering and shouting. Your only chance to get an open casting spot around here is to get to it very early in the morning—I mean get here by three am!" Today, I got up early enough. There was no one else in the hotel restaurant. I poured a bowl of cold cereal and a cup of hot coffee at the self-serve nook. I sat down to mull Malinda's advice. I decided to try the quiet place first, at a pool near the outflow.

Now, standing in the Salmon River, I have nothing to do but rhythmically pick up the line, backcast, and lay the line back down on the water to drift a fly over the waters—where—it appears, there are no fish waiting to break up any reveries. This is fly fishing at its best—minimalist. No need for a boat or any more equipment than I carry in a vest.

Yet, at this moment, my daze breaks! A sharp pull, a splash on the surface! And—alas! A fish—probably a salmon—spits out the trash taste of my fly and the line goes slack. With a shout, I throw back my head in frustration. My hat flies off. I grab it wet out of the water and feel the drops on my ears as I put it back on my head. When this happens, it is always like that hollow feeling that comes from getting a rejection notice in the mail. It could have been a big rainbow trout or a brown trout that also ascend the river to gorge on salmon eggs—and then lay their own. Afterward, unlike the moribund salmon, the big trout swim back into the lake to grow some more and live to return and breed again. But I hadn't hooked one of those either, so why wonder?

The two anglers who had been downstream on the Salmon River have walked up, adjacent to where I am standing. They whoop at the take and laugh at the miss. And I shout at them in mock dismay, "You scared it away!" All three of us laugh and shake our heads, conspirators in the knowledge that sport fishing is mostly failing to get anything. As the two men walk away, I am comfortably alone with my thoughts again. Starting with a laugh is always the best way to start waxing nostalgic—you descend into the melancholy of times past with a smile on your face.

I certainly can't complain about a lifetime on, in, and around surging waters as embracing as Long Island Sound down the street from where I grew up, and here—at a remote remove in the state of New York in this clear strong Salmon River. Today, the dull late fall leaves appear silver as they reflect the overcast sky floating on the strong blue current. There's the rich smell of decay wafting off the forest floor and down the riverbank near where I am standing. The water gurgles around the knees. Geese honk. Gulls squawk. But not because they have anything to say to me.

My breathing is labored, as much from savoring the wet rank

smells of the decaying leaves and, even incongruously, the sharp smell of unseen fallen apples coming through the riverside trees as from the effort to stay standing in one spot as the current pulls at my knees. I keep picking up and laying down a fly line on the surface of the river that apparently is sterile down below. Cold drops of water flick off the loop in the line as it passes over my head. A sudden sharp gust of wind blows drops into my eyes. Cold tears. I shiver. The small shock of cold water on my face reminds me of once sailing on Long Island Sound, homeward with my childhood friend Donna. A school of porpoises had surfaced around the boat. They blew spray breathing through their blowholes.

But then I admonish myself sharply, "Stop having second thoughts for once. You're here to fish!"

I decide that's enough fishing in vain on what Malinda had dubbed "the quiet section of the river." Time to head upstream to the crowded fishy place. I dig a wading stick into the bottom, turn toward the bank and start wading out. I stumble, inadvertently kicking up the decaying carcass of a spawned salmon. I can see several others under the clear water. Adult salmon of course rotted after spawning. This one came to the surface with dozens of crayfish hanging by their claws on its belly, having their fill. I watch for a while. It gets raucous. Gulls from the lake that are always opportunistically up over the river during spawning season, dive down and start splashing round the salmon carcass, tearing off hunks from the top.

For a moment the swirl on the surface swirls in my mind too. It reminded me of Donna watching the splashing of bluefish scattering the mackerel we saw together sailing in my small sailboat *Flotsam*. Also, the intensity of the mating horseshoe crabs on the sandbar we had sailed to, swirling around each other. Nearby, young Jesuits running, playing basketball; whose game I later joined.

Now it was a frenzy of gulls feeding off a salmon carcass—but part of the same cycle of life and death and life again. *Not pretty*, I think. *But Donna taught me not to flinch at creepy things.*

Death in the river—as at sea—was one smooth transition to new life. In the river, the nearly invisible bacteria from the rotting carcasses would feed microorganisms the newly-hatched salmon fry would eat after hatching from their eggs in the spring. Once they grew strong enough, they would eat larger food like the crayfish who had once fed on their parental flesh to gain the heft needed to continue to swim down the river to the lake—there to fatten and strengthen for their return mating runs years later.

Donna had told me she wanted her ashes scattered "on places where you fish. So that when you find yourself in these places you love, you'll think of me." Mark had sent me a packet at her request.

I decide this was a good place to scatter the ashes I'd carried to the Salmon in a small plastic sandwich bag tucked into my fishing vest. I had another pinch of ashes. I had burned one of the last letters Charlie wrote me typed on paper that his hands had touched—before we switched to ethereal emails in our fifty years of correspondence.

I empty both bags of ashes right into the swirl of the river around the carcass, the crayfish, and the gulls. *Maybe some small piece of them will come back to the river again in a fish I'll catch on the rebound*, I think.

"That's what I could say I came here for, whatever else happens upstream," I say out loud to no one.

With melancholy thoughts of Donna and Charlie stirring my mind, I drive through the village of Pulaski to go toward the second spot recommended by Malinda—closer to its source waters—where she said the fish were. I tried to keep my mind clear of purpose as I run the distracting gauntlet of the "Salmon River circus."

Official government notices are stapled on telephone poles warning about the industrial and agriculture chemicals suspended in salmonid bodies from rain run-off pollution in the lake. *Don't eat your catch*. But on the same telephone poles are stapled other signs offering to clean and smoke your fish. *Bring home fish ready to eat*. The New York Salmon River was working-class salmon fishing, unlike hiring for the day a private beat on the Scottish river Spey.

There are signs on old derelict buildings offering rooms for "$35 a man" (women apparently need not apply); on the main drag there is a long strip of cheap motels, and of fast-food restaurants—Long John Silver's for fish food if you wanted it deep fried in fat—and tackle shops scattered on side streets. The most prominent is Fat Nancy's, a big-box scale tackle shop on the main drag visible from I-81 several miles coming.

And what is almost worse, if you know anything about why the salmon run up the Salmon River in the fall, it's clear the fish themselves have been recruited for the circus. There's a state fish hatchery situated in the midst of their headwaters' breeding pools. Cement canals siphon off thousands of fish to strip the females of billions of eggs. And to isolate the males in holding tanks to spread clouds of gray sperm over the eggs. Later, workers release the fertile eggs in such a way as to fix deep in their embryonic brains or souls a memory of that part of the river for its mystic natal destination to return to when their primal urges push them back. Industrialized fish sex.

For all the river's wild trappings in many secluded pools along the run, and the savagery of anglers fighting fish (that's really the right word for it—certainly from the perspective of the fish), and the opportunistic big brown trout and steelhead eager to eat their eggs and young, salmon fishing on the Salmon River—as indeed most stocked salmonid fishing everywhere—is truly fishing in a great big artificial barrel. The industrially shaped wooden staves and steel hoops of recreational fishing commerce remain concealed in the trees. As Barry Lopez points out in his wonderful book *Arctic Dreams*, not even the remote frozen poles are untouched by human designs—and plastic.

The hullabaloo advertised on the route upstream extends to the river by her shop where Malinda had said I might actually find fish. Wherever I look upstream from the Altmar Bridge, anglers stand shoulder to shoulder, just as Malinda predicted. It is like a teeming village as seen from the air—or, the annual flounder fishing tournament in East Norwalk as seen from a camera drone. Anglers stand very close to both banks in ankle-deep water, as the current is very strong. In their dark waders and vests, they look with their swishing lines like segments of a centipede with wiggling legs. The smell of cigar smoke; beer cans flashing in the opening sunlight. But here, indeed, some anglers are catching fish. Perhaps every five minutes an angler shouts, "Fish on!" A rod makes a profound bow of worship to the water. An angler in a blue jacket threads his way up or downstream following a fish's run, while other anglers hasten to pull their gear out of the way until just the precise moment when the hooked-up angler with the blue jacket moves just out of casting range. A little later, the man with the blue jacket catches another fish. I take care not to give in to a prick of jealousy.

What Malinda had told me was that the mob was here because the fish were here. Early in the fall, salmon fill the river and can be cast for all along its run. But by November, the diminishing number of fish bunch up into separate groups that appear in fewer and fewer pools—and one of those groups was now hunkered down upstream of the Altmar Bridge along with the anglers who'd come to hook them. By regulation, in this zone, anglers had to use flies, and they had to release any fish they caught. It was close to the upper parts of the river where female fish (who'd bypassed the breeding canals) would form their redds (the technical word for "fish nests") in the sandy gravel, over which the males would shoot gray puffs of sperm where the females had deposited their eggs. It was like the horseshoe crabs on the sandbar.

I dig a thermos of coffee out of the back pocket of my fishing vest, along with a russet brown apple, and sit down on the bridge to enjoy the sun, to watch the action, to transition between the quiet place and the circus place.

One thing I discovered during decades of fly fishing, is that its core lies deeper down than awareness. I always set the hook on a suspected take before my mind says to do it. Like a baseball batter facing an incoming pitch, the fly angler strikes instinctively—before any sign from the tug of a strike indicator, or a hesitation in the line's drift.

My next step in analyzing this instinctive moment is to expand the contexts. The fish too acts instinctively without deliberation. To illustrate, imagine the water is transparent, as it often is in fly fishing waters. Because fly fishing usually takes place in the same water that the fish swim in, and the distance between the angler and the fly is limited by the skill of the caster and the quality of the gear, the angler often sees the rise of the fish to the fly at the same moment the fish rises to the fly. Each desires the take. But for opposing motives. The angler wants to fool the fish; the fish wants to feed itself. At the moment of the strike, two opposing motives collide, critically—instinctively—faster than either angler or fish can calculate.

This is the zen moment of fly fishing. An event occurs outside of time and space that cancels conflicting desires to zero. Everything you do or feel or think about fly fishing follows from this moment of nothingness. It resembles my lifelong practice of reflection as "reminiscing," or "composition," that is, drawing together images or scenes or actions adjacently to allow them to give rise to thought or insight not implied in either individual image or scene or action in itself but rather as only as the product of the comparison. And then, to consider the emerging understanding as just the beginning of the mind's play. In other words, the zen of fishing is that moment just before the fish's desire and the angler's desire cancel. And so, too, is the moment as the mind moves from one image or scene to another, prior to giving rise to thinking—to play the fish as it surfaces and dives.

For me, fishing happened inside this silent, quiet place regardless of any ruckus of other anglers nearby. That space was as vast as between the telescope and any distant star. Or between *Flotsam* and Dwayne's boat, or in the beckoning space between the story lines of Herod's birthday party and Jesus's picnic at the lake, inviting the viewer to take whatever time it takes to take it in.

Ultimately, Gospel guidance brought me to sit still on Altmar Bridge—an appropriately symbolic place I thought—to cross over the bridge of Jesuit life between my childhood life and my now elderly adult life. I mourned Charlie and Donna, my parents, and many friends along the way, many of them fellow former Jesuits, and even older men who had remained Jesuits with whom I kept in touch. My friend Richard, who once played a burned-out cigarette in one of my skits, said recently, mournfully, "The contact list on my phone reads like a graveyard."

But now, from my elevated perch over the river, I notice a man with a large black mustache doing something different from every other angler. Because of the strong current, the mass of anglers upstream from the bridge stand close to the bank, with the heavy current only up to their ankles at most. They are casting into the river from the bank. In contrast, the man with the mustache is standing in the middle of the river and casting toward a part of the left bank thick with brush. This looks risky; I can see him leaning against the push of the current against his knees.

But—it works! The man hooks and plays a fish. To do this, he needs fancy footwork to keep his balance as he works his way into a shallower part of the run where he can reply to the way the fish swerves.

That looks interesting, I muse to myself, *let's have a closer look*.

I am careful climbing down from the bridge and wading out into the strong current, relying on my wading stick, to meet the man with the large mustache. Who, it becomes clearer as I close the distance, is a Black man—perhaps the first one I have ever encountered fly fishing.

The man introduces himself as Sean Bennet, from Connecticut. I tell Sean I was born there. Then after chatting for about five minutes, Sean says, generously, that he'd reveal a secret.

"Follow me."

Like Brubeck's Black bass player, Eugene Wright, did for the blind White drummer, Joe Morello, Sean holds my elbow and carefully leads me along a hidden underwater path where the current is weaker. Both stop. Sean makes a short cast toward the bushy bank a short distance from the edge. Here, just clear of the bank, is a stretch of slower, smoother water approximately five feet square. I twist my studded boots in the gravel firmly and join Sean in casting.

Pausing for a moment, Sean turns to me, then points to a large tangle of multicolored flies and monofilament fishing line hanging from the branch on one of the trees of the thicket hanging over the spot.

"Behold," he says with a rhetorical flourish, "a melancholy monument to the failures of fly-casting finesse."

"It looks like a big wasps' nest."

Sean warns, "Watch out for that tree limb!"

"Thanks. I've had a bad experience with wasps in trees." Sean doesn't respond, and I feel no need to elaborate.

After a while, for a moment I stop "watching out" and snag another fly in the nest.

"The nest proves other people did fish the spot," Sean says with a chuckle. "Maybe when the current was even slower than today. But I never saw anyone else try for this five-foot square spot any time I was here."

Sean adds with a slight smile, "One of the advantages of being Black is that White fishermen—and everyone else on this river always are—don't like fishing next to you, so you can carve out your own space."

Sure enough, Sean also snags several flies in the hanging, prickly, entangled nest while we fish together.

"Sean, let's pull it down."

We steady each other while wading into heavy, faster water right under the branch. I use the reel on the rod as a hook to pull the branch down where Sean can grab it and hold it down while I cut the branch off with a knife. Both of us wade with the nest across to the shallow part of the fish run (on the opposite side) and onto the bank. We scissor flies out of the tangle of monofilament.

I recall cutting the ball of rope off a propeller when Donna and I were eight years old. Sean laughs heartily when he gets back about a half dozen of his own flies of yesteryear. We divvy up the "catch."

It is like sharing a Christmas morning for fly fishermen! There are many green and red ones—with tinsel. Using the harvested flies, we fish for a while longer. Sean hooks a few, but I don't have any luck.

Sean says it is too late in the day to be any good. As the day darkens, Sean says he'll be back on the river at 8:30 the next morning, and we can try the spot again.

"You don't have to get here real early. Nobody else wants it. They think the water's too fast, and, maybe they think, 'It's the Black guy's spot.'"

When I return to the hotel room, despite what Sean had said, I still hanker to get one of the good spots on the right bank—where it looked very comfortable to stand near the bank in the slow current, only up to your ankles, and where you could see anglers hooking up on a regular basis. I desired the sweet spot taken by the man in the blue jacket.

Malinda had advised me about starting early and I set the alarm for 2:30 a.m. Again, a quick cardboard cereal breakfast and a cup of coffee. But when I get to the river about 3:15 a.m. I am flabbergasted. The right bank is already packed with fisherman standing cheek by jowl, wearing headlamps, guarding their sweet spots like light posts along a highway. It is exactly the same number and density as yesterday in the middle of the day. Apparently, these men hadn't gone to sleep at all. Now it is raining and windy, and many men are huddled under tarp shelters that they tied in the trees, smoking and drinking coffee. There are red dots at the end of cigarettes among the white beams from the headlamps.

The scent of cigars floats down along with light whiffs of marijuana. Salmon fever is already raging, and it is almost three hours to sunrise and the official beginning of the fishing day! The man in the blue jacket already stands defending his precious spot.

I trudge back downstream toward Sean's personal spot. I am startled by what for a moment is an optical illusion—or a dream fragment—of a dead fish coming back to life. On the path lays the exact outline of a coho salmon shimmering in the faint early morning light. I kneel down to look closer. It is the flattened carcass of a coho salmon teeming with slimy wiggling maggots having their fill. I reached a hand out to touch, as Donna had the horseshoe crab, but flinch. I still lack the instinctual tolerance for creepy things Donna had. It had been her way of demonstrating an understanding of the beauty and purpose of even the more initially repellant scenes of life, reproduction, and the death that links them. I relent and press a hand down into the swarm of maggots. They feel cool and wet, as if caressing my palm with soft fingers like the horseshoe crab had done.

Rotting fish radiate the sacredness of life renewing itself. Build a philosophy of life on that—and live right with the world. The thought fastens my knee to the ground as if in prayer just for a moment.

I stand up abruptly and walk back and sit down directly across from the fishing spot I had shared with Sean the day before. I am alone with my thoughts again, awaiting the three hours to go before official sunrise and the official beginning of the fishing day. I'm wearing waders, again with heat pads in the socks, and a thick sweater under a waterproof rain jacket, and a Gloucester fisherman's style yellow hat with large drooping sides that sheds rain efficiently—but of the sort you'd never see advertised in an Orvis catalog. It is pleasant enough to wait while listening to the rain patter on the hat. I am inside the small sound that makes a private space. The wind shifts to blow the anglers' smoke another way, and now I breathe deeply the fecund odors of wet leaves settling into the expected decay—which includes a whiff from the dead coho salmon the maggots are feeding on.

Occasionally there is a brief puff of cold air on my cheek, giving advance notice of the long winter to come. The natural world is forever going about educating anyone who took the leisure to watch and listen and smell its messages about the meaning of life—which is, in a single word, *reproduction* and all the changing of one life form into another upon which it depends.

I feel snug—maybe even a little smug—in my warm clothes with a premonition of some good fishing to follow my patient waiting.

By the time the morning sun has risen above the clouds and the rain, everyone who looked at a watch could tell the official fishing day has begun on the Salmon River. Sean still hasn't shown up.

I'll start without him, and when he turns up, I'll let him choose wherever he wants to stand near his spot.

In Sean's honor, I use a tinselly spotted little brown hare's ear fly Sean had found in the fly hook nest we harvested together. Sean chuckled when he handed it to me and said it was one of his old flies that he was happy to share.

Oh, happy day! I get one on with the first cast. The fish hops and jumps and runs for the middle, causing me to stagger a little—turning around in the heavy current. I pivot on my wading stick (the upper part of an old hockey stick with a rubber crutch cup on the end). I hold the rod sideways and bend, until the footing of the shallow side comes up. But magically I get the fish to the shallows and find it is a coho salmon, the season for which is supposedly past. This one without any maggots on it yet. I carefully perform all the holy rigamarole of letting it go, and then sit down on the bank stones, take a drink of water, and start eating a russet apple.

While I am recovering, the man in the blue jacket works a large fish into the shallows at my feet. He introduces himself as John Miletich. Like peers, we two anglers congratulate each other on our successes with smiles and waves and "good lucks."

See? I think, *It was silly yesterday to be jealous about the success of another angler like the man in the blue jacket.* Success at fishing breeds magnanimity in any angler. I get up again and wade back to Sean's spot.

By my fourth or fifth hookup, working unsteadily down the rapids, I look back for a moment to get my bearings. I see dozens of anglers up in the traditionally good spots watching me. They wear that concerned blank look anglers have when they wonder why it's that guy—who's not of their party—who's catching fish and they aren't? It does no good for them to stare like this as I had admonished myself yesterday. And certainly no one should gloat for the moment he or she is on the good end of the stare. Good luck fishing comes on silent cat feet, like grace. Enjoy it while you can. Stay within yourself.

And so, well fortified by the warm feelings of camaraderie with my new friend John, the man in the blue jacket, I refuse to look back again, lest the stares ruin what was starting to feel like a sacred day. It gets better.

As if a reward for thinking proper second thoughts, I next hook and play and draw into the shallows a steelhead trout thirty inches long, with a dark back and lovely thick red band down the middle. I have never caught one so magnificent. As the great fish fins in my hands in the shallows before being released, a small hole opens in the clouds for the sun to spotlight just the two of us. The wind that blows in the trees faintly conveys a hint of the sound of an angelic choir chanting, "Hallelujah!" and blows the smell of cigar smoke away. The red body band of the steelhead flickers with rainbow colors.

"This release is for Charlie," I say out loud. "We would have liked to have had you with us longer . . ."

All frustrations of the previous days—in fact of my entire life—are forgotten. I have achieved the nirvana of angling. "God gave Moses a rainbow sign . . ." as the old hymn has it.

Sitting back down for a moment again on the stones of the shallows across from Sean's spot, I think of Wordsworth's lines: "Our Souls have sight of that immortal sea, which brought us hither."

I decide since it is still well before noon, and I can get back home to Christine driving in daylight if I leave within an hour. I have time to try for one more fish.

I wade back into the strong current, and my feet set and legs bent, start casting again. I must look like I am about to lose my footing since a tall, thin young man wearing a black watch cap wades over. He holds out a hand. He says his name is Max and, perhaps responding to my white beard and unsteady posture, says sweetly, "We don't want to lose you."

Max remains at my side while I hook and play what will be the final fish: a big female brown trout. Its brown sides are tinged with gold, with a pattern of small yellow dots freckled along the lateral line. The fish lays out almost still on the sandy river bottom, cradled in white froth, as if in patient, expectant ease, with its gills working slowly under the covering luster of the shallow river water.

I undo the hook and, with wetted hands, gentle the brown trout away from the shallows, toward the flow of the river. The bright brown-gold speckled trout slips into the cold, dull gray current on its pilgrimage upstream.

Epilogue

This story answers the question a fervent Christian woman asked me several years ago, incredulously, "How could you, who had given your whole life to worshipping God, come to decide you didn't have to? What about Pascal's Wager? Either God exists, or he doesn't. If he does, it's vital to believe in him. If you say you do, and it turns out he doesn't exist, nothing is lost. Why can't you take that chance?"

My answer, unsatisfying to her, was, "What if God does exist, and I come to decide, that as far as I can honestly determine, he or she or it does not—or at least that it doesn't matter. Isn't it likely he or she has the sense of humor and sympathy to say, 'It hardly matters what you believe. You worked at it. Come see if there *is* a promised land.'" (Genesis 12:1).

Acknowledgments

I am grateful to have had friends willing to read parts or all of this story in manuscript form even before they said how to make it better. Sandy McCloy, Robert and Marla Niederer, Lee Perron, Neil Myers, Robert Astle, Natalie and Ferd Leimkuhler, Maureen O'Leary, John Miletich, Meg Mellan, Ben Hamelin—I thank you.

My hope now is that there are five thousand other readers like you at the lake.

www.ingramcontent.com/pod-product-compliance
Lightning Source LLC
LaVergne TN
LVHW041741060526
838201LV00046B/876